W9-BAX-558

THE NEW ART EDUCATION

BY THE SAME AUTHOR

FIFTY PRINTS OF THE YEAR

John Day Co., N. Y. 1925

HOW TO SEE MODERN PICTURES

Dial Press, N. Y. 1925

EXPERIENCING PICTURES

Harcourt, Brace & Co., N. Y. 1932

CRITICAL APPRECIATION COURSE

Design Workshop, Nyack, N. Y. 1940

EXPERIENCING AMERICAN PICTURES

Harper & Brothers, N. Y. 1943

CRITICAL APPRECIATION COURSE II

Design Workshop, Nyack, N. Y. 1951

Comprising a series of 50 articles on

"THE MODERN RENAISSANCE IN THE U. S. A."

Articles

A MODERN VIEWPOINT

A column running in *Art Digest* since January, 1945.

A Mural for the Provo, Utah Post Office, by EVERETT THORPE.
A former professional student of Ralph M. Pearson.

THE NEW ART EDUCATION

REVISED EDITION

RALPH M. PEARSON

FOREWORD BY EDUARD C. LINDEMAN

HARPER & BROTHERS Publishers
NEW YORK

To my wife

L.H.P.

THE NEW ART EDUCATION—REVISED EDITION

Printed in the United States of America

Library of Congress catalog card number: 52-12046

CONTENTS

FOREWORD

by Eduard C. Lindeman
Professor Emeritus of Social Philosophy, New York School of Social Work

The esthetic impulse expresses itself through the medium of at least four types of personality. There is, first of all, the professional artist who expects to be compensated for his work; his attitude toward his productions is one of self-consciousness; he has in more recent times developed also a craft-consciousness with respect to his relation to society. Wherever there are professional artists there will also be customers, collectors, patrons, and critics, persons who may be called appreciators; their functions are intermediary, although, as in the case of the genuine critic, they may so far elevate their functions as to become artists in their own right. Next in order, are the teachers of art and of these there are usually three varieties: the true teacher who understands both esthetic and pedagogical principles, the pseudo-teacher who transmits from one generation to another the standardized practices of conventional art, and the artist-teacher who may have been lured into teaching because of his desire to reproduce himself through disciples, or who may teach for economic reasons, or who may be one of those rare persons who is at one and the same time a creative artist and a creative teacher. Last of all are the amateur artists who enjoy "playing" with materials upon which they place such designs as correspond with their natures, and hence derive recreational values from experiences which are essentially esthetic.

The respective roles of these four types of persons are, or should be, complementary; but, alas, they are not. The recreational experiences of the amateur artist invariably end when he comes in contact with the teacher of art. He, the teacher, is preoccupied with professional standards and is scarcely able to comprehend the function of art as recreation. He fails to understand that these amateur artists might some day become the kind of audience which the true professional artist needs. Likewise, the relation between the professional artist and those who announce him to the public, select his works for exhibition, or become his customers is not a happy one, but this is a situation with which I shall not now concern myself.

My primary interest centers about the relation between art and democratic culture. My zeal on behalf of art in education and in recreation does not in any sense detract from the respect and honor which I freely give to the professional artist. I doubt whether any society could maintain a progressive culture without dependence upon professional artists. But, it does not seem to me inconsistent to believe that a society which is by declaration democratic might not also furnish an environment in which all the people could participate in esthetic experience. This end cannot be brought about, however, until there occurs a radical reorientation with respect to the teaching of art.

Ralph Pearson enters my equation at this point. What I have so long theorized he has actually done. He is a genuine teacher of art who has practiced what he believes. I first became acquainted with his work when we were both teaching at the New School for Social Research. In my class there appeared a student who was well known to me; his chief occupation in life seemed to be "taking courses"; he possessed a good average mind which he was intent upon filling with knowledge. His education appeared to follow an inverse ratio: the more courses he pursued the less wisdom he revealed. But now something had happened to him; for the first time in our acquaintance he expressed dissatisfaction with the mere accumulation of knowledge; his mind became inquisitive rather than acquisitive; he even began the hazardous enterprise of self-expression. The transformation was so startling that I made an inquiry into his recent experiences and discovered that he had been and was a student in Ralph Pearson's Workshop.

It was thus that I discovered what I had so long sought, namely a teacher of art who began with the assumption that design is inherent in human nature. I shall go no further in describing Ralph Pearson's point of view and his methods. He has achieved this purpose in his book. His style is provocative, at times even belligerent, and his language is plain. What he says he means and what he means he says. He speaks primarily to teachers, those whose office it is to introduce children, youth and adults to the world of art. If they heed his words, we may discover that art will ultimately find its true place in that cluster of experiences and values which may be called democratic culture.

PREFACE

THIS book challenges certain widely accepted theories and practices in art education. It substitutes for these certain other theories and practices. The cleavage between the two is deep and wide and not always understood. Lack of understanding means confusion. It is part of my purpose to clarify the issue between the two opposed ways.

The way herein challenged may be roughly summarized as the school of skillful copying, the one advocated, as the school of designed creation.

If there are root qualities in works of many different eras which endure through long periods of time, these qualities certainly go far beyond craft as a criterion of value; they tend to deal with the visions of man and the welding of these visions into symbolic concepts which he, the *creator*, has added to the material of his subject. It is with this plus quality, this something added to subject by man as artist, that we are here concerned. This is the quality that has been left by the wayside in the art and art education mainly concerned with craft. It is this quality that the new art and art education must recapture, assimilate, and apply.

If the creative powers of man have in a general way unified the art of the ages, it follows that in any one period these powers must also be a unifying force in the people of that period. That is to say, creative power can and should interweave with man's life in two directions—in the long warp of history and in the short woof of contemporary life. It has done so in varying degrees.

If this assumption is true it means two things. There will be, or should be, a folk art as well as a professional art in all normal cultural periods. Art, in other words, should not be esoteric, the special property of the few. It should be widely rooted in the general life with a flowering of concentrated power on the highest level of professional achievement. Today we do not have such a widely rooted art; therefore, we are not a normal period. To urge the creative process back into such a healthy functioning is a prime responsibility which the new art education must assume.

The new art education, then, has responsibilities which are impressive in their range and their social importance. It must train professionals with a new vision, purpose and value emphasis. It must equip students to meet with high courage and self-confidence the inevitable conflicts in ideology which await them on every side. With equal energy it must attack the problem of winning an ever-increasing adjustment by society to the ideals back of the new art vision. To abandon youth to this heavy task without institutional support is a cowardly escape from an obligation inherent in the nature of the new teaching—as reprehensible as is the current surrender to average standards of taste wherever this occurs. Beyond these responsibilities lies the one to people in general—to give them opportunity to participate in the art experience.

Creative art can transform the environment of man. It can refurnish the mind and the home. It can change dull routine to emotional excitement. It opens the door, through participation, to the art of the ages. It touches all things of use which make up environment. It makes you and me and the leading artists of our time copartners in the art production which will measure our culture for future generations. And beyond even these weighty matters it can mean that personal and elusive thing—joy in living.

This book is written for all adult students. Just where the line can be drawn between child and adult in creative art is hard to say. Adults should become children in creative painting, in its early stages at least, and children need to be encouraged by adults, under present conditions, to have the courage to remain themselves. Teachers of young children will have to translate the experiments here presented into simpler terms or use them only now and then as direction finders for the unquenchable self-assurance of tender years. Art teachers must practice in some such program as this in order themselves to be creative artists and so inspire their students to parallel but different production. No teaching should ever limit itself to the methods or experiments here or elsewhere presented. These should blaze the trail to and along the creative tradition of the ages, delineating its boundaries, defining its basic standards and suggesting the directions which the creative mind of today, as that is present in some degree in all people, may take.

Those in whom creative power is not developed may be blind to the expression of that power in a work of art because they are chained to a literal attitude of mind. If such blindness is realized and the values involved are guessed at, the very lack may induce a desire for growth. If not, the lack may well take the self-defensive line of attack and ridicule. The art world, unfortunately, as well as the general public, is divided into two such camps. Some understand and value the creative expression of their time. Some ridicule, condemn, or ignore what is beyond their personal horizon.

In the world of art education the same division occurs. Many authorities including certain art education magazines are mainly technical, literal, stereotyped, naturalistic, or intellectualistic in their approach to art and art education. Many large and influential art schools or art departments in important institutions of learning are limited to a teaching which, by its very nature, ensures creative sterility. Within such institutions, however, and scattered within and without all types of schools, there are often individual artist-teachers who have the spark and philosophy of creation. These are importing the new art education into the lives of a minority of students. For the few this means growth. Against absurd handicaps this is increasing the art fertility of the nation. The educational tragedy lies in the needless conflicts and confusions which devastate the mass of students—conflicts which only the strongest can overcome.

The creative way does not meet the specifications of existing curricula in all school systems. Where these are based on skill as an end or on imposed adult standards of excellence or where they are intellectualized (even when labeled "creative" or "modern") the new way definitely breaks with the old, making the creative emotional experience the dominant value and skill the secondary one. I want the argument here presented to be a direct challenge to such noncreative practice.

Where the creative values are recognized and encouraged, as they have been increasingly in recent years, the method here presented will aid development by dividing up the creative process of building a picture or sculpture into a number of single steps each of which can be dealt with and assimilated separately. The comprehension of a single step—color, for its infinite possibilities, space as a concrete element and its relationships, line and line relationships, planes, form, texture, etc.—can and should be mastered before the development of skills and before the complications of combining it with subject. This facilitates easy and rapid growth. After such assimilation both skills and application to subject, if desired, can progress normally as a by-product of that growth.

While this plan encourages a student to "do what he wants to do," it does not leave him faced with the immense problem of solving all production tasks alone and unaided. It gives him an insight into many ways and means of carrying out his own visions and of building them into pictorial or sculptural form.

To analyze and develop pictorial and sculptural *form,* or design, is another major purpose of this book. Creation mothers design. The instinct to organize color, space, and form into design is, like the power to create, in human blood. The wide distribution of design in works of art of all ages and degrees of civilization, its emergence in the works of young children and amateur adults as well as its supreme development in the masters of many ages, prove the point. Design may not be listed by the psychologists as one of the instincts of man; nevertheless, there it is in man, an indelible part of him, ready to be used whenever he looks at or deals with color, space, and form.

Comparisons of this teaching with others which have been influenced by, or are a direct expression of, the French Modern Movement should be made first with the purpose of severely appraising foundations to see if they are harmonious. Then, where harmony in basic point of view and values has been established, there should be considerable tolerance of divergent ways and means. This does not mean that analysis and as concrete a statement of values as possible should be avoided in kindly forbearance. Disagreements in ways and means of applying any fundamental knowledge will always exist because of varying personalities with their different experiences and interests. Conflict on ways and means is healthy—if the same roots nourish divergent opinion (or, perhaps, if they do not). Among modern or expressionistic schools, however, the foundations should be on common ground to make the divergencies healthy.

In this teaching, creation and design in their elemental meanings and values are developed as human capacities on the assumption that when assimilated they will work on any material in any situation in many directions and that all these will be rich in their rewards to the individual—and through him to society. The leeway so granted ensures the student from being held within any one conception of *right* design.

In various places throughout these pages I have made comparisons with other schools and writers which are, I believe, in basic agreement on foundations but will disagree with me and I with them on some methods and some results. In Chapter III there is such a comparison with several representatives of what I call the intellectual branch of the Modern School. In Chapter XI there is one comparison, coupled with additional explanations, with Moholy-Nagy of Bauhaus fame; in Chapter VII, with Hans Hofmann; in the bibliography, with Morris Davidson in relation to his book, *Painting for Pleasure,* with John Dewey, and in various places with Sheldon Cheney and his excellent explanations of Expressionism and plastic form. Each of us who is teaching or writing in this field should look well to his foundations in relation to others, should correlate where possible and should at the very least try to agree on terminology: the present confusion in the use of such words as "design and composition," "naturalism and realism," etc., is needless and confusing. I have learned from them; I have tested my experience against theirs. I am fairly sure that some of the foundations which I have been able to lay in students would apply to and perhaps supplement their teaching. The ground to be covered by the creative powers of man is so vast that many valid approaches are needed to tap the full potentialities of the multitude of those who wish to learn. Intramural, and extramural, comparisons, therefore, should be exacting, intelligent, and frank.

My general purpose, then, is one of reorientation in art education—a reorientation based on the findings of the Modern Movement in art which say that the dictates of the human spirit are the important matters, that skill is craft and useful only as a means to a spiritual end.

This book is written from the point of view of an artist-educator who has learned through practice plus theory rather than through theory alone. Such practice has included production in several media over a period of twenty-five years and teaching the new findings for fifteen years. The philosophy and method back of the teaching may be called functional because they have largely grown out of experience.

THE DESIGN WORKSHOP

The specific field in which this teaching philosophy and method has been developed is the Design Workshop (probably the first modern school in this country to be called a workshop rather than a studio), a School of Modern Art for Adults, started by the author in 1924 at Valley Cottage, N. Y. A year later the Workshop moved to New York City, then into the New School for Social Research where it inaugurated the art practice in that school's program, then into its own quarters six years later in the building of the Cooperative School for Student Teachers where, for five years, the entire student body took its courses. In 1937, with a backlog of over three thousand students who had taken lecture or practice courses in New York City alone, the teaching enlarged into correspondence courses in creative painting, modeling, drawing, and critical appreciation. Students carried out instructions always free to follow their own instincts in interpreting them, sent in the work by mail, and received a personal criticism and the next lesson in return. Results, during three years, have been constantly surprising in the originality, creative power, and speedy development of the people working regardless of age, profession, or previous training. Enrollment has grown steadily and has included ages from twelve to seventy-seven, occupations from housewife to orchestra leader, from a coal miner in West Virginia to a farm girl in Minnesota, from art supervisors to art teachers in many types of schools, from businessmen to college students, from professional artists with years of academic training to be counteracted to beginners who had never wielded brush or pencil.

The Design Workshop has never been a full-time art school training young art students in a one or four year professional course. Instead it has always given short basic courses which lay the foundations on which future study and practice can be built. Most of its courses in class sessions have been once a week or for six weeks in summer. The wide diversity of its students would have imposed this kind of program even if such did not fit into its general purpose of training and re-training adults. Adults are busy people who have other responsibilities and often little spare time. For this reason the Workshop has less mature, advanced work to show than the full-time school should have. Such work from other schools, therefore, is included and honored when it is the outgrowth of a similar philosophy and method.

This book does not duplicate the specific lessons used so successfully in the courses by mail. It lays down basic essentials and assumes that each student or teacher will work out his or her own applications. Student or professional work reproduced shows one application. There are untold numbers of others. It is part of the responsibility of the creative mind to find and practice its own way. Work from a number of different schools is included to show the diversity possible when creation and design are the common root-source of practice and philosophy.

The economic history of the Design Workshop during the fifteen years of its pioneering teaching has considerable social significance, for it is probably typical of all advanced independent enterprise in a highly institutionalized educational world. Among large educational institutions subsidy is always assumed as a normal necessity. That individuals who break new ground for institutions to follow many years later may also need subsidy is rarely admitted. Through fifteen years of difficult growth the Workshop received loans and subsidies totaling $450. That is all. Never in its history did it have any funds aside from these for working capital, for promotion, for enlargement of facilities, or for overhead beyond its own ability to pay from earnings. That it endured is due solely to the support of its students—well over four thousand in total number during the fifteen years. Their support must measure its worth.

Nyack, N. Y. RALPH M. PEARSON.

PREFACE
TO THE REVISED EDITION

THE main reason for a major revision of *The New Art Education* is to survey and appraise events of the past decade in the art educational field for the purpose of a mutual testing of the argument here presented and the events, each in relation to the other.

That such a survey is timely and may have considerable importance is indicated by the recent incidence of a movement which is one of the weirdest throwbacks ever to invade a national culture. Heretofore there have been slow advances and slow declines of the cultural curve in one or all of the arts; today we are witnessing, in certain quarters of visual art, a relatively sudden abandonment of both content and form—which constitutes a retrogression to pre-Stone Age levels of achievement to find its inept equal. This debacle and its relation to the argument of this book is discussed as part of its survey in an added Chapter 14.

The preceding Preface to the First Edition, written in 1941, still holds, except for needed corrections of facts. The Design Workshop is now (in 1952) twenty-eight years of age and the Mail Courses fifteen years—with a corresponding increase in the number of students. But, in spite of its slow and steady growth, the Workshop is still a one-man, experimental school with individual instruction; it is not and never will be an impersonal institution. The total of its subsidies remains the same.

Three major and several minor changes have been made in the text for this revision. The end of Chapter 7 and all of Chapter 11 have been rewritten in order to substitute reports on two schools at the college level giving professional training of the type herein proclaimed as being the education of the future. The main body of the text remains unchanged because its arguments are not dated even though the illustrations thereof inevitably are. If the latter serve their illustrative function, the dating will not matter. A considerable number of new illustrations either replace or supplement old ones. Stars after a name indicate a Design Workshop student, as explained on page 69.

RALPH M. PEARSON

Nyack, N. Y.
September, 1952

PART I
MODERN THEORY

"It is the obligation of education to train the minds and talents of our youth to improve, through creative citizenship, our American institutions in accord with the requirements of the future."

FRANKLIN D. ROOSEVELT.

1. THE OLD AND THE NEW ART EDUCATION

ONE day recently I drove onto a Hudson River ferry directly behind an empty furniture van. The endgate of the van was down and out of its gloomy interior spilled a galaxy of old-fashioned comforters. Gray, faded and dirty, these comforters had obviously descended in the social scale from the dignified role of warming reclining human beings to the lesser dignity of saving furniture from scratches.

My eyes roamed idly over the jumbled mass as I thought and talked of other things. I was not particularly interested in old comforters. I was not collecting them. They were not a new experience. There was nothing surprising in them to attract attention. There was no tangible reason to think about them.

But suddenly my conscious mind was jerked into a realization that I was enjoying these old things, that my eyes playing over them were awakening somewhere in me a response that was definite pleasure. Thus awakened, my conscious mind became curious. What was I enjoying? Dirty old comforters—the fact of these, was it that? No. Definitely not. I had no interest in the existence of dirty comforters. What was it then?

My eyes began to observe more consciously. Each comforter was a different color and design. Stripes, large flowers, small flowers, diamond shapes, and checkerboard squares—all in a tumbled chaos. Ah! A harmony of grayed and subtly different colors. Yes, come to notice, it was such a harmony. Extraordinarily varied. Repeating colors. Different colors. Motifs of flowers and stripes repeated all over the array but in different sizes, positions, directions. I realized that my eyes were playing over this material and picking out chords of colors, shapes, and repeated motifs. It was as if this were a piano keyboard on which I could play harmonies, only the music was seen instead of heard. I had been enjoying the experience *unconsciously*—thrilling to visual sensations. And when I did become aware of what was happening, did *think* about it, the experience was not killed; it continued in the realm of feeling supplemented by the act of thinking.

It was a certain alertness to the quality of environment that made me sense the harmonies in this pile of old comforters. John Dewey[1] argues that sensitive awareness to environment is the beginning of aesthetic appreciation. He sees the rudiments of such appreciation in the animal world—in the dog when his keen ears respond to every sound, in the cat watching for its prey alert to the slightest move. In primitive man, with his very life dependent on a quick response to a dangerous environment, this alertness and keen observation continued—probably with dwindling sensitivity as safety increased. In modern man, with his senses dulled by lack of use, the capacity for this alertness is present but undeveloped. When developed it becomes a sort of radio antennae ready to receive. Broadcasts do not register unless there is that slender wire to catch ethereal waves. Both nature and works of art are broadcasting to us steadily through the days and years and we are receiving or failing to receive the many strange messages according to the sensitiveness of our aesthetic receiving sets.

Why do some people see *only* a pile of old comforters, *only* broken-down old buildings, *only* the ugly old woman as they look about them at "dirty" or so-called "ugly" things? Why do they miss the sensations of pleasure I have described? Because they observe only material facts about tangible things with practical or literal vision. They fail to see the qualities of things which go beyond the hard, bare fact. They may respond to the more obvious and familiar beauties around them—a sunset, a butterfly, a flower, a handsome girl—but they do not see the unfamiliar beauty on its

[1]*Art as Experience*. Minton, Balch & Company, New York, 1934.

own merits wherever they look—even in sunset, butterfly, or girl.

Harmonies perceived in environment exist partly in the natural scene and partly in the observing mind. In this case the harmony of grayed color was in the scene and could have been observed by all comers with even the slightest degree of awareness of their environment. The harmony of related spaces, motifs, movements, was in the observing mind and would probably have been perceived only by the relative few who had trained themselves to be aware of these qualities. And only the creative-minded, design-conscious artist would be able to create added harmonies out of the material he saw.

All people have the hidden power to see and enjoy such harmonies and the right to that enjoyment. Also the power and right to create harmonies of their own. That only the relative few among our millions have developed their powers and claimed their right as either appreciators or producers is one of the cultural tragedies of our time. To point out how these inherent powers in people can be developed and this aesthetic enjoyment extended is the major purpose of this book. And because these powers do exist in people in general the argument is addressed to all—not merely to the specialist, the artist, art student, critic, or historian. We can have no genuine civilization in the finer meanings of that term until our extraordinary development in science, technics, and knowledge is balanced by a like development in the arts and a wide distribution of the experience-values inherent therein. The Government Art Projects have done more to achieve that goal than any other single event in American history. But we Americans, in this field, are as yet far from being a civilized people.

DESIGN

The word in English which comes nearest to defining the harmonic qualities I have described is the word "design." But the meaning of this word has to be greatly extended beyond its familiar limits to include these new-old values or qualities. Ordinarily when we say "design" we think of applied design—familiar patterns in wallpaper or textiles. But the Moderns have stretched the meaning of the word far beyond these narrow limits. To them it means organization of all the elements of the picture into visual harmonies—into

Fig. 1.—*Phantasy*. A drawing by SOUTHER BUTTRICK.*

a visual symphony, if you like—and the reorganization of subject to fit the demands of that organization. Design in this sense, as related to pictures and sculptures, is a rediscovery of our time. Cézanne and Van Gogh were the pioneer explorers; they rediscovered and added to a function of man that has existed through all of human history. Primitives of the Stone Age unconsciously designed their pictographs. The early Mediterranean cultures knew and practiced design. The Egyptians, the Chinese, the Greeks of the early and the Golden Age were masters of design. Then, after the Roman decadence into naturalism and the complete fade-out of the Dark Ages in Europe, came the ressurection with the early Byzantines and the great Renaissance of the Middle Ages where design reached a climax of richness and complexity. Then again the decline into naturalism and now the developing rebirth.

Since the great Armory Exhibition in New York in 1913 our rebirth has been in full swing as its revitalization of the art of the picture has penetrated further and further into the consciousness of artists and public. Design, more than any of the changing attitudes toward subject, has been the home of the rebirth, the source of the new experiences offered by pictures, the rich vein of ore from which we are again mining the values of the spirit covered by the word "aesthetic." Design is the least common denominator of all the arts. It is the element which, more than any other, unifies the arts of all times and places where it has been known and used.

Perceiving the qualities of life and things about us, then, from old comforters to cathedrals, sunsets, smoking factories, flowers, animals, landscapes, and human beings is the beginning of the aesthetic experience. Creating, out of any materials in any medium, our own expression and building that expression into the harmonies of design *is aesthetic experience.* So, too, is the response to the expressions of others—to a simple creation of the child or amateur artist and to a complex creation of the master artist of any age.

THE OLD ART EDUCATION—NATURALISM

The art education which we have inherited from the nineteenth century missed practically all of these new-old values. Creation had been discredited. Design had been forgotten. Truth to the actual appearance of things, facts reported with skill—these had become the main and often the only concern. Pictures should mirror nature, should be a replica of actual things, should "look like" their subjects, should be handmade color photographs of the beauties of the world. Beauty was thought of as existing in nature and the task of the artist was to report that beauty so faithfully that the observer thought he was seeing and responding to the original beauty. The artist personalized his report; in fact latitude in the personal interpretation was welcome. But he was not a creator of beauty in his own right and according to his own lights; he was a reporter of the beauty created by God.

The school devoted to this practical philosophy and more or less mechanical process is the Naturalistic School.

The art education which was the product of this factual attitude was a reflection of the prevailing standards. Skill was the goal. Developing skill in reporting facts—in copying the physical aspect of things as they actually appeared to the physical eye—was the object of four long years of "academic" training (in art schools) or of whatever training was given in many other types of schools from the secondary through high school and college. Design and so-called "fine art" were separated in such academic training, the two departments usually having no contact with each other. "Fine art" students looked down on "design" students as being practical, commercial people studying design as a future business occupation. And the design students thought of fine art as unrelated to design. Since design in its universal applications, including the field of the picture and sculpture, was not then, and still is not, understood by the naturalists, this division was to be expected. The design taught in such schools was the conventionalized, intellectualized type. It followed stereotyped formulae, sometimes adopted or adapted from the past,[2] sometimes adapted from nature into set patterns of decoration (see Fig. 2).

Such has been our art education in this country since official art

[2] Best-Maugard, in his book *A Method of Creative Design* (Alfred A. Knopf, New York, 1926), took seven types of line—spiral, circle, half circle, double half circle, wavy, zigzag and straight—from decorative motifs of past arts and used them in new combinations as a way of making decorative designs of today. The result was too limited to have more than a superficial, experimental value.

2.—Stereotyped design. A conventional, set
rn, stiff, tight, learned by rote. No per-
expression, no feeling, no tie-up with life
rience. An academic design. Contrast to
pposite type on all counts in Fig. 3.

Fig. 3.—A fourteen-year-old girl in Erasmus Hall High School, Brooklyn, made this textile design based on the subway which she knows from daily experience. Mary Ragan, instructor.

STEREOTYPED AND CREATIVE DESIGN

schools began to be established about the middle of the past century. It has settled into a convention. It still is the dominant way.

Art education of this academic type is an externalized thing; the work produced comes from an outside source, is assembled, so to speak, through the thinking (not the feeling) process into the picture or sculpture by skill of hand. There is no genuine *creation* in this process. There is no felt organization of all elements into a personal expression which grows out of individual life and experience. The entire procedure is barren of aesthetic experience and values. It is frozen art. It is craft. Regimented by such materialism, the normal creative spirit in child, youth, or adult withers and dies.

The Naturalistic School, not understanding design in the modern sense, uses a terminology which either fails completely to include the enlarged meanings of words like "creation" and "design" or which confuses, distorts, and nullifies such meanings. Also it speaks of "art training," "principles of design," and "art" as if there were one accepted standard in this great field instead of two diametrically opposed ones. To correct this confusion, to accentuate the fact that the Naturalistic School is the direct opposite of the School of Designed Creation, which for lack of a better term we call Modern, is the first task of the new art education. The words "art" and "art education" must be qualified wherever used. Naturalistic art and art education. Creative art and art education. This is the minimum definition. The word "academic" will not serve for the former school because there can be academic modern art as well as academic naturalistic art—a distinction which I shall later explain more fully.

THE NEW ART EDUCATION—DESIGNED CREATION

The new art education born of the Modern Movement in Art[3] reverses this trend and its processes and substitutes different goals, methods and values. Its philosophy is a continuation of the general art philosophy of the creative past with a shifting of emphasis in many places and a new dress for old concepts but without basic change.

The new methods also can be evolved from past creative practice or they can grow functionally out of the empirical needs of the creative philosophy by a kind of inevitable logic discovering themselves as they go. Again it is conceivable that they could be worked out on a purely negative basis determined by their effectiveness as an antidote to the naturalistic methods which they supersede. All of these sources have contributed to the following program.

[3] Sheldon Cheney, in *Expressionism in Art*, argues for the term "Expressionism" as the title best fitted to describe the Modern Movement. He recounts the term's first use in Germany, the opposition to it in Paris—partly for that reason—and its gradual spread and acceptance by writers in this country.

Granted that we have no word adequately describing the Movement. Granted that Expressionism may be nearest to adequate of any word in sight. My objection to it is that it does not cover or imply design as an ingredient and that it runs the risk of becoming dated, as many other "isms" have. The term "Modern" has come to include design by informed usage and it is sliding in application. For many years to come it will mean a break with naturalism, designed creation, and elastic adaptation to contemporary growth. For these reasons I continue its use.

GOALS

Summarized as briefly as possible, the goals of the new art education are: Development of the design sense and its application to the making of pictures, sculptures, and things of use. Adventure of the spirit, experiment, new experience. Creation. Expression, both of the self and of external reality. Application of the creative mind and the sensitivity to design to life and environment.

THE DESIGN SENSE

The quality in historical art which is least understood today is design. Logically, therefore, design presents itself as a field of study which is most important both as a means of getting back within the Grand Tradition[4] and of counteracting naturalistic standards. To develop the design sense will be our first objective.

This granting of priority to design contradicts the program of some educators within the Modern School who place awareness of subject and its expression as tempered by personal experience first —design being thought of and developed as a means to that expression. This places content of the picture before form; it rates form (or design) as of secondary importance.

When content is given first place it is reasonable to think of design as a means to effective expression. Design is that. It dramatizes and makes effective, through omission, selection, clarification, emphasis, and *organization*, all the elements of subject. Also in this case subject determines the character of design; the design is functional in relation to subject. A building, an elephant, a flower give their character to the lines, spaces, colors, and forms which are the building materials of the design. Content can be given first place, of course, without the buttressing of design, as has happened in Fig. 4. This is creative expression, not mere naturalism, and it is an effective dramatization. But its effectiveness would be increased and aesthetic satisfactions added by design.

Genuine self-expression has deep values which authenticate this process. Each human being, regardless of age, is a unique personal-

[4] The Grand Tradition implies the enduring qualities of great art. These are the creative reorganization of subject into symbolic expression and design.

Fig. 4.—*Gossip*, by DAVID KENNEDY, student of Colorado Springs Fine Arts Center. Boardman Robinson, instructor.

A forceful expression of life with no design sense whatever. Dramatic expression of subject has been the first and only concern.

ity with different interests, capacities, sensitivities, loves, hates, visions, dreams, and grouches. He sees the life around him (or should so see it if free from the blinders of convention) through the prism of this unique personality which is his self. He sees it differently from every other unique personality. For him to choose the particular aspect of life or things which interests him, to digest its essential qualities, to dream dreams about it, to see his dream or vision take shape in his own mind as a re-creation which is his own interpretation of reality, to translate the mind-vision into a concrete thing in some medium, to create a new entity called a picture —this creative act is a tremendously important achievement. It is important to the individual and should be so recognized by the teacher regardless of any crudities, limitations, or imperfections of technique. It is a using of his faculties, a testing of his potentialities. It is an exercising of the muscles of the mind. It is growth through exercise. It is creative health.

Such a process is rightly called creative and so has its important place in the creation of a work of art. *But the art lies more in the way such a vision is expressed* than it does in the recording of the inner vision itself. The capacity to express in some medium a concept in the mind is more within the usual range of used abilities than is the power to weld that concept into the qualities we call art. Take the concept, Child Skiing. This can be set down in a picture literally —a near copy of a photograph which freezes some one pose into a "still"—or it can be expressed as a riot of hilarious action true to the essential experience and an exciting color and space harmony —as a twelve-year-old has done in Fig. 5. The former process has its constructive values but these may be entirely outside the realm of art. Furthermore, the virtues of the process are equally effective when the order is reversed, when the sensitivity to relationships of parts is developed first and so is able to control expression as it deals with subject. A house is not "expressed" (or built) without a plan. Design is the emotional plan.

The value of design as the major source of aesthetic emotional experience is the deepest and richest value in the picture or, to be more conservative of statement, is a neglected value which is at least of equal importance with the interpretation of subject and which, because of the neglect, should be stressed first in compensation.

Design is universal in its applications; it can be present in all things produced by man out of color, space, and form including pictures, sculptures, crafts, merchandise, decorations, costume, gardening, architecture, and town planning. This universality gives it precedence over one department of its use—the picture dealing with tangible subject.

Design, on all these counts, should be understood, assimilated, and used.

ADVENTURE, EXPERIMENT, NEW EXPERIENCE

Perhaps these are the three most potent reasons why all people

Fig. 5.—*Skiing*, by GLADYS DANIELIAN, age 12.
Paterson, N. J., Public Schools. Helen Stanley, teacher.

FREE, EMOTIONAL CREATION

should practice and enjoy the arts. All human beings of all ages need adventure. Experiment is an awakening, a stimulating, a building process. New experience provides an excellent justification for living from day to day throughout the years. Without these three vitalizing forces life may become somnambulism, the daily routine a bore. The arts are probably the most certain way to provide such living insurance. Adventure should be the door through which the child or the amateur adult enters into the art experience.

CREATION

Art should never be a remote thing associated with long-dead masters or famous living "artists." It is something which every human being, including famous living "artists," can experience and practice. The child and the grownup can create pictures. They can sense harmonies of space and color. They can express an idea or a subject. If they copy these from others or from nature, or if they merely repeat recipes learned from an outside source, they are technicians. If they express these things in their own peculiar, personal, different way, then they are creating. They are building. They are expressing. They are getting the vital experiences which only a creator knows. Differences between one person and another's expression are inevitable (when there is no copying) and are one of the important reasons for an observer's interest in the work. Children should be praised for differences and for self-assertion in defending them. The six-year-old was right when she rebuked the snooping art supervisor who looked at her painting and then asked the silly question, "But, did you ever see a purple cow?" "No," came the indignant answer, "but this is the way a purple cow would look if I ever did see one." Divine courage that. May it never fail. Six-year-old artists are not afraid to remake nature to suit their tastes and the aesthetic demands of their picture. Would that all ages above six had a similar courage. The personal vision and expression, then, are prerequisites to genuine creation in art. In the next chapter we shall explore more fully the meaning and possibilities of this vital process.

EXPRESSION

Expression of the self and of reality as interpreted by the self is the logical role of creative expression. This term, it is frequently said, has been sadly abused in the past decade by such indiscriminate application to all manner of human activities that it has ceased to have any real meaning. Everything was creative expression or self-expression from throwing an exhibitionistic fit to painting a bad picture or running to school. Well, are they not just that? Is not every act we do, every gesture we make, every word we utter *self-expression?* And in a sense *creative expression?* Imitation is the expression of a poverty-stricken self. Exhibitionism, tantrums, moods, pretenses, deceits, destruction, building, walking across the room, talking, singing, dancing, playing a part, buying merchandise, going to a movie (or the choosing of the one to attend)—all are expressions of self. Just how "creative" some of these expressions are is another matter and a debatable one, but the power to create is in all people and there certainly is or can be some percentage of it in most human acts including the destructions of war. The words are not worn out; they never can be. They are as staple as sugar and salt.

Expressing reality means expressing essentials rather than superficialities. What are the realities of a dog or a man? Are they hair and clothes, the parts seen by the physical eye? Or are they the bodies under the outside covering, the disposition, the intelligence, the loyalty, the past experiences which make one individual different from another, which are the essence of the one? There are many realities; some can be seen, some must be inferred or known by other means than sight. The creative artist finds a way to see through the clothes to the man and to express unseen qualities. El Greco did that in painting the very spirit of religion reflected in the flamelike bodies of praying men. Bruno Krauskopf, modern German, has done it in his moving painting of the spirit of The Last Supper.[5] Naturalism in pictures copies surface facts. Realism portrays essentials.[6]

APPLICATION OF THE CREATIVE MIND TO LIFE

The creative mind and its agent, design, should function in all the activities of man. This is a broad statement and exceptions to it can doubtless be found. War, murder, intrigue may be called exceptions but the argument that design, in its functional rather than its aesthetic capacity, makes these acts effective certainly has validity. Our interest, however, is limited to the aesthetic. Within it comes the quality of man's environment—the quality of the houses, cities, merchandise which he produces and uses in everyday life. The environment man produces reveals the degree of the civilized life he has achieved. The arts as they are applied to life measure the national culture.

Every individual has considerable latitude in creating his own personal environment. He can use his creative mind in choosing that environment or he can abdicate his personal throne and allow

[5] Illustrated in *Experiencing Pictures* by the author, where it is contrasted to The Last Supper of Leonardo da Vinci.

[6] Sheldon Cheney makes no distinction between the two words "naturalism" and "realism"; he uses them interchangeably. This is unfortunate.

the average standards of a materialistic society to impose on him the average taste of his time. To do the former is to assume responsibility, to make his own decisions, and to act in accordance with them in spite of any outside difficulties. These are invigorating experiences; they imply life and growth. To escape them by evasion of the difficult way, by swimming with, rather than against, the current, by accepting the average trend is to dissipate one's potential powers, to go to sleep on the job of living, to miss half the excitement which that job may imply. We have creative capacities. They should be used.

If this responsibility is granted, then it becomes the duty of art education to recognize the universality of design and to encourage and teach applications of it to life. We shall suggest some of those applications as we proceed. In Chapter X a number of typical examples are recorded. Ways and means of achieving these goals will be discussed throughout the balance of this book.

The values to the individual and the nation which are inherent in using our creative powers in many applications to life and things should be experienced rather than talked about. Sufficient for the moment to say that these activities of spirit, mind, and hand tap the deepest and richest veins of human experience. They are the kind of activities which are furthest removed from the animal, most characteristic of man as man. They allow man to achieve the civilized life.

2. CREATION

"We live in a world in which there is an immense amount of organization, but it is an external organization, not one of the ordering of a growing experience, one that involves, moreover, the whole of the live creature, toward a fulfilling conclusion."

JOHN DEWEY

HAVING established a psychological atmosphere of emotional awareness, the first step of the art student (and under that title I shall hereafter include all people regardless of age, stage of development, or occupation who wish to participate in the art experience through doing) is to *create*. The subject does not matter. The medium does not matter. The degree of skill is irrelevant. So is the simplicity or complexity of the work. The thing that is relevant, the thing that is one of the two ingredients of pictorial art which are of supreme importance and without which the work does not exist as art, is that healthy process called *creation*.

THE WORD "CREATION." WHAT DOES IT MEAN?

To create means to produce, to bring into being from nothing, to cause to exist. An object like a chair may be created mechanically by following patterns or outside directions—physical production. Or it may be created pictorially as the result of a vision and an organization of past and present experience into an *expression* by the individual who does the producing. It is axiomatic that a work of art must be such an expression. It is the doing something with his materials in the unique way dictated by feeling, sensing, and visioning that causes the work to become art.

COPYING IS CRAFT, NOT ART

Albert Sterner, a distinguished artist of the Naturalistic School, expressed his standards in a session of the Town Meeting of the Air recently in these words: "Content is the important thing, not how we say it." Then he stressed craftsmanship as a means to telling a story. "The artist is a craftsman," he said, "creating beauty." And he meant re-creating the beauty observed in nature, not beauty *created* by the artist. Subject and the skill to portray it faithfully were his goals. Ours are the exact reverse.

Copying of any type, from nature or from another work of art, is not a creative process. It is a craft process. When, in a picture, we copy what the physical eyes see before them, the thing copied becomes the source and the picturemaker becomes an instrument which, with more or less skill, reports or records facts. A mirror is such an instrument. So is a camera. The Naturalistic School of art believes that an artist should be little more than such an instrument.

If from our total experience we can admit that the source of a work of art must be Man, the creator, and that he must weld subject, whatever it may be, into his own expression, then we are ready to admit that art must be creation and expression and that the two functions together, plus the amalgam of design, define the Grand Tradition of the ages. It is creative art which we are concerned with here.

THE ACT OF EXPRESSION

In pictures the building materials of the creator are subject, and the means, to its expression—line, space, color, light-dark, texture, planes, and form. Additional means are stone, clay, paint, ink, or any other medium. From all these materials the picture builder aims to present a new object with its own unique meaning—not merely the meaning of the portrayed objects as these may be observed in the actual scene and not merely the tangible evidence of emotional turmoil in himself which may have been aroused by his reactions to those objects—but rather a fusing of the two into an expression of just that meaning which he wishes to convey to the observer of his work. It is a process of spiritual distillation. He distills or abstracts from all the forces at hand, within himself and without, a purification of meanings both practical and aesthetic.

The above implies the maltreated term "self-expression." But self-expression is by no means the objective with which we are concerned. Rather, it is expression of subject as interpreted through the prism of self. It is the self acting on material with the emphasis on the end product, not on itself, which gives the subjective interpretation we are after. The self, in other words, is not an end; it is a means.

The genuinely creative artist does not want to find his aesthetic expression ready-made in some "beautiful" scene or object. He wants to do his own distilling of the purified essence from the medley of materials which surround him. He wants to observe, study, reflect, select, re-create, and organize. Also he shrinks from following the path laid down by another—from imitating another style, from repeating another recipe, even a former one of his own. If he is sensitive, the myriad of kaleidoscopic impressions constantly beating in upon him will inevitably affect any particular impressions, with which he may be dealing in a given work, differently at different times. Thus, if he were painting Man Sowing, the various conditions under which a man may sow—rain, sun, wind, dust, gloom—and the shifting of his own moods or interests would automatically condition each of a dozen interpretations differently, one from the others. This impact of outside and inside forces, if allowed to work on him, ensures originality as an automatic thing. Merely to copy nature or another artist means a shutting down of all the dynamos which generate the art within expression.

The act of expression must be prompted by an urge from within, by an emotional reaction to some stimulant. As has been said, however, it is not enough merely to have an emotion and to record it by some sort of objectified palpitation with brush or pencil. This process might create an interesting abstraction with art lurking just around the corner. Expression which rounds out to full formal meaning implies much more than that. It must be clarified and ordered by taking into itself the findings of past experience. It must overcome obstacles. It must remake the juxtapositions and meanings it may see or know in actual life. Take the woodcut by Lynd

Ward in Fig. 134 as an example of this purifying and remaking process. The girl has seized her violin to play for a father who has just tried and failed to commit suicide as an escape from his many defeats. Out of the mingled impacts of tragedy, pathos, hope, and despair the artist has wrung a masterly expression of human drama. Not one distracting detail. A perfect blending of content and form. A mature creative work.

When the creative artist studies nature he does not merely see actual colors and forms as does the layman. He unconsciously imposes on the elements he sees his own sense of order or form, as I have tried to show in the case of the old comforters of my opening chapter. Out of the natural scene he whips chords of color, space, plane, and form which reverberate in his own consciousness, which play their visual music on his sensibilities. His expressive task is to coordinate these with such aspect of subject as he wishes to stress or to impose them on his own concept of a subject which he may not actually see. Organization is the blanket word which covers this process; design is the more specific word. Emotion guides both.

Concern with expression rather than with fact and skill immediately frees the creator to play his harmonic chords of color, space, and form. The instinct to design can then function; it is not thwarted by conflict with an opposed objective.

Expression, as will be shown in the next chapter, can be a product either of the conscious mind or of feeling and sensing. Or it can grow out of a healthy blending of the two. Because conscious mind tends to limit its products to what is already known, can be thought out, remembered or seen, it is a severe limitation more than likely to result in tight, familiar, and usual work. A highly imaginative mind may partially escape this charge because it will range farther afield in the knowable and seeable but it will still remain within the concrete limits of conscious thought. The illustrations of Arthur Rackham, so popular a score of years ago, were of this type.

Feeling and emotion, on the other hand, are more elemental. They are a release into new and unknown pastures. Expression based on feeling automatically, because of the urge to organize thereby released, becomes art. Feeling plus thinking taps man's full expressive power.

The primary lesson for the student who accepts these statements as outlining the foundations of the art of expression is that he must shift his attention and study from the objective material all about him to this subjective interpretation. It is this process which is infinitely more important than skill in recording fact.

METHODS

The simplest possible step in pictorial expression is to set down a two-dimensional symbol in line, space, or color of some subject. Figure 87 shows such symbols of woman, monkey, and tree. The next step shifts from objective to subjective by saying something about subject; in Figs. 115 and 116 the artist says Man Runs and Man Swims. Primitive artists always said something about subject in their symbols. The deer is running, wounded or startled. Men kill bison. Men fight. To say something about subject in addition to naming it pictorially is the beginning of complexity—a complexity which can grow without limits to all manner of story or fact interpretation in limitless combinations of three-dimensional form design. The student of today can learn much from the primitive artist in this matter of having something to say about subject. Once adopted as a guide to creative practice, all mere painting of landscapes, posed models, and still life, where portraying of subject is the objective, will be superseded by an interpretation which includes meaning added by the artist. The child of today, if unspoiled, attacks this complex creative process without fear because he is unhampered by technical demands; the amateur and professional artist should, from the beginning, do the same.

Eastern philosophy in China and India assumed that the artist should lose himself in contemplation and a resulting identification with the thing to be expressed. To paint a fish he must, in his mind, become a fish; only so could he intimately know its character and movement. In both these civilizations through two thousand years this identification released artists into functional design—a design which grew out of the nature of subject; never did it abandon design for formless expression, never did it design without subject meaning. Always there was the perfect synthesis, the perfect blending of content and form achieved through this feeling of identification.[1]

[1] For an explanation of Indian philosophy see *The Dance of Siva,* by Ananda Coomaraswamy. Sunwise Turn, New York, 1924.

It is interesting to note that the nineteenth century degraded this great philosophy by giving all importance to subject and forgetting design. Thus Ruskin defines great art as that which includes the largest number of great ideas. And our recent worship of naturalism is a degradation even of that degradation.

DRAMATIZATION OF SUBJECT

The moment we are free to translate subject into our own interpretation it is almost inevitable that such an interpretation will play up, accentuate, or *dramatize* some one aspect which we wish to make the dominant interest of the picture. A skyscraper is tremendously high. We wish to accentuate that quality. We exaggerate it; we dramatize it. We ignore other lesser qualities or facts like texture of stonework or the thousands of windows. We get the *feeling* of great height. The freedom to dramatize is granted in other arts—the stage, poetry, the novel. Old habits have prevented the pictorial artist from free use of this liberating quality. Figure 6 is a dramatic picture. Total interest is centered on the dog's unethical act.

SYMBOLISM

When subject is re-created and designed it cannot be treated naturalistically. It cannot be copied from nature as seen by the physical eyes. It cannot be the mere factual record or replica. It is changed, rebuilt into a new entity which stands for or expresses subject.

A symbol is a sign by which one implies a thing or meaning. It is a token or emblem. Subject in a creative painting, then, becomes a symbol for the actual thing it represents. The difference between this function and that of a replica is far-reaching and must be clearly understood.

To use subject as a symbol in painting or sculpture is a great liberation. Instead of centering all his energies and skill in a faithful report of fact the artist can write his own meanings in a kind of pictograph language of his own invention. His symbols can be abstract like the Greek egg and dart, the swastika, the Hopi Indian pottery symbols; they can be semiabstract as in Fig. 3; they can

Fig. 6.—*Dog Stealing Hot-dog,* by JOSEPH PATRIZZ, age 12.
Paterson, N. J., Public Schools. Helen Stanley, teacher.

A DRAMATIC PICTURE

be realistic as in Fig. 19. In all these different degrees of abstraction (the realistic picture of a subject can be called an abstraction, for it is changed from the superficial to the fundamental truth or reality) the artist can make his symbol have special meanings which he wants to emphasize. Thus if he were painting a symbol for Man he could stress the strength or weakness of man, his bulk-weight, weariness, gaiety, or craftiness. The external surface of man's clothes, which is the part seen by the physical eye, has little to do with any of these qualities. Therefore, in the symbol, they can be subordinated to bulging muscles, a drooping position, cutting capers, slinking movement. The symbol can stress any of these meanings and still say Man. Also it can say Negro, Indian, Chinese, fireman, soldier, and countless other types.

The naturalistic picture also, of course, can say all these things and so may be called a symbol in a pictograph language. But it has limitations which can never be overcome as long as it remains a record of actual fact. It is more facsimile than symbol. It is tied to the literal, all-there statement; there are no added meanings, no poetry, no dramatization or exaggeration of facts to give heightened meaning. And there is no possibility of design.

Design is facilitated by the symbol. The symbol can be built into design. Being a sign, it can add to the function of meaning that of pleasing the eye by its *decorative* quality. When an artist designs he must rebuild subject into the different entity which fits his purpose. The act of so doing is in effect the changing of subject into a symbol. The two processes really are one. To translate subject into a symbol, to think of it as a symbol is a natural and effective step in the process of creation and design.

An artist at any stage of his development may be moved by many different stimuli to create a picture.

DESIGNED ABSTRACTION AND NONOBJECTIVITY

One artist may be interested primarily in the aesthetics of his art and, like Bauer and Kandinsky, paint nonobjective improvisations with no subject implications whatever—with the entire emphasis on design (see Fig. 7). Another may play his visual harmonies with abstractions taken from subject with their symbolic meanings, as in Fig. 40. In either case visual music is the chief concern.

REALITY OR NATURALISM

Another artist may be deeply conscious of the quality of things about him—the character and movement of human beings, animals, clouds, water, fire, the color, texture, form of a landscape or city street, of grass, rocks, flowers, weeds, sand, and be driven to express that quality. If he copies what he sees literally he is a naturalistic artist. If he expresses essential, rather than literal, truth he is a realist creating realistic pictures.

PROPAGANDA

A third artist may be conscious of the drama of human life—the social problems and injustices, the tragedy of war or crime—and have a burning desire to interpret these so that others will understand and, perhaps, improve conditions. So obsessed may he be with conveying meanings that all refinements of aesthetics are forgotten or discarded; we then have the propaganda picture.

DESIGNED REALITY

Finally, the more mature artist may combine the two; that is, he may be interested in the social scene or any subject but equally absorbed in building his interpretation into plastic design. In this more rounded out personality art is welded with subject and great art may be the result. Orozco is an outstanding example of this mature type.

The abstract, or nonobjective, picture may also be great art. The marriage of content and form widens the range of experience values but it is impossible to say with any other validity than that of personal opinion that the one is greater than the other.

* * *

All these motivations, if the artist belongs to the Modern School, will have at least two characteristics in common—the artist's drive to make tangible his vision, his feeling, his interpretation, his *expression,* and to build this into design.

NONOBJECTIVE PAINTING

The Soloman R. Guggenheim Foundation at its museum in New York City presents to the American public a constant but changing exhibition of nonobjective paintings, mostly by the German, Rudolf Bauer, and the Frenchman, Vasily Kandinsky. This exhibition is of great importance and should be studied and enjoyed by everyone who is alert to the art movements of his time. The museum itself is a masterful harmony in warm gray and music.

The Baroness Hilla Rebay explains nonobjective painting for the museum both in lectures and in the forewords to the various catalogues. Out of some hundreds of lines of such catalogue explanation she devotes perhaps a dozen lines to the relatively tangible qualities of color, line, and space harmonics and the remainder to romantic, verbal rhapsodies about "elevation into the cosmic beyond," "spirituality beyond comprehension," "elating beauty," "elevation and blissful oblivion from earthly reminiscence," "beauty in unearthly pictures," etc. The main trend of her argument is to the effect that the aesthetic experience is remote from daily life, a higher and purer ecstatic state, a supreme heavenly good in contrast to the baseness of the common way, an aristocrat of the spiritual world.

From this exuberant explanation emerge two significant facts. Nonobjective painting breaks all contacts with tangible objects and tangible meaning; it is not symbolic of the objective world. The experience offered by Nonobjective painting is above and distinct from ordinary human experience.

The first of these facts is verifiable in the paintings of Bauer and Kandinsky—unless one wishes to argue that the circle, triangle, and square which they so frequently use are symbols with acquired human meanings (as they certainly are). But no symbols of tangible, objective objects are used; that is obvious. So any meanings read into the works are entirely subjective. It is from these subjective meanings that Baroness Rebay has opened the floodgates of her own imagining and poured forth a torrent of word-symbols which give ample evidence of her own emotional excitement but have little other tangible meaning. Why, if the paintings themselves abjure all "meaning" of a practical kind, must she pour over them heavy layers of meaning of a spiritual kind? Why not merely observe and enjoy the works as sensitive visual symphonies, in the same alert way in which one enjoys music? It is the privilege of any individual, of course, to indulge in verbal rhapsody but it is most unfortunate to impose rhapsody on others as the authentic way to appreciation with the weight and dignity of an exhibition foreword.

The paintings of Bauer and Kandinsky are sensitive creations in line, space, color, texture, and movement harmonics. Some are dominantly intellectual, some dominantly emotional. Bauer tends to the intellectual or the severe geometric motif as shown in Fig. 7 *c*, and I think it is fair to say that geometric motifs are intellectualizations. Kandinsky tends to the emotional, as in Fig. 80. Bauer also taps pure emotion, as in Fig. 7 *c* and *d*, and both artists, like Leger in Fig. 8, combine thinking and feeling as these must be combined in a mature and rounded work of art.

The assumption that aesthetic experience is remote from ordinary experience has been effectively refuted by Dewey, I. A. Richards, and other philosophers and I think most creative artists will agree that, though it releases strong emotional power, it is a sharpening and an extending of ordinary human capacities rather than an

Fig. 7.—Nonobjective painting, by RUDOLF BAUER.

Fig. 8.—Nonobjective painting, by FERNAND LEGER.

All on this page are from the Solomon R. Guggenheim collection.

Note the extraordinary complexity of the harmonic relationships of line, space, texture, dark-light, and form. Color harmonies are equally complex and subtle.

NONOBJECTIVE PAINTING

Fig. 8A.—Nonobjective painting, *Pointed and Round*, by MAURINE BUSH, Taos School of Art. Emil Bistram, instructor.

One of a series of nonobjective paintings planned with Dynamic Symmetry proportions and directions as taught by Mr. Bistram.

escape from them into an ideal heaven of the "spirit" as distinct from the mundane "body." The two are inextricably interwoven in the pattern of human experience.

Emil Bistram, in his Taos School of Art, has been teaching nonobjective and abstract painting, as well as realistic, for a number of years. All his own painting is based on Dynamic Symmetry, of which he is a master because of his long study with Jay Hambidge and his subsequent research and experimentation in collaboration with Howard Giles, and all his teaching includes instruction in the use of its principles. Beyond this Mr. Bistram's school, in his own words, "features a technique based on the understanding and mastery of essential forms, spatial interrelationships, color values, balance and integration of motives and all problems of handling of materials." Such a program obviously indicates a direction "away from the mere representation of sense-perceived objects and from a photographic consciousness of the outer world." This is the kind of redirection of student energy needed in art education and the mathematical precision which Dynamic Symmetry can give to felt design is an extension of design potentialities in which I have complete faith. Provided only that the mathematics is used as a tool instead of a crutch and that feeling and sensing direct its use instead of only conscious mind. Intellectualized design can go dead even when it conforms to Dynamic Symmetry laws.[2]

The organization of circles and directional line movements in Fig. 8A is a sensitive and fairly successful combination of felt and mathematical design. The feeling here has authenticated the mathematics.

ABSTRACT PAINTING

Abstract painting, as distinct from nonobjective, does tie up to reality, does have references to subject and meaning, can be used as a symbol for such references.

The word "abstract" means to lead out from, to deduce from. This can be interpreted by the artist as taking suggestions from or essential meaning out of. Thus an abstract painter can extract some one quality of an object—say the color from a lemon—and use that quality to stand for the object or to become a new entity in its own right to be joined with other such entities into a new conception. Or he can select from the obvious realities around him whose surfaces are seen by the physical eye deeper realities which are not visible. A human being has surface truths—clothes, skin, hair, etc.—and inner truths—character, moods, habits which cannot be seen by the observ-

[2] In *How to See Modern Pictures* (Dial Press, 1925) I have shown in diagrams the basic principles of Dynamic Symmetry as it relates to pictorial design. In *Experiencing Pictures* (Harcourt, Brace & Company, 1932) I have commented briefly on the virtues and dangers of its use, stressing how a lack of design knowledge with a resultant attempt to impose mathematical proportion on naturalism can only give hopeless confusion to a picture.

The complete presentation of the principles was presented by Jay Hambidge in twelve issues of the *Diagonal*, a magazine published by Yale University Press in 1920.

ing eye, except as they are revealed by signs or actions. Certainly it is possible to paint in some symbolic way a mean disposition, deceit, conflict, hate, love, kindness. The abstract painter can explore such fields, paint the unseen realities which are just as *real* as the observable ones. There is a vast mine of possibilities in such delving into the inner nature of man and things which stirs, challenges, and arouses curiosity and interest. These possibilities should be used by the artist and welcomed by the observer as a rich addition to the concrete and matter-of-fact. We need abstract works of art in many media.

The symbol is a way of expressing such nontangible meanings. Stuart Davis in his mural, Men Without Women, in Radio City Music Hall (Fig. 37) has used such symbols to tell his story. Playing cards, barber's pole, the ponies, yachting, cigarettes, machines are among his symbols—each telling its implied story of compensating activities. The symbol is a necessary means to abstraction as long as any tie-up to reality is intended. Abstraction means generalization. As meanings depart from the specific to the general they expand, they have growing implications which the abstract symbol alone can express. When meaning has become so general that it loses all specific communicative function then the emphasis will normally shift to design and pure aesthetics. The meaning and aesthetic power of pictures can greatly expand through the use of abstraction.

SURREALISM

The Surrealist Movement, born in the disillusionment of a group of French artists at the insanities of war, was such a widening of pictorial experience. It extended the field of the picture from the known to the unknown, from conscious to unconscious mind. In the beginning it barred all exercise of reason and every aesthetic and moral consideration. It symbolized the chaos of human life by deliberate chaos in the picture. The Dadaists, who immediately preceded the Surrealists, would stage an evening entertainment with two lecturers shouting meaningless words at the top of their voices accompanied by the beating of tom-toms, discords on a piano, and a prize fight all at one and the same time. As the movement developed, Arp, Ernst, Miro, Pierre Roy, and Dali returned to some degree of order by exploring within the general confines of Thought or the Concept, either conscious or unconscious. Gradually the bar on aesthetics fell away—an interesting side light on its necessity—and Picasso, Klee, Miro, and Chirico, design-conscious artists all, brought design and with it aesthetics back to the visions of the subconscious mind. What matter how weird or "crazy" these pictures are with their dripping watches and grotesque distortions? It is just this picturing of the unreal that is their main value. They break with the obvious. They offer a world of startling new experiences in the departments of both subject and design.

Creation involves the ordering of a growing experience, one that involves the whole of the live creature, toward a fulfilling experience.

3. THE EMOTIONAL VS. THE INTELLECTUAL APPROACH

> Emotion is as the sunlight to the seed of art, and the seed in time is fruit.
>
> MAX WEBER

ALL art and art education, as has been said, can be divided into two general schools—the Naturalistic School and the School of Designed Creation, which at the moment we call Modern. The Modern School, however, is by no means a unity in its understanding of basic principles; within it are several subdivisions. The two most important of these are the divisions whose motivation and methods spring dominantly from feeling and sensing, in the one case, and from intellect, in the other. These two divisions both rightly belong within the Modern Movement and the Grand Tradition because they have progressed beyond the craft of copying, because they do re-create subject into their own interpretation, and because they can know and practice design. But the differences in their understanding and practice are at opposite poles, as we shall discover. Another subdivision within, or on the borders of, the Modern School may be called the School of Confusion. Its members, and they are numerous, have sensed the inadequacies of copying and have floundered into more creative ways without comprehending where they are going, how they are to get there, or what is the meaning of the conflicts in which they find themselves.

Producing and experiencing works of art are not thinking processes. They are not matters of skill. They go much deeper within human capacities than these functions of conscious mind and hand. They are more mysterious, less possible to explain. They root in sensitivity. They are intuitional in the sense of not being reasoned. We *feel* that certain colors are harmonious. We respond with emotional excitement to the harmonies of music, movement, color, space, and form. We cannot adequately explain why we like certain harmonic chords of sound or colors; they move us, we enjoy them, that is about all we can say in words.

The urge to create, as has been said, can spring from the emotional excitements of design with no reference to content or it can grow naturally out of deep feelings about life experience—sorrow, joy, love, hate, or any other reaction to human or inanimate environment. In either case the drive to create may be authentic.

No art teacher whom I know of has developed the latent powers of students to express their emotional reactions to life as potently as has Florence Cane and nowhere in print, perhaps, can one find a better brief explanation of this process than in her article in *Art Education Today* for 1937[1] on "Possibilities of Integration through Art."

The only difference between Mrs. Cane's point of view and the one here advanced is that she ignores design and its emotional values even though it springs from the same subconscions sources she knows so well. This argument includes hers, adds the great field of design to it, then gives precedence to that design on the well-proved theory that the developed power to organize will facilitate expression of any urge or subject. She lists "composition," her nearest approach to design, among the skills and argues for free, emotional expression as the beginning of the art experience—the skills to develop later as a means to clarification and amplification. I agree on this last point but do not list design, or even composition, as a skill. If Mrs. Cane included design in her sound emotional approach she would complete the wholeness for which she argues. Without it the work of her students would be expected to fall to pieces through lack of an integration similar to that which each one has achieved in the department of the concept itself. Here is a pretty paradox of wide importance to art education. *Design is of equal importance to concept.* Both must be authenticated through emotion. Free emotional expression without the discipline of design is unbalanced confusion.[2]

---

[1] Published by Teachers College, Columbia University.

[2] An interesting light on this issue is revealed by the illustrations of student work in Mrs. Cane's article. Since nothing in the article shows that she teaches or values de-

Once this sensory, or feeling, approach to works of art is granted, we can bring into play the conscious mind as a supplementary force. We can examine our emotions and their causes; we can be as aware as possible of the how and why of them—even, perhaps, to the extent of finding their roots, not in the art of the work, as they should be, but in some extraneous matter associated with subject or in a personal liking or disliking of the artist or his wife or even in our own particular mood. To be conscious of our own emotional reactions is intelligent. To be limited to intelligence in the response to a work of art is to miss the richest vein of human experience.

To attempt to acquire "art appreciation" through the study of art history based on dates, places, personalities, trends, and other related data may be useful or interesting for other reasons but it can completely fail to find the art in a work of art. For the only authentic contact with the art in a work of an old or a modern master is through this same kind of emotional participation in the sensations it offers—a two-way radio exchange of stimulation and response. The student whose learning is limited to an intellectualized field is losing his birthright to a share in the art of the ages.[3]

---

sign, it would be a fair assumption that her students would ignore it or show ignorance of it in their work. Three examples, Nos. 1, 2, and 5, show such ignorance. One, No. 3, has a crude but authentic design sense and one, No. 4, is well integrated with a sense of design that even leans strongly toward the propriety of the intellectual. This outcropping of design in spite of neglect proves its universality. It is in all men. It cannot be downed by ignorance or neglect—even though the grasp on it be lost by some individuals and some historical periods.

[3] Art criticism that is not based on an emotional contact with the art in the work of art becomes as aesthetically barren as any intellectualized production can be. This is true no matter how erudite the critic may be or how much information he may give about other matters.

Thomas Craven is a critic who has attained eminence by an unremitting attack on the aesthetics of the French Modern Movement and on aesthetics in general. No invective has been too raw for him to use—his definition of Surrealism as "the culminating rot of European gadget-makers" is typical, rather than unusual. Let me quote from my review of his *Treasury of Art Masterpieces* (Simon & Schuster, New York, 1939), published in *Forum Magazine* for November, 1939:

I have called Craven a healthy irritant in contemporary art criticism because he challenged the anaemia of some studio pictures and the snobbishness of aesthetic sham. This needed to be done and the deliberate vulgarity of Craven's attack, used apparently as effective publication and reader insurance, did gain an outlet for art writing in popular magazines and the Hearst press. Also his preoccupation with the American scene was healthy; artists did need to return to life as a source. On other aspects of criticism Craven is ignorant, destructive and negative.

His ignorance is spotlighted by his generalized sneers at all aestheticism instead of at the patently "pseudo"; by his talk about pictorial form and his general failure to

(*Footnote continued on page 36*)

Of these three main types of art and education the naturalistic way is still probably the one most widely accepted and practiced (even though definitely on the decline). The intellectualized modern is the most widely accepted and used in the general progressive field. The way which roots in the emotions is the least comprehended and applied. This is the inevitable result of our materialistic civilization and practical, literal habits of mind. To counteract these tendencies of our time, to free the spirit within us of these fetters to the literal fact, is another tremendous responsibility of the new art education. Emotion—the faculty of feeling and sensing, as the word is used in psychology—is the food and language of the spirit. Emotion is the way to emancipation of spirit. It is the way in which we can feed and cause to grow powers within all of us, powers which alone can break the bondage to materialism.

Differences between the emotional and intellectual ways of working are not always easy to distinguish in a given work. Obviously they overlap; a genuine creation will have both, the conscious mind can and should guide the emotions. Extremes in both directions—the cold-blooded, tight, thought-out work and the free, wild, emotional spree—can be easily recognized. But, as the two forces merge, all we can do in an attempt at intelligent criticism is to decide that this work is dominantly intellectual or dominantly emotional. Or we can say that the blending seems right. The main necessity is to

(*Continued from preceding page*)
apply it; by his constant, indiscriminate sniping at the "Paris School"; by his one-sided standard of values, with all the emphasis placed on the artist's (healthy) identification with "localism"; and finally by his definition of style.

On this last point he quotes Taine's definition of style as "environment affecting form" and then goes on to interpret this definition in these words: "Taine stressed, as the most important element in the formation of style, the artist's response to the substance and color of his environment."

But Taine did not stress this as the most important element. He said style was environment affecting *form*—a diametrically opposite conception. Here *form* is the dominant matter; environment gives it specific character. Craven sees through colored glasses; he bends Taine to conform to his more limited vision.

When Craven talks of form and design it is always as a means to an end (where he admits its utility) or as decoration, which he tolerates as trimming. Never does he reveal comprehension of its (hated) aesthetic function. Craven would not hate aesthetics if he knew through experience the emotional content of the term. Americans are a practical people, he says. Artists should conform to the "group feelings and attributes of their people." So does he define for us the limits of his own practical vision.

* * * * * *

Craven has discarded aesthetics from art criticism. That is his great destructive contribution to the public which reads him—a contribution that is dangerously amplified by this impressive book.

have the emotional base on which conscious mind may act. *Art education must be built on the solid foundation of this emotional approach to doing and experiencing.*

THE INTELLECTUAL APPROACH

What is meant by intellectual art?

An art in which the source of concept and method is conscious mind. Conscious mind is limited to what is *known,* to what is definite and tangible, to what can be thought out and set down with precision. The tremendous limitation of this process can be better realized by shifting to another art, music, where a thought-out composition or a thinking appreciation would obviously be absurd. With visual art the thinking process, if we only know it, is equally absurd.

One of the millstones around the neck of art education in this country today is the fact that the cerebralists do not comprehend sensory experience or the emotional reaction to *form,* even though in some cases they may more or less speak its word language. Since they are in the numerical majority, have the widest following and influence, it seems important, at this point, to join issue with them and get into the record the extreme opposite character of the two approaches.

Mr. Francis H. Taylor[4] becomes a spokesman for intellectualized art teaching in an article in *Art Education Today,* published by Teachers College of Columbia University in 1935, when he explains that the Worcester Museum, in its children's classes in "creative design," uses "simple derivative systems similar to those described in the books of Prof. Eggers and Best-Maugard" and then goes on to quote and register agreement with the following statement by George Biddle. "Art," says Biddle, "is the individual's critique, or reaction, or reconstruction of life expressed in certain design or rhythm in a given medium. One cannot, then, postulating this approach, place any great value on child art. A child's critique of life, expressed in painting or sculpture, no matter how interesting it may be from the angle of education or child analysis, has no more importance than a child's critique of philosophy or science."

---

[4] Former director of the Worcester Museum of Art, now director of the Metropolitan Museum of Art in New York City.

Since Mr. Taylor acknowledges that he used a "derivative" system, I do not need to argue that point; I only comment that all such systems are obvious intellectualizations. And when Biddle tests a child's work by its capacity as a "critique of life" instead of as a harmonic creation he, too, reveals his intellectual bias and his apparent blindness to the qualities of design and rhythm which he mentions. The fact that he does include design and rhythm in his definition of art is interesting and typical of the Intellectual School. Design qualities, to the intellectual artist or teacher, are useful as a means to making the expression of subject more effective but they apparently see in them no emotional values over and above this utilitarian one. When authorities so limit themselves to an intellectualized art and pass on their own limitations to children, or any students, the aesthetic barrenness of our dominant national attitude toward the arts is perpetuated and the children and students lose their natural inheritance of joyous creation. Child art is important *as art* when it is that, and the Lord of Creation knows (if we do not) that aesthetically starved adults need all the art they can find in life—even that of little children.

Mr. Charles J. Martin, Professor of Fine Arts at Teachers College, wrote in *Art Education Today* for 1939 an article on murals done by his students for Russell Hall of the college. This article is another and excellent exposition of intellectualism in art education—both in the article and in the murals described and illustrated. I quote:

> The style for this mural was arrived at . . . after a study through reproductions of successful decorations by contemporary masters. It was a style which might be described as semiabstract, combining almost flat areas of color with geometrically simplified lines.

No creative artist with a *feeling* for the quality of things would choose a style for his work, *at any stage of his development,* by the external method of studying and adapting the work of any other artist. He would evolve his own style through self-reliance in his own powers and philosophy and through the needs of the task at hand. A man's style in any medium is a part of the man. To borrow a style is a confession of spiritual poverty. Just a few paragraphs back Martin had said, "Style develops unconsciously out of work."[5]

In the main body of his article Mr. Martin asks a number of questions with the purpose of "directing the thinking of art teachers toward the clarification of a philosophy with respect to the teaching of design." Among them this:

"What proportion of teaching time should be devoted to free expression and how much to the discipline of abstract design?" And a bit later: "How can we reconcile free, creative expression with the more or less abstract character of modern design?"

But why separate free expression and abstract design? Free expression, I am arguing, is the one and only means to all authentic, original design including the abstract. Design means organization of elements—colors, spaces, lines, planes, and forms. Whether these elements exist with or without subject is relatively unimportant. To call abstract design "discipline" is as good as labeling it intellectual. Discipline by mind to control emotion is necessary, of course, but such discipline is merely a means to an important end. The power to organize felt harmonies is the important matter.

Martin calls modern design "more or less abstract." Again, why so limit it? Design covers all art creation—abstract or realistic. Later he amplifies this: "The nearer the new design approaches a pure state of abstraction the more the design must conform to the laws of geometry." Why so, in heaven's name? It can be geometrical. It can be mathematical with definite, measured space intervals. It can be pure emotional improvisation. Or it can combine the two—the emotion authenticating the mathematics. Hopi Indian pottery symbols are not geometric or mathematical; they are freely drawn, felt designs.

Mr. Martin admits that what he labels the Free Expression School may be "valuable to the untrained student in the first stages of his art education" and then goes on to say, "the weakness of the

[5] The fact that this mural was a group product and had to be produced within a limited time may be used as an excuse for the specific event. Granted that group sensitivities may be difficult to synchronize within set time limits, the difficulty cannot justify, in my opinion, either the event or the method. Even conflicting free improvisation would have avoided the barrenness of the conventional, thought-out pattern.

method lies in its failure to provide a continuity and progression into new and increasingly difficult problems." Why assume this lack? Why assume that free expression does not do just the reverse—gain in complexity and call on mental discipline with continuity and progression into increasingly difficult problems? If he includes sensory experience in his definition of free expression—and it should be so included, for free expression releases sensory powers from their enslavement to conscious mind—then he should know that sensing and feeling must apply on all levels of complexity and that to lose them is to sink into the aesthetic sterility of intellectualized art.

By the statement of such theories Mr. Martin places himself within the intellectual branch of the Modern School. The issue between this and the emotional branch is clean-cut and important. Obviously there are values in each, and many overlappings. But the emotional is the more authentic and should dominate the picture. This is my argument. The reader will make his own decision.[6]

One more instance of intellectualized teaching comes through the students of a certain school which shall remain nameless because the report is secondhand. The method of having the students understand the various "isms" within the Modern Movement—Cubism, Futurism, Dadaism, Surrealism, Impressionism, Cézanneism, etc—was to have them paint for some two weeks like Cézanne, then two weeks like the Cubists, the Futurists, etc., the assumption apparently being that understanding of an art comes through imitation of style.

Against such copying of a style I would have students understand and practice the qualities which *are* the Modern Movement—qualities which include all valid isms within them—creation and felt design. This means assimilation, participation from within. It means self-confidence to be oneself within a vital movement. It develops and gives importance to a personal style. It allows one to observe with interest and comprehend other styles. But it would disdain copying as irrelevant, as a waste of time, as superficial, and as a thoroughly bad educational goal.

[6] Teachers College, with its large and varied staff of instructors, has done important pioneer work in breaking down the old copying traditions and establishing the new. Arthur Dow was the first to start this process long before the official art schools even guessed there was an issue. The college publication, *Art Education Today*, is ample evidence that the process continues today.

Under the head of intellectualized art education I think it is fair to list the many valuable studies in personality development through the arts which, stemming from Dewey, have gained increasing statement and currency in recent years. Caroline B. Zachry, Director of Research, Commission on Secondary School Curriculum, Progressive Education Association, states the case excellently in her article in *Art Education Today* for 1937 on "The Role of Mental Hygiene in the Arts." Says Dr. Zachry:

> In order to understand the function of mental hygiene in the arts it becomes necessary, then, to re-evaluate the relationship that exists between the two. It is important to recognize that they are inextricably bound together. Both are concerned with the "ordering of growing experience"; both involve the whole creature moving toward a fulfilling conclusion. The artist asks of the individual that he make an order out of chaos, that he take what he perceives in imagination and convey relationships of ordered form and content within some given medium. The mental hygienist asks of the individual that he make a related order out of the disintegrated experiences of which his life is composed, and through his action or behavior find the fulfillment of his growing experience. Both have the same struggle for coherence in an incoherent society. Both seek the same fulfillment.

This recognizes the need for organizing chaos both in art expression and in personal experience. The rest of the article stresses the mental hygiene benefits from such ordering. So far so good.

But, and this is a tremendous *but,* nowhere does Dr. Zachry show that she recognizes the aesthetic emotional experience of formal organization (design) in the arts as a positive value that goes far beyond the practical values of organizing and expressing human experience. The article continues:

> There are two aspects of an art product which must be considered in criticizing its quality. First, the content—that is, the originality, insight, sensitivity, imagination and richness of ideas which the student has to express. Second, the technical skill, which includes the mastering of such things as color, form, composition, light and shade.

Composition is here listed as a technical skill. The word "composition" is often confused with design even by some modern artists. Or it is used by the Naturalistic School to mean arrangement without any design implications whatever. Since Dr. Zachry does not mention the aesthetics of design at any time, the assumption is natural that she either accepts the confusion without investigation or is a victim of the widespread ignorance in this field.

According to the evidence of this article, the one by Mrs. Cane and many others by able and progressive educators, all the values of the organization and expression of experience are recognized *except the one greatest value.* It is an incredible omission. It seems to indicate a blind spot in highly developed intellectuals. If they are not blind to aesthetic emotional values how can they fail to stress them? Everything they say is right; in what they fail to say lies the great lack.

Intellectualization, then, of the art experience is not necessarily "wrong"—its devotees obviously have a right to play in that field if they wish—it is a limitation and a missing of deeper emotional values. As a limitation it is most unfortunate.

When modern ideology and practice settle into routine, when forms become stereotypes, when a fresh vision fails to penetrate the always encircling fog of the obvious and familiar, when the modern picturemaker becomes a creature of habit instead of a creator, then the motivation must shift from the emotions to some branch of the realm of intellect. Habit must dwell at least in the suburbs of the conscious mind; the habit-ridden artist certainly is not responding with emotional alertness to sensory impressions. Rather, it is the going to sleep of such awareness which degenerates into habit and its clichés.

Such going to sleep at the switch is a human weakness and as likely to strike within the modern ranks as within those of any other school. Except that the Academicians are more conditioned to professional sleep; that is what the word means. Academic practice is that which has become standardized. The Moderns can fall into standardized ways; there can be and is academic Modernism.

4. DESIGN

The old painter Demetrius greatly injured his glory because he was more zealous in catching resemblances than in attaining beauty.

LEON BATTISTA ALBERTI 1484

UNIVERSAL DESIGN

THROUGH thousands of years of human history there has been in man a strange sense that has compelled him to create order out of chaos. Design is one name for that sense of order.

Man's sense of order, or design, may be practical, that is, concerned with efficiency, neatness, economy of time, space or money. Or it may be concerned with function, as in a machine, to get effective operation of all parts in performing a certain task.

Again, design may go beyond practical order into a kind of order or relationship of parts which acts on our sensibilities as we respond to them through the senses of sight and hearing. To give pleasure through playing on human sensibilities as on a musical instrument is an inadequate way to state the purpose of this ordering of parts. The effect of it goes deep within us to the very roots of the capacities, which are of the spirit rather than of the body. Yet the ordering is not detached from body functions, from everyday experiences. It is a crystallization of them into a purified form. It is a kind of spirit language with universal human meanings that go far beyond the limits of the concrete and the particular—which cross all superficial boundaries of language, nationality, and time. It communicates the rhythms which are native to man by building them into a form which should be understandable by all men.

The design sense is inherent in human capacities. All persons *can* share, if they will, in its excitements through both practice and appreciation. The ability so to participate can be developed and its range of applications endlessly extended. When once developed in any person it comes into play automatically whenever he deals with or responds to certain combinations of sounds, movements, words, thoughts, lights, lines, spaces, and forms. It is in human blood to dance, to listen and beat time to music, to sing, to write or respond to the rhythms of poetry, to act a part on a stage, to enjoy the harmonics of color, space, and form.

Design applies to all the arts. Drama could not be an art without the application of design to the play itself, to its acting, and to the living picture on the stage. Music is design of sounds in chords, repeats, accents, variations, interweavings, and time intervals; subject, when implied, is definitely incidental, submerged in the design. The dance is design of movement. Poetry is design of thoughts and words. The essay, the novel, the oration, and the verbal or written argument are designed both for practical and for aesthetic reasons. Design permeates all the arts. It is their lifeblood. It gives cohesion and effective meaning to the vision and expression of the universal artist. If our education in the arts were thorough—if it were a national objective to assimilate and use the arts in the national life —we would study universal art before any particular art just as we now study the English language before any special department of learning. And the study of universal art would have to start with the study of design.[1]

DESIGN IN THE PICTURE AND SCULPTURE

Design has dominated the art of the picture and sculpture throughout human history except in those relatively few periods when the quest for truth facilitated the decline into the factual statement. The late Greek and Roman were such factual periods. Both are now commonly called decadent. Our own recent past is such a period—but its similar decadence is not generally understood or admitted. In most other periods and in practically all civilizations in both

[1] I should like to prophesy that the day will come when there will be a genuine school of Universal Art and that the idea, once demonstrated, will spread throughout this and other nations. The directors of such a school would have to be masters of creative design in each art field who could work out an integrated program. This would start with the universal aspects of design—organized rhythm and harmony—and advance into the particular field. Progress is now being made in this direction; there are schools which correlate several arts. But our knowledge of universal art is so incomplete that, in such a school, one is more than likely to find designed music and the dance but naturalistic painting and sculpture. Or one finds teachers who talk the design language and mainly miss its application in practice. Perhaps this will be the next and the most important of all steps in the development of art education.

Eastern and Western Hemispheres, from the earliest Stone Age paintings on the walls of caves up through the flowering period of the European Renaissance, creation and design have been the means to an immense diversity of works of visual art. Today the modern renaissance developing in us and among us is continuing that flowering. It is opening long-closed doors. It is discovering in us and in history the experience and values of universal art.

Design, as has been said, makes a picture effective in portraying subject. It dramatizes subject content. It brings order out of chaos, that is to say, for practical reasons. But it also adds a new dimension to pictures—an aesthetic dimension; it plays harmonic chords of all the elements with which the picture is built. And the values so contributed validate the practical values connected with subject and its expression.

The building materials of design in pictures and sculptures are subject, medium, line, space, color, texture, dark-light, planes, and form.

There are several ways in which design works on these materials when it organizes them within the picture frame or within the total mass of a work in sculpture:

1. It crystallizes a specific order out of the confusions of the physical and mental environment and so contacts the cosmic order of the universe.
2. It controls the choice and placing of objects in the picture field. This function is covered by the word "composition" and can apply also in the naturalistic picture.
3. It controls directional movements of objects into positions which carry the eye into and through the picture field with some one position, if so desired, dominant in size and place. This also is covered by composition.
4. It creates a different kind of *movement* totally distinct from the directions of lines of movement in a subject (as in a leaning telephone pole) or the rendering of physical movement (as in a dancing figure). This movement is induced by relationships of planes, colors, forms. It is a kind of vibration acting on the sensibilities; it leads the eye to leap from one color or plane to others which complement it as part of a chord. It is self-contained movement operating within the limits of the picture field. It is the dynamics of interacting relationships. It is called plastic movement.

   Recorded natural movement would destroy this plastic movement just as the intrusion of any natural or copied material from the actual scene would destroy design in general. The Brueghel painting of a dance in Fig. 19 is a masterly example of such plastic movement.

5. It organizes subject and each pictorial element—lines, spaces, colors, dark-lights, textures, forms, and planes (the surfaces of forms)—separately into harmonic chords and at the same time integrates or harmonizes each with all the others.

   This organization can be in two or three dimensions.
   It can be simple or immensely complex.
   It results in what the Moderns call PLASTIC FORM.

The designed picture becomes an entity in itself instead of a recorded fragment of nature. It creates its own world, it has its own laws, it becomes a source of experience and gives forth its own values which are different from the values experienced from nature. It serves the spectator, not as an illusion of actual objects, but as an expression of a human soul which concentrates its vision of cosmic order in the universe into the pristine glory of a creation called a work of art. The recognition of this break with the actual appearance and the substitution for it of a source of new and different experience is the first requirement both for producing and for comprehending a designed work of pictorial art.

COMPOSITION

The familiar term "composition" means merely effective arrangement. It includes selection, omission, balance, emphasis, dominance—all qualities which can exist in the natural scene and be transferred to canvas with little if any intervention of the creative or design sense. The naturalistic artist, when he goes out "sketching," tends to hunt for ready-made pictures of a "beautiful" scene which he can then copy without disturbance of or demands on his creative will. Or he will select, omit, and arrange by calling on the fringes of his buried organizational powers with skill alone as his main reliance. As an aspect of the picture composition is a first step toward the larger function of design, it is included in it but lacks all the dynamics of formal harmonies. It is a static thing. It belongs to the material world. Its range is limited to concrete effects.

ART PRINCIPLES

Throughout the duration of our recent dark age of naturalistic art the Academic, or Official, School has honored and presumably applied a set of what it calls "art principles" including the following:

Rhythm
Harmony
Dominance
Subdominance
Balance
Transition
Variation

All these words, it should be noted, with the exception of rhythm, can be applied to the naturalistic picture. There can be objects in a landscape painting—trees, houses—which are arranged or composed with one dominant, others subdominant, all of which objects can then be copied from nature more or less as they are actually seen. Balance, variation, and transition can be applied in the same way. These imply shifting of positions, change of size, omission or selection; they do not imply remaking or complete reorganization. Rhythm, however, is different; it does mean a thorough reorganization into controlled relationships. A picture that is rhythmic must eliminate all extraneous material; the chaos of nature must be synchronized.

Harmony is a versatile word. A naturalistic picture can copy the harmony of nature and so be harmonious. Or an artist can create his own harmonies in any degree of deviation from those of nature. The term straddles both schools.

These words are intellectualizations of the most obvious characteristics of design. They are characteristics which can be thought out, it should be noted, and put into a word with definite meaning. The fact that they are stressed and *design* as a basic necessity is ignored indicates the narrowness of the vision which calls them "principles." They describe concretely the intellectual fringes of the deep emotional experience of design.

The word "design" as used by the Moderns includes all these meanings as a matter of course, but as some among many *qualities* characteristic of its processes. Other qualities are integration, interplay, color chords, space chords, opposition, etc. But all such, like the so-called "principles," are not principles at all; they are aspects of the process of organization called design. None *in themselves,* with the exception of rhythm, have a value which is a vitalizing force. The creative mind must deal with them and give them life before they become significant. Principles in modern practice go much deeper. A principle is a fundamental truth, a law from which others are derived. Design is a fundamental truth in human nature, a law dictated by human sensibilities which endures. Design is a basic principle of art. And design is validated by *feeling,* not by conscious mind.

The most familiar method of analyzing design in pictures is to point out directional movements of bodies, roads, or any forms. This movement may be of two kinds. It may be inherent in the objects themselves—as a body may lean and an arm may be flung upward and back, as a road leads back into deep space, etc.—or it may consist of movements which the eye may take in leaping from object to object—from house in foreground, to dancing figure, to tree, to distant hill and back—in, through, and around. The hackneyed triangular designs so often pointed out in the old masters are of these types with their broad bases and groupings which rise to a triangular apex. Designed pictures dealing with reality normally use both these kinds of organizations of movement and they can be studied as part of the total design. But they are only a part and their analysis can be entirely a cerebral experience; in themselves they are the lesser part of the design experience.

Emotional design and the response to it go far beyond this control of movement. Observe carefully the reproduction of Cézanne's painting in Fig. 10 and the photograph of the actual scene from which he painted it in Fig. 9. The secret of all emotional plastic design is here revealed—if one has the eyes to see. I shall attempt the near-impossible task of explanation of what has here occurred under the heading Plastic Form.

PLASTIC FORM

In its physical aspect a picture is a flat plane (of canvas or paper) definitely limited by its frame. On this flat plane color or some other medium represents objects or plays color-space harmonies, or both. Objects may be represented as an illusion of reality—as if the picture were a pane of glass through which one looked at the actual scene (the naturalistic picture)—or they may be represented by symbols which perform the double function of standing for subject and at the same time taking their place in a color-space harmony. In the latter case the surface of the painting, instead of being violated by an illusion of deep space, is frankly admitted as a concrete element to be decorated and enjoyed.

In a two-dimensional plastic picture this process is at its simplest. Subject, if any, is translated into flat color spots which take their places with other color spots in a flat pattern mosaic. Figure 26 is such a decoration.

In a three-dimensional picture, subject, say a house, has front and side planes. The front plane may be parallel to the picture plane and so take its place normally within it. The side plane retreats into deep space away from the front plane. This plane, in the plastic picture, will be painted as a color spot which has the *sense* of retreating into deep space but does not give the *illusion* of so doing, at the same time that, as color-shape, it fits into the pattern in the picture plane. Sky, as a curved plane like the inside of a bowl, must be treated in the same way. So will irregular planes of hills, foliage, ground, or any other element of any subject. The planes of a human head or tabletop all may conform to the same law. These movements back into deep space and out again and across and up and down may be infinitely complex with all manner of repeats and countermovements.

THE PICTURE FIELD

The picture field is the total space within which the organization

The Arts Magazine

Fig. 9.—Photograph of the actual subject from which the painting on opposite page was made.

of elements works. The controls of design imply limits; to escape limits would be to escape control. In two dimensions, length and breadth, the frame provides the very tangible limit against which movements, lines, planes, and spaces play. When depth is added there must also be a limit against which these elements may act. Indoors, walls or draperies supply this limit; outdoors, the extreme limit is sky and distant hills. The distance back to such extreme limits is too great, however, for the major forward and back movements; these should take place with a reasonable compactness of interplay for the main drama with, perhaps, one counterpenetration to the extreme of distant sky. The picture field thus becomes like the inside of a box, a room, or a stage within which and against which the pictorial drama unfolds. The painting by Cézanne is such a plastic picture.

The Arts Magazine

Fig. 10.—Cézanne's version of the subject on opposite page.

FUNCTIONAL DESIGN

Tangible subject, when it is present in a picture, must be amalgamated with design to achieve the plastic picture. There are two ways of doing this. One is to impose design on subject, bending subject to conform to the empirical needs of that design. The other is to let subject, by its character, determine the character of the design. This last is functional design. In the portrayal of reality functional design is logical and inevitable. It accentuates character. It is the type of design used by such old masters as Raphael, Tintoretto, Michelangelo when dramatized reality is the chief concern. As an artist departs from reality toward abstraction, design may gradually dominate subject-character imposing its own harmonic laws on reality till complete abstraction becomes pure visual music entirely liberated from factual truth. Such design becomes subjective instead of functional. In it the language of the spirit finds liberation and free emotional range. Both types of design are logical and necessary. Figures 47 and 48 of the paintings by Henrietta King illustrate the two types of imposed and functional design where subject realism is preserved. Figures 29, 35, and 38 are typical of design domination in abstract and semiabstract works.

INTELLECTUALIZED DESIGN

Design, like the portraying of subject in general, can be intellectual or emotional in character. It can be stereotyped and barren of any personal vision or spark of creative life or it can be full, rich, warm-blooded sensory expression. Intellectualized design, including all the usual and familiar conventionalizations of subject, all copies or adaptations of historical styles, and all *thought-out* patterns, which may even come under the title "creative" or "modern," are foredoomed to such barrenness. The art of the picture—and again I stress the point—cannot be a cerebral process. Figure 11 illustrates the point.

DISTORTION HEIGHTENS EYE INTEREST

Distortion of subject in any picture or sculpture has several important functions. It can be humorous, as in a cartoon, or grotesque. It can accentuate some one quality like suffering, weight, lankiness, ugliness, beauty, evil, good, and so increase the effectiveness of the story as well as manufacture humor, gloom, fear, or any desired psychological atmosphere. It can facilitate design. The animated cartoon has built its popular success and is significant as an art form because of such distortion. Religious painting and sculpture definitely make use of distortion to heighten effects; note the exaggerated human and animal figures in primitive symbolism to inspire awe, fear, or reverence for the unearthly. Note the stressing of emaciation of the Christ figure in Christian symbolism to express suffering, also the overstatement of human beauty to express the perfection of the ideal in their god-forms by the Greeks (which is a kind of distortion up the scale from normal instead of down) and many other like emphases.

Fig. 11.—A painting using obvious decorative stereotypes—the lowest level of pictorial decoration.

STEREOTYPED DESIGN

The third type of distortion is that which increases eye interest in a form by making it unusual and thereby adding to the interest of design. Increased eye appeal may result from a shock of surprise when a familiar form or shape is twisted out of normal but it also results from the more lasting and innate satisfaction with variety. We have all seen thousands of houses of normal shape—both in nature and in pictures. One more normal picture of a normal house, therefore, can have no thrill as an experience; there is nothing to waken the imagination, nothing in particular to get excited about. When that house is slightly distorted, however, it becomes a new experience; there is a refreshing realization that this is not an actual house or a mere record of one; it is something new—an *expression* of that house, a peculiar and different way in which it is seen by this picturemaker. Such a realization arouses flagging spirits. This is a valid reason for distortion (see Fig. 12).

METHODS OF STUDY

Since the range of free, emotional design is as wide as man's sensibilities, no one way of studying or practicing is right as against other ways which are wrong—provided originality and feeling are protected and their normal functioning assured. The important matter is to develop sensitivity and the power to organize all materials. Our present study of design, therefore, must point out ways and means of organization of elements and show examples, each of which illustrates one way. The student should strive to assimilate the basic process, not the specific result. He should then practice *organization* as such, should exercise his sensitivities to the relationships of all elements with which he deals. In such a direction of energy lies growth of creative power.

There is one exception to the above tolerance of method. As stated in Chapter I, there is one working plan which long experience teaches is more effective than other ways:

The study of design in painting, modeling, and drawing should start with abstract creation in order to eliminate the conflicts and complications of subject. As the design sense grows applications to subject can begin and continue in slow and easy stages of complexity, always keeping that sense dominant.

In Chapter I three important reasons were stated for giving design first place in all art education. It is the least understood, it is the major source of aesthetic experience, and it is universal in application. To these I now add the argument of effectiveness. Design studied separately can be more easily and quickly assimilated.

MISUSE OF TERMS

The words "design," "rhythm," "harmony" are constantly being

Fig. 12.—Drawing by NELLIE M. JOHNSON.* Note added interest in house because of distortion, also the free, emotional type of drawing.

DISTORTION

used by laymen, some art teachers and artists who do not know their meanings in the modern and classic sense—whose appreciation is limited to, or who practice, naturalistic art. Since words are as free as air and since each person's definition of them is normally limited to the range of his personal horizon, it is not strange that there should be conflict and what, to one with a wider horizon, seems misuse. Such conflict and misuse in this field of art, though normal, are decidedly unfortunate as they add to the popular confusion.

One of the most extraordinary examples of misuse of these terms which I have ever seen occurred in a recent issue of *Art Instruction Magazine* under the article heading,

DESIGN
THE CORNERSTONE OF PICTORIAL ILLUSTRATION

The article and its illustrations were by William Oberhardt. In the first three paragraphs of his article Mr. Oberhardt says (the italics are mine):

> Design deals with *abstract* qualities of art. It is the *organization* of pictorial essentials from nature to a given space. The public appreciates art for its story telling qualities, the artist for its *design* qualities only. The latter is fascinated by *color harmonies, relationships of space*, the *rhythm of line*, the form.

The entire article is illustrated by naturalistic sketches in which *not one single aspect of design in the modern sense is even remotely hinted at.* They are straight sketchy imitations of the chaos of nature.

5. A LOOK BACK INTO HISTORY

SINCE it is obviously impossible to condense a history of the creative mind and its products during some six thousand years of man's history into one short chapter, I am going to serve our immediate purpose by merely showing a few examples of such products selected almost at random down the centuries. These examples are chosen as illustrations of the thesis that the creative mind and the sense of design have been part of man's equipment through all recorded history. If they are unique examples in each period, the thesis will not be proved. If they are typical, it will—at least in a general way. I shall attempt to choose such as are, in the main, typical.

In any general survey of the painting of the European Renaissance one outstanding trend is clearly discernible. Free, creative design with its sensory enrichments was in the ascendency over subject from the twelfth to the fifteenth century.

Then gradually design became more and more functional—that is, it was assimilated into subject for the purpose of increasing the effectiveness thereof rather than providing aesthetic enjoyment. And finally the concern with skill and truth which had started immediately after Giotto in the early 1400's gradually became a debacle; verisimilitude was achieved and art was lost in the process. The dark age of naturalism became the vogue.

No definite time limit can be placed on the recent decline. It has been gaining momentum slowly and unevenly since the first mental rumblings of the search for truth and the technical means of portraying it began to distract the followers of Giotto from the symbolic

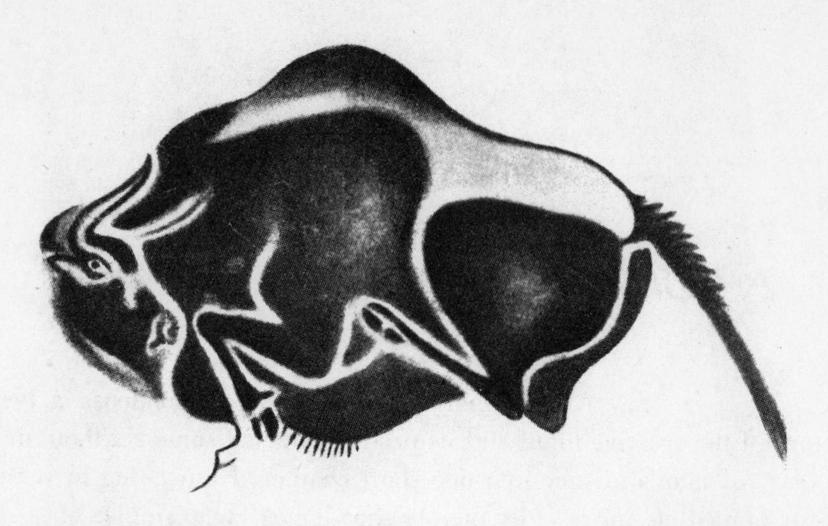

Fig. 13.—Bison from the cave at Altamira, near Santander, Spain; Old Stone Age; about 20,000-10,000 B.C. One of the earliest known pictorial creations of man. Here, in the very dawn of man's history, the power to re-create subject into a symbol and to harmonize its lines, spaces, and dark-lights into design is present in remarkable degree. It would be a most interesting study to explain how a sensitivity which existed in man some 22,000 years ago has been lost in our "civilized" age.

DESIGN DOMINANT OVER REALITY

expression of meaning and the intuitive harmonies of design. Giotto (1266-1336) preserved the art of the primitives in his more human characterizations. But Masaccio (1401-1428), his immediate follower in Italy, deserted and, as much as any one man, started the momentous abandonment of art for truth. There were many breaks and reassertions of the design instinct and many glorious achievements culminating, perhaps, in the supreme emotional organizations of El Greco (1542-1614). But in general it was in the fourteenth and fifteenth centuries that design dominantly enriched subject; in the sixteenth the conflict was in full swing; in the seventeenth truth had won. From then to now the tide of battle has shifted continually but truth has held steadily to its gains up to the initial revolt of Whistler in the 1870's with its daring challenge to the accepted way. The Modern Movement picked up where Whistler stopped. It has arrested the decline. It has returned art to the Grand Tradition of

Lent by The Buffalo Museum of Science

Fig. 14.—*Pre-Achaemenian Pottery (Persian);* about 1500 B.C.

Simple, freehand, geometric design. Emotional in quality, no mathematical rigidity. Note square motifs as a foil for curves and the top border of parallel verticals as a subtle contrast to the bolder elements.

LINE AND SPACE PATTERN

Fig. 15.—*Etruscan Bronze Plaque* of about 700 B.C.

Note subject translated into sensitive space design with variations in the two animals—movements of legs and tails, shapes of the same parts, etc. Also note that space around animals is a definite part of the design and that border is a contrast to the simpler forms with greater decorative richness.

FUNCTIONAL SPACE DESIGN

Fig. 16.—*A Knight and a Woman (Engraving)*, by MASTER E. S.

Design of line, space, texture and form which was typical of fifteenth century art in Europe. The exploitation of folds in drapery into decorative pattern was a convention of the time which held up through Dürer and the early 1500's till it gradually dissolved into the portraying of reality and a more functional, less decorative, design,

DECORATIVE LINE AND SPACE DESIGN

Metropolitan Museum of Art, New York

Fig. 17.—Chinese stone carving, first half of sixth century. A human head simplified to express universal woman (even though it is a portrait) and organized into exquisite form design.

creation and design. It started and is continuing our contemporary renaissance.

If we compare the master paintings of the Modern Movement with the early and late masterpieces of the European Renaissance, an-

Fig. 18.—*Madonna and Child,* by AMBROGIO LORENZETTI.

A Sienese painting of about 1330 showing the Byzantine inheritance of rigidity and stylization. The simplified spaces and colors are thoroughly integrated into a design that is fluid and sensitive in spite of the formality of subject. Note long, vertical curve of the edge of the dark coat as an instance of sensitive variation.

Fig. 19—*The Wedding Dance*, by PIETER BRUEGEL the Elder.
The physical movement of the many forms is built into a plastic movement of form, space, and color. Note how body forms are clarified, how each color shape counts definitely as a color shape, the variety in size and importance of both forms and shapes and the weaving into organized relationships.

THREE-DIMENSIONAL ORGANIZATION OF PHYSICAL MOVEMENT INTO PLASTIC MOVEMENT AND DESIGN

other trend which rarely receives notice stands out with dramatic importance. Modern masterpieces, generally speaking, in contrast to the old masterworks of the later and more technically developed periods, show a vast growth and enrichment in the emotional, sensory, or purely plastic qualities of design. The contrasting of a Cézanne, a Van Gogh, or a Chirico to a Raphael, a Titian, or a Botticelli will illustrate the point. The latter are more skilled as technicians, they achieve more detailed character, they express form through color with greater finesse and objective realism and their design is undoubtedly more complex and polished. But the modern masters gain different goals with a power that is startling in contrast. Their technic, though not so polished, is adequate. Their characterization is powerful. They express form through color with a dramatization of essentials which seems to get down to the roots rather than the externals of physical reality. And finally their design frankly plays harmonic chords of color, space, and form which are the more exhilarating because not chained to surface verity. The design of the realists among the old masters was primarily functional; it mainly contributed to the dramatization of subject and story. That of the modern masters is both functional and plastic—the great gain being in the latter field.

These comparative results were strikingly in evidence at a recent exhibition at the Museum of Modern Art in New York City when Italian old masters were shown on one floor and modern masters on another. To this observer Botticelli's Birth of Venus, Raphael's Madonna of the Chair, Titian's Portrait of Pope Paul III, and the many lesser works were a definite letdown of spirit, whereas the Cézannes, the Van Goghs, the Chiricos, and the Lembruck were a lift, a thrill, a warm sense of rich rewards. It was as if the spirit, released from the need for specific statement of obvious reality, could speak its own language more effectively. It is so easy to forget that the range of the spirit is extraordinarily wide—much wider than the range of the physical eyes and the things which they perceive. Masters such as Raphael, Rubens, and Van Dyck, because of their concern with and masterful expression of the realities seen by the physical eyes, tend to confine the observing spirit within those concrete limits even though the human drama they portray so well tends to extend their range into all manner of psychological profundities. We respond to the profundities—if we can penetrate the veil of an historical drama characteristic of the age in which the work was produced and with which we of today may have lost all personal contact. Certainly madonnas, crucifixions, and last suppers hold less sway over the mass of people today than they did in the age of unquestioning belief.

But with the compelling hold of subject lessened and with the plastic means of the artist usually limited to the expression of reality, the spirit of us who observe is more or less thwarted in its hunger for experience beyond the real by this confinement to reality. It is such a releasing into new fields to conquer far beyond the real which the Moderns give us to satisfy our emotional hunger. Study the Van Gogh of Fig. 21. Study the Cézanne of Fig. 10. Both are rich with sensations beyond obvious reality.

Giotto and El Greco, outstandingly among the old masters, did escape from the confines of familiar reality—the one through the liberating effect of a more primitive technic (and primitive works do normally gain in emotional power as they lose in verisimilitude), the other through a spiritual fire which burned away all unessentials. Through them the new and the old come close together, the cycle of history is more nearly closed.

The Moderns belong in, and have added to the Grand Tradition.

Fig. 20.—*Madonna of the Chair,* by RAPHAEL.
An example of design by an old master absorbed into external realism.

DESIGNED REALITY

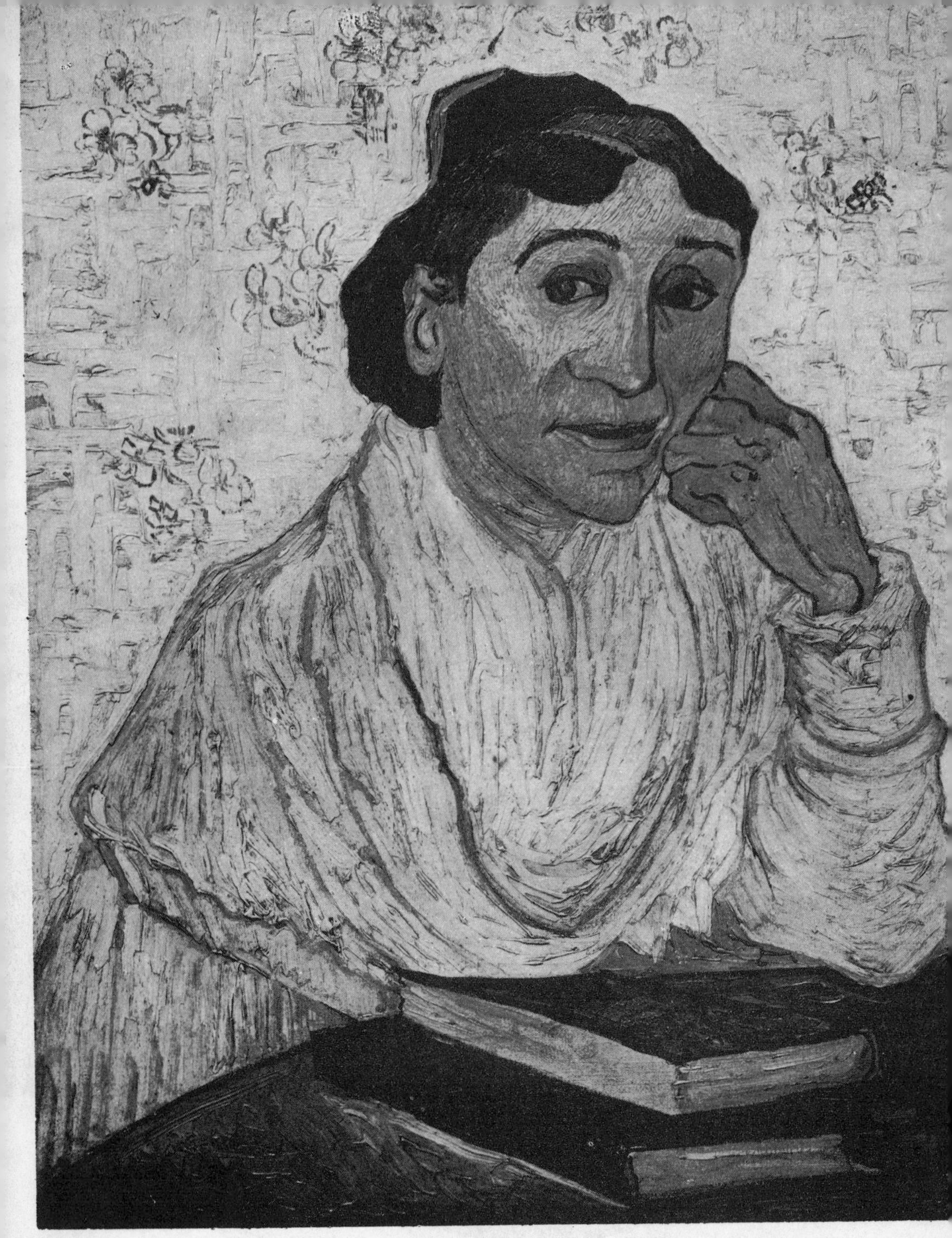

Fig. 21.—*L'Arlésienne,* by VAN GOGH.

An example of the different goals achieved by the Moderns without loss of character expression.

DESIGNED REALITY

Fig. 22.—*Birth of Venus,* by BOTTICELLI.

A harmonic blending of realism and design in which the design still functions as design. Note texture and movement of hair and conscious and definitely related space arrangements in head, neck, shoulders, and hand. Every single item is controlled; nothing is copied from nature as it actually appears to the physical eye in its chaotic details.

DESIGNED REALITY WITH EMPHASIS ON
DECORATIVE QUALITY OF LINE AND SPACE

PART II

PRACTICE—TEACHING METHOD

Illustrated by student and other works from many sources.

EXPLANATION

THE ILLUSTRATIONS

The illustrations of student work are chosen from students of the Design Workshop and other schools where similar standards and practices are in force.

The inclusion of one example from a large school does not imply that all standards and practices in that school are in harmony. On the contrary the work selected may be the exceptional revolt of a single student. (One selection which I have honored herein was apologized for by the director of the school in these words, "Oh, that lad's a misfit. We can't do anything with him.")

Design Workshop present or recent students are indicated by one star (*).

Former Design Workshop students are indicated by two stars (**).

6. CREATIVE PAINTING

> "The emotions are sometimes so strong that one works without knowing one works, when sometimes the strokes come with a sequence and a coherence like words in a speech or a letter."
>
> VINCENT VAN GOGH, 1888.

CREATIVE painting, with the initial attention given to color, can be the logical starting point of all art education because color is the most universal and obvious element both in nature, things, and pictures and the one with the widest appeal.

Creative painting, with or without subject, can develop awareness and control of color freely and fluidly and so provide the power to deal with it wherever used by man. If a student can create color harmonies with paint on paper he can create them also in textiles, room decoration, costume design, gardening, or any other application to his environment. Color has vast potentialities. The painted picture provides the richest possible proving ground for these potentialities.

OBJECTIVES

The objectives of creative painting can be summarized as follows:

1. A relaxed freedom and sense of power with the medium.
2. Sensitiveness to the relationships of color—emotional design.
3. Combining both these powers with subject.

To gain the above objectives of creative painting:

1. Skills and copying should be forgotten. They are craft, not art.

2. The thinking mind should be temporarily discarded (as thoroughly as that difficult act of emancipation can be achieved); the senses should be alert.
3. Along with the discarding of conscious thought should go all systems of dealing with color which are thought-out or scientific.
4. A spirit of adventure and experiment, of alert sensitiveness to the quality of things including color should be given free rein.

COLOR

Many treatises on color assume that the child or older student should learn color through analysis, or "knowledge." Even color harmony, it is assumed, can be studied and learned consciously. "The color problems then," says one book on *Art in the Elementary School,*[1] "show a need for *knowledge* of color mixing and an *understanding* of the three color qualities—hue, value and intensity." I thoroughly disagree with this thinking process. The conscious application of knowledge is science and science is not art. Knowledge shifts emphasis and directs energies away from surprises, adventure, and emotional experience; it clamps its devotees within the tight, practical limits of known facts.

When the liberation of sensing and feeling has been made part of one the conscious mind can be called into consultation to control emotion, for both are needed in mature creation.

The physical properties of color will not be gone into here because they have been adequately presented in a number of books of which several are listed and described in the bibliography, page 248. These properties may be studied when well along in the experience of painting; they should never even be mentioned to the young child or to the beginner at any age. They are technical problems and such should be ignored until emotional power over color and self-confidence in the free use of it have been highly developed and a wide exploring of the sensory potentialities has been achieved. Then gradually the student should become conscious of techniques and skills, *as these are needed to implement creative powers.*

[1] By Margaret E. Mathias. Scribners, New York, 1929.

A METHOD FOR BEGINNING CREATIVE PAINTING

It would be educationally unwise to set down in book form a series of specific exercises covering courses of study in creative painting, modeling, or drawing. They would be too specific, too unmalleable. They would not allow for individual and different ways of achieving the same general goal. They would deny full range for the implications of their title, creative. In the classroom or in a printed course by mail, instructions can be specific and follow a prearranged plan, for in the personal contact between student and teacher there is plenty of elbow room for the diverse way. In these pages, therefore, I shall be less specific than in the Design Workshop courses by mail; I shall try only to establish the minimum foundation, by means of several typical exercises, on which future diversity can be solidly built. The following exercises in creative painting will set the stage, so to speak, and implement in a sufficient degree the objectives above stated. Examples of additional experiments by many students will serve as charts for future growth.

Paper or canvas, brushes, and color are ready. Any color medium may be used but opaque water colors (show-card colors) are best for early experiments because they are low in cost and can be used either as thin color (transparent) or as thick color like oils (opaque). Paper should be large, at least 22 x 28 inches. Brushes for water color should be large, No. 12 is excellent. Work may be done standing in order to get full arm and body movement—the paper on a drawing board standing on an easel or the paper may lie flat on table. Color should be like thin cream. A muffin tin makes an excellent palette. To start use any three colors.

FIRST STEP

First paintings should be done with *no subject and no conscious design*—just free, happy-go-lucky adventures with color. The wilder and freer the better. Thinking and remembering should be discarded. For one experiment paint an *explosion in a paint factory*. Use any device that will liberate from knowledge and skill. Dip a single brush, without washing, into any or all colors so fast that you don't have time to *know* what you are doing or what mixtures you are getting. First paintings should be a galaxy of accidents. No planning, no fears, no inhibitions. They should be finished in five to ten minutes each and eight or a dozen made in one session. The object is to *find out what can happen with color.*[2]

SECOND STEP

Once complete emotional abandon is gained, with its resultant sense of power over color, then a number of experiments can be undertaken more slowly and consciously. The brush can dip into a color and spread it idly over the paper. Pure red. Too violent a color, some instinct says. The brush dips into red again but also into another color to modify the redness. It paints the two blended colors (they blend partially as they flow from the brush) beside the former red, then leaps to another section of the paper to repeat this color. But the repeat should be different. Another touch to palette for another color or a white that will soften the red. These flow onto an enlarging area, jump to a third section, then back to the original red, taking their places alongside colors already down. Always the new area should be different; repetition of size, shape, or color is monotonous. The eye likes variety. The colors now on the paper call for opposites—red for greens, blue for orange, yellow for purple. So mixtures of these take their places. *With no thought-out plan* colors merge and flow and surprise.

COLOR CHORDS

Color should be played in chords. One color demands others as foil or complement. The eye should be sensitive to qualities, should react to the effects which hand and brush create. Are there too many all-dark colors? Is contrast needed—a delicate tint against a heavy dark? Do groups of dark chords need groups of varied lights? Mixed colors make gray or neutral color (an even mixture of red, yellow, blue makes a perfect gray). Is grayed color richer than fresh unmixed? Are the straight primaries too simple? A pure color is accentuated by neutrals around it. Cool colors (blues) are the opposite of warm colors (reds and yellows). These opposites make strong

[2] Finger painting is a happy experiment which fits in at this point but, after emotional freedom has been gained, the brush becomes the much more versatile tool.

contrasts. The eyes watch all such events as they occur. The conscious mind sits on a fence, so to speak, perceiving and studying events in a world other than its own, intrigued by happenings it cannot dictate or explain. If the liberation is complete and courage to do and dare does not fail, the result of such painting will be rich with all manner of surprises and adventures. Harmony, rhythm, balance, variety, dominance—all these qualities of design will have happened unconsciously. Unguessed creative power will have been unleashed. Paintings of freshness, spontaneity, and lively interest will have been created.

The most important single thing to remember about such liberating exercises as these is that the ultimate test of their worth lies in the pleasure or pain they give the embryo artist who produces them. If their contribution is sensory pleasure, they are justified. If pain, it is then necessary to question why. If the pain lies in objection to new ways or to lack of subject or to technical crudity, it is not justified and the stretching of awareness to cover new experiences should continue. It is conceivable that appreciation of pure color harmonics may take as much as seven days of taste development. It is worth that cost.

BRUSH EFFECTS

Additional eye interest is added to color by varied brush effects, by a handling of the brush to give different movements, twistings, jabbings, groupings, etc. Such effects diversify each color area and can be repeated, varied, or played against and with each other as can the colors themselves.

COLOR-SPACE

In such free, emotional painting, space as color-shape can logically be ignored; colors may blend and interweave with vague and undefined limits. But, vague or clear-cut, a color does have limits. It meets another color or the frame. These limits define shapes. Shapes may be interesting or uninteresting. They may be familiar and conventional—circles, triangles, leaves, etc.—or they may be unfamiliar and surprising. They may be monotonous in size and character repeating one size or character over and over again, or contrasts of both

Fig. 23

Fig. 24

DEVELOPMENT OF A DESIGN WORKSHOP STUDENT, VIOLA DON, IN SIX DAYS OF CREATIVE PAINTING.

Fig. 23, her first painting, is tight, frightened, and intellectual. Fig. 24 was done on the second day and shows a loosening up with complete emotional freedom with color for its own qualities; there is no concern with any other matter. Fig. 25, a third-day painting, shows consciousness of color shapes and their relationships. Fig. 26 adds subject treated as flat color spots added to the color-space arrangement.

Fig. 25

Fig. 26

may be varied and arresting. Space in a picture is as definite an element as color. It can be played in harmonies as color can. It is another keyboard on the color organ. The creating artist plays space harmonies as he plays color harmonies and at the same time.

At this stage spaces, like colors, should be accidental—free and easy, experimental, unthought-out. A sensitive brush should flow in free arm movement, should twist, turn, jab, dot, play groups of lines into constant space adventures. Fig. 29 shows a simple space arrangement and Fig. 68 a complex one.

COLOR-SPACE HARMONICS

How are color and space harmonies, either separately or together, played? By playing chords or groups of one or both which "feel" right to the observing eye. Chords of this kind have no predetermined, mathematical intervals, as they do in music; they are determined

Fig. 27

Fig. 28

DEVELOPMENT OF A DESIGN WORKSHOP STUDENT, VIOLA DON (CONTINUED)
In the fifth-day painting of Fig. 27 easel motifs were taken from the environment and played into a color-space arrangement—the colors being improvised, not the actual color of the actual easels. In Fig. 28 the same has happened with roof beams and a window as motifs. Note how the distortion of the square window adds to eye interest.

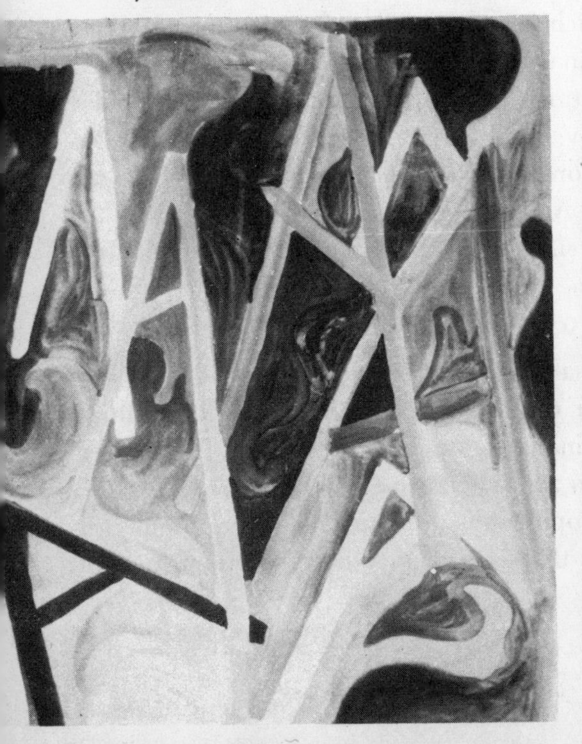

solely by the sensitivity of the artist and are right (for him) if they feel right to him. Because taste differs in different people there will always be wide differences of opinion as to what is right and what is wrong in such harmonization. But in spite of all such personal differences and the lack of any specific law of harmonic rightness, in general, human sensitivity seems to have a least common denominator that holds good through the ages. A space arrangement in an early Egyptian relief still looks right today as do all manner of other arrangements from all periods of history. Individual sensitivity is a part of this universal sensitivity. Each validates the other.

The capacity within us which does the validating—which guides the brush which mixes and applies color—is a peculiar unconscious power. "When I paint," says Elizabeth Erlanger (see Fig. 64), "there's one thing I know. The only time I do something worth while is when I don't think and can't tell how I did it." Picasso, in explaining how he worked, once said, "At the actual time I am painting a picture I may think of white and put down white. But I can't go on working all the time thinking of white and painting it. Colors, like features, follow the changes of the emotions. You've seen the sketch I did for a picture with all the colors indicated on it. What is left of them? Certainly the white I thought of and the green I thought of are there in the picture, but not in the places I intended, nor in the same quantities." Which is another way of saying that feeling, rather than thinking, was in command of his brush. "A picture lives a life like a living creature," Picasso added, "undergoing the changes imposed on us by our life from day to day. It is never thought out and settled beforehand. While it is being done it changes as one's thoughts change. And when it is finished, it still goes on changing, according to the state of mind of whoever is looking at it."

SUBJECT TRANSLATED INTO COLOR-SPACE

The foregoing suggests a way of painting that depends entirely on feeling, or sensing, for quality. It develops power to organize color and space into original two-dimensional design. The power to do this is the foundation for all creative painting.

The next step in development is to translate subject into this color-space design, a step that is probably the most important of all single steps in dealing with subject. Also it can, but need not, be difficult. The difficulty arises from an inherent conflict between the functions of subject and of design. Subject, in a picture, is a record or presentation of fact; design is a playing of harmonies. To amalgamate the two subject must be changed—the colors, spaces, and forms which are the means to its representation must be reorganized to serve the double duty of the two functions. It is comparatively easy to do either of these two things alone; it is quite hard at first to do them together.

The simpler the expression of subject the easier the double task becomes. The first step, therefore, is to reduce subject to an abstract symbol which is only one or several color spots, then to integrate it freely and easily with other color spots some of which are subjects and some of which are not, into a color-space arrangement (see Fig. 33).

In such arrangements subject can be made important by strong contrasts or unimportant by a subtle harmony. Dark against light, pure color against neutral, warm against cool, and large against small are means to such contrasts. The crucial thing to remember in this important step is that, so far as the visual harmonics are concerned, it is the colors and spaces as such and their relationships as such that are to be given prime consideration—the subject submerging itself in the design. In this sense every space and every color works and so is vital to the whole; the whole is the sum of all contributing parts.

A STAINED-GLASS WINDOW OF ABSTRACT COLOR-SPACE

After a number of paintings have been made with two-dimensional color-space arrangements which please the eye, an especially interesting one may be chosen and the color shapes outlined with a uniform line of black paint to represent the leads of a stained-glass window. This should be done first without subject, Fig. 29, then with subject simplified into flat color spots, Figs. 31 and 32. The black lines heighten the intensity of the colors they enclose, giving a rich effect. The main value of this step is the accenting of color shapes, making the student more conscious thereof. Such paintings can be

Fig. 29.—By AMALIE ADLER*
A stained-glass window of abstract color-space.

Fig. 30.—*Telephone Operator,* by WILLARD BEECHE

BEGINNER PAINTINGS

OUTLINED COLOR-SPACES AS STAINED-GLASS WINDOWS.

Below: left. Symbols from sea life. Below, right: Symbols for girl, dog, and tree have been integrated into a sensitive design—in spite of the crudity of subject rendering. This can be called an honest primitive painting because the artist, as a beginner, is a primitive in this field.

Fig. 31.—By FRANCES PERRY.*

Fig 32.—By ROSE STUDNITZ.*

varnished after they are dry, thus becoming more transparent, and actually hung in front of a window, giving to a room a subdued richness.

A STAINED-GLASS WINDOW WITH SUBJECT TRANSLATED INTO COLOR-SPACE

Adding a black outline to the color-space treatments of subject described above not only accents color and space but does give a decorative arrangement which can be called a stained-glass window even though it may not be used as such. The idea may be developed ad infinitum and applied in many ways to actual situations. A school class, for instance, can paint such decorations for one or more of its windows for Christmas or Easter—the painting being either on paper or on the glass itself. The same method applies for stage sets or murals. Also, it would apply to lanterns or shades around electric lights. Subject can be simple or develop into the utmost complexity. The illustrations hint at the endless possibilities.

MORE COMPLEX APPLICATIONS OF COLOR-SPACE TO SUBJECT IN TWO-DIMENSIONAL PATTERN.

Fig. 33.—*Subway*. A painting by MARGUERITE N. PADDOCK.*

Fig. 34.—*Circus*, by AGNES SLAYMAKER.*

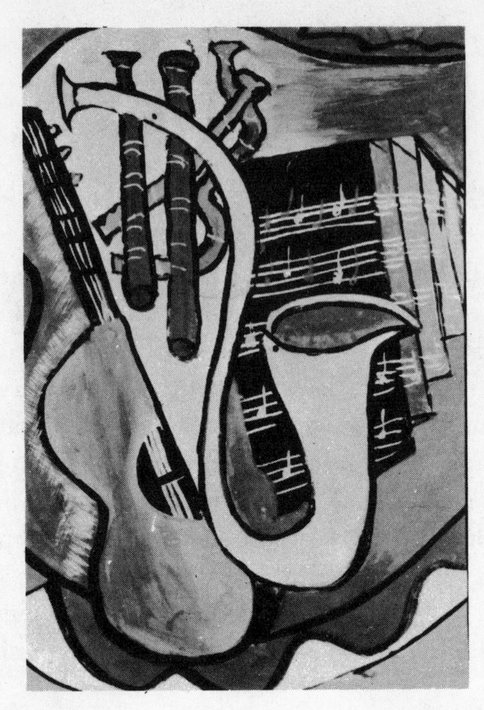

Fig. 35.—Symbols for music in a line, color, and space two-dimensional harmony. By EDWARD WALDEN, age 13. Art Teaching Division of the New York City WPA Art Project. S. Sulkwitz, instructor.

SEMIABSTRACT COLOR-SPACE DESIGN

THREE-DIMENSIONAL COLOR SPACE ARRANGEMENTS

Three-dimensional arrangements of color-space harmonies with or without subject carry the processes just described into plane movements that recede into deep space instead of lying in the single plane of the picture's surface. Relationships in deep space can be infinite in variety and so add immensely to the complications of movement and interplay. A color plane moving back into deep space is stopped by another at an opposing angle. The eye moves along this till it is switched to another at a different angle moving in a different direction. This can be forward around some object which becomes the pivot of encircling movements, simple or complex. Such planes or movements can be chaotic as they are in nature or they can be controlled to cause the most agreeable eye sensations.

Fig. 36.—*Voltige Aerienne*, by ALBERT GLEIZES.

Abstract design harmonizes its lines, spaces, textures, and colors as does a Beethoven symphony. The organization is both emotional and conscious. Study the repeats and variations of each element—dots, squares, diamonds, crossed lines, single lines, and the angular and curved spaces.

ABSTRACT, PLASTIC DESIGN
THE BEGINNING OF THREE-DIMENSIONAL ARRANGEMENTS

This directional movement of planes, however, is only one aspect of three-dimensional design. A planned movement around a pivot or in, out, and across a picture plane may plot a design which is vibrant with harmonic life or it may fall flat as an inept attempt which fails completely to attain harmonization of all elements. I heard Diego Rivera spend an entire evening some years ago explaining the murals he had just finished for the New Worker's School in New York City and the only explanation of the design he gave was concerned with these directional movements. Whether he was ignorant of deeper meanings or was simplifying his explanation to suit his audience could only be inferred.

Harmonization of planes, or tension of planes as Hans Hofmann calls these interrelationships, cannot be adequately described in words. The reference to music, therefore, seems to be the only way, here as elsewhere, in a design discussion, to convey specific meaning. A melody in music can flow up and down the scale, as directional movement can flow in and through the picture field, but the fact of this movement does not constitute the melody; the quality of the relationships of the different notes does that. It is this quality of

Fig. 37.—*Men Without Women.* A mural by STUART DAVIS in Radio City Music Hall. Subject translated into semiabstract color-space arrangements in two dimensions.

SEMIABSTRACT COLOR-SPACE DESIGN

THREE-DIMENSIONAL SUBJECTS IN COLOR-SPACE ARRANGEMENTS

By students of The American Artist's School, New York. Carl Holty, instructor.

Fig. 38.—Semiabstract arrangements of subjects into line, space, texture, and color harmonies. Note how three-dimensional objects have been woven into two-dimensional patterns of color shapes. Take the white plane under black jug in central picture as an example. Also the rug in picture at right. This is a simple form of plastic, subject painting.

relationships which decides the quality of design and all the powers of genius (at any level of complexity) are needed to achieve that supreme quality which is right on every count.

PLASTIC PAINTING

The word "plastic" as explained in Chapter IV, is used by the Moderns to describe the interweaving of all elements in a painting into a two-dimensional decoration which frankly acknowledges and decorates the picture surface.

PAINTING REALITY—THE STILL LIFE

When the sensitivity to the relationships of color, space, and plane are developed sufficiently to come into use automatically whenever a student uses color in the art of painting attention may then turn to the interpretation of real subjects. In this important transition subject in the painting becomes less the abstract or semiabstract symbol and more the expression of the real object. Such an expression should still be thought of as a symbol rather than a replica but emphasis shifts from the sign to the reality. Here lies the danger point. In spite of this necessary shift the design sense must still remain dominant, controlling every element. If it does not, if recording subject facts gains the upper hand, a hole is torn in a

Fig. 39.—*Improvisation*, by MARIE BARTON.*

Fig. 40.—*Oil Painting*, by MARY DREHER, University of Washington. Ambrose Patterson, instructor.

THE COLOR-SPACE SENSE APPLIED TO OBSERVED OBJECTS IN THREE DIMENSIONS

Students here observed actual subjects, sensed the qualities they wished to use—receding planes of tables, roundness of vases, color and space character of flowers and their relationships to each other, and all other elements. Then with such data they created their own improvisation on each theme.

delicate structure, design crashes, discord destroys harmony. The shift from design to subject dominance can happen easily and quickly if sensibilities slumber. But the consequences of the slip are not slight. They are catastrophic. The art of the picture is destroyed.

A still life is useful to student and artist both for practice and for mature creation because it gives a chance for thorough study of all aspects of real objects over a long period of time. If design can dominate such study, then all is well.

On a recent visit to a naturalistic art school I was taken into the "still-life room." All around the room still lifes were set up with the utmost of refinement and care. Each was an obvious harmony—a pleasing arrangement of objects varied in size, color, texture, and character. The extreme concern with arrangement was verified by

Fig. 41.—*Circus*, by BERTHA N. ENOCH.*

MORE ADVANCED APPLICATIONS TO SUBJECT

Fig. 42.—*Art Class*, by ANNE RAMUS GREENE.*

Fig. 43.—*Picasso*, by FLORENCE L. CHAPMAN

Fig. 44.—*Helen*, by MATISSE.

Here design is dominant over subject. It is a free, emotional design stressing space and color harmonics and linear movement. Note the wavy line around throat and bosom as it delineates the white space and plays against the flowing line curves and the leaf shapes in background. Here is a space chord of three types with face and hair different in character and the center of interest because of that difference.

Fig. 45.—*The Unsuccessful Man.* A still life in oils with human meaning by ELIZABETH N. ERLANGER.**

the instructor who explained that each student set up his own group, sometimes giving an entire morning to its planning before he began to paint.

But this *planning* is really *designing;* the thought struck me forcibly while he talked. It is designing in materials. And the resulting creations can probably be called works of formal art.

Then came the great contradiction. *In his painting the student merely copied this designed material.* He himself, as a painter, did not design. He did not do in paint what he had done in materials. Instead, he reproduced with skill data before his eyes. The fact that such material had been designed did not mean that his picture was designed. Copying designed objects or copying the chaos of nature both spell naturalistic art. Both depend equally on skill. And skill is craft, not art.

This incident reveals the inherent weakness of naturalistic art education as effectively as any single incident can. It shows that even the naturalistic artist has an innate design sense which he can use (in materials) and would use in his productions if he had not been thrown off the design track by established mental habits growing out of the misconceptions of our art decadence. Skill as an end is the greatest of such misconceptions.

Against this absurd and needless contradiction I pose the following:

There are three main ways in which a still life may be painted with all subject material designed *in the painting*.

1. Semi-abstraction. This is the simplest way where design can dominate without interference or competition from subject.
2. Reality built into design. The posed objects can here be painted as they are arranged and more or less as they appear but every color and space is designed, as it is painted, in relation to the whole of the picture.
3. Arbitrary rearrangement of real objects.

Of the first method Fig. 40 is an excellent example. Here motifs have been taken from observed objects—vase, checker pattern, rug,

Fig. 46.—Two still lifes in oil, by MARY NEWBERRY.**

These are spirited paintings in bold, thick color. Done after a year of study of such preliminary exercises as those here presented with a thoroughly assimilated sense of design.

THOROUGHLY INTERGRATED THREE-DIMENSIONAL DESIGNS

picture, and built into an entirely original semiabstract harmony. The freedom to create and to give major attention to the aesthetics of painting makes this an invaluable field of rich experience for both artist and observer. There is pure joy in abstract and semiabstract painting.

In the second method there can be a balance between the values inherent in subject, including the artist's interpretation thereof, and the values of design if and when it is amalgamated with subject. Figures 46 and 48 are examples of this amalgamation with a fine balance between the realities of subject and the harmonics of related colors, spaces, and forms. The books, table, vegetables, and flowers of Fig. 46 are all real—in fact, more real than if they had been copied naturalistically (of which copying there is none whatever in any of these works). But each color and space at the same time is played into harmonic relationships. The great realistic art of the past is in this idiom; it amalgamates subject and design. Fig. 50-A is an outstanding illustration.

The third method of designing a still life—and perhaps the best

Fig. 47.—Design imposed on flowers, with loss of flower character and subtlety.

Fig. 48.—Design taking its character from character of subject with extraordinary subtlety. Functional design.

Two Paintings by HENRIETTA KING.

IMPOSED AND FUNCTIONAL DESIGN

one for practice in dominating subject with design—is one which liberates the still life from its stillness. This method scatters a medley of objects on a large table or around a room with no arrang-

Fig. 49.—*Pussy Cat and Roses,* by THOMAS BENTON.
Textures are here stressed above all other plastic qualities.

DESIGNED REALITY WITH EXAGGERATED TEXTURES

ing whatever. A group of textiles can be hung from a wall or thrown over a table or chair, each with different motifs, textures, and colors; a vase of flowers, rugs, chairs, can be the normal decorations of the room.

The student studies all these objects and begins to evolve his own pictured creation taking suggestions from hither and yon. Here is a yellow pot. Where does he want such a shape and color in his picture? What size in relation to the frame? What color does he want as a foil to its color? Ah! This drapery. What other color to complete a chord? An angular larger object is then needed against this small round one. He searches till he finds the object that fills this need. What movement into and out of the picture plane does he enjoy? What objects will carry the eye in such movements? What textures against this smooth, hard glass? Shall he rest his pictured objects on a table or float them in air—*as pictured objects can float*

Fig. 50—*Cut Glass Bottle*. A still life by HENRY L. McFEE.
A masterly blending of reality and design. No single object or color is "copied" from nature as it is seen; all are reorganized into color, space, and form harmonies.

DESIGNED REALITY

without gravitational complications. A revelation, this simple fact? Had he never thought of this—of the picture as a liberation from fact? What a new world it opens! Why not float objects in space? Books above eye level, seen from in-under, a new experience. A table upside down. A sphere playing against the planes of table

Associated American Artists Galleries, New York

Fig. 50A.—*Winged Victory,* by ROBERT E. TINDELL.
Student of Kansas City Art Institute, Thomas H. Benton, instructor.

A STILL-LIFE WHICH EMERGES FROM THE STUDIO INTO LIFE.

and books. Textiles waving in the breeze just where needed. What a sense of command over material! The artist is Lord of all he surveys. He can build his own order out of the chaos around him. He can *create.*

In this kind of organization the real object is at hand to be studied and used or changed as needed. If a color or texture fits into the design, it is used; if not, a hint is taken and improvisation bends it to the creator's will. The drawing, St. Louis Blues, by Laura Woolsey, Fig. 107, is such an organization of forms floating in space.

The foregoing presents the rudiments of a way of painting that is basic in the philosophy and practice of those modern artists who know the plastique of painting and whose control over their expression is sensory before it is intellectual—who feel before they think.

The intellectual artist does not work this way. He gives primary attention to subject and its conscious *planning*. With him design, if he knows it, is a means to an end—a way of making subject more effective in his picture; it is not in itself an end fully equal in importance to subject as such. I was shocked recently on a visit to an advanced high school art class to find that a group of students working on a large mural project had been deciding on subject, looking up historical matter, planning arrangements of figures and backgrounds—all in charcoal sketches—for a total of eleven weeks and had not yet even begun to consider color and space harmonies as an emotional, aesthetic language. They were doing a factual illustration with technical proficiency and modern flavor and totally missing the aesthetics of the art experience. They were blind to the spiritual eloquence of *form*.

BROKEN COLOR

Broken color is a way of painting. It is not the only way. It has certain virtues and, when freely used, no defects. It is the opposite of flat or premixed color painting which many artists prefer. Its virtues are vibration, sparkle, liveliness. It dramatizes the all-pervading grays of nature by releasing the colors which compose grayed color.

Broken color was used by the French Impressionists as a means of approximating the effect of sunlight in nature more effectively and vibratingly than had ever been done before. It was in 1874 that Monet, Sisley, Pissarro, Renoir, Cézanne, and Degas held their first joint exhibition in Paris, after having been rejected by the Salon of that year, and shocked both public and critics with this departure from the decorous facsimile in premixed color. Their preoccupation with light, however, and what amounted to a color-photographic view of nature limited them to the role of trail blazers into a new world of pictorial art. It was the Postimpressionists who explored that new world; it was the application of broken color to the vibrant expression of form as revealed by color and to all the complexities of design that earned for this method a place in the Grand Tradition. It was Cézanne in his forty years of heartbreaking search who, more than any other man, welded the old and the new—who brought pulsating color life into the pulsating design of the old masters and so fathered the renaissance of our day. To enrich the Grand Tradition of the masters is no mean achievement. It does not happen every quarter-century. Cézanne so achieved.

The Postimpressionists made wide use of the great discovery—Van Gogh, Renoir, Seurat, Picasso, Matisse—each grasping the potentialities of the new-found design and applying them in his own way, each using the vitality of broken color in greater or lesser degree.

All color in nature outside of bright sunlight is grayed by some degree of shadow. Any color area seen half in sunlight and half in shadow proves the point—the difference in color intensity is a familiar fact.

Gray in pigment is the result of a mixture of the three primaries—red, yellow, blue. An equal mixture makes a perfect gray in which can be seen no single color. An unequal mixture results in a preponderance of one color and gives a red-gray, a yellow-gray, or a blue-gray. All color seen about us outside of bright sunlight is reproduced in paint by some mixture of red, yellow, and blue.

Broken color breaks colors seen in nature into these component parts and paints them in dots or brush strokes as red, yellow, blue. Each dot or stroke as painted is scattered, others then of different colors come between till the paper is covered—each dot or stroke theoretically (but not so literally as to become mechanical) being different from its neighbor. This contrast is what gives vibration and sparkle. Colors can be pure with a different brush used for each (which gives a limited effect) or they can mix on a single brush used without washing so that each primary color is modified by the mixture on the brush and comes off with an immense range of variations (giving a much more subtle effect). To get such mixtures the one brush is dipped into two colors at once and then, as the painting continues, into one or another color—the mixtures occurring on the brush and so being transferred to paper. Always in this process one color will be dominant, which is all that is needed to get the broken effect.

As a first exercise a large sheet of paper can be covered with

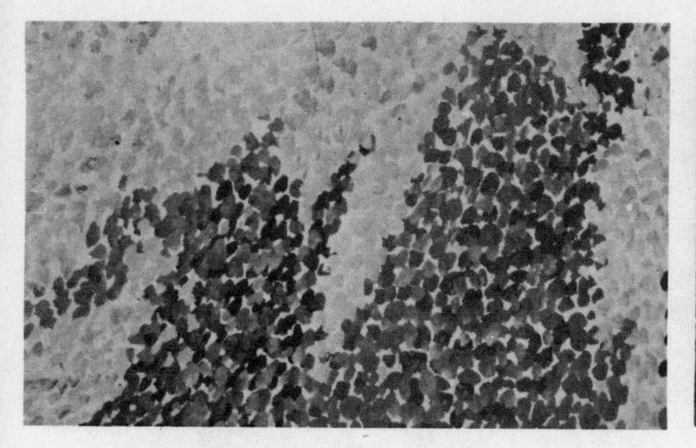

Fig. 51.—Exercises in the basic principle of broken color. At left, the dot method. At right, dots and strokes.

dots of the three primaries—red, yellow, blue—with or without the above mixtures, the aim being to get constant change from dominant blue, to dominant yellow, to dominant red or green but always with the three colors in all color. Then the same can be done with strokes. Then white can be added to the palette and a much greater range obtained with delicate tints at one end of the keyboard and the

Fig. 52.—Still life, by MARIE CLAUSSENIUS* in broken color with a free and emotional handling.

Fig. 53.—Close-up of same showing free brush handling.

Fig. 54.—Broken color painting in dots, by LUCY D. WELLS.*

Fig. 55.—Broken color painting in dots by MARGUERITE N. PADDOCK.*

REALITY PAINTED IN BROKEN COLOR

Fig. 56.—Broken color painting in brush strokes, by DOROTHY BRAKE.*

Fig. 57.—A combination of broken and flat color painting, by KATRINE C. PERKINS.*

heaviest darks at the other. After experimenting with all possibilities, actual colors in draperies or in any group of objects should be approximated as nearly as possible in the painting—this requiring practice for so many days or weeks till the student can see the colors which make up color and quickly and easily break them down in this way. When such power is developed it is time to break away from the rigid system of dots and strokes and to improvise on the basic process with all manner of variations and combinations of different effects. This broadening out is absolutely necessary as the literal method, as shown in Fig. 54 is monotonous in technical or texture effect. The variations can.go so far as to include broken color *areas* (each area painted in one color) or even to contrasting premixed color areas with broken ones—as Van Gogh has done in some of his works. Figures 52 and 57 show this broader handling.

THE PORTRAIT

The foregoing applies to all types of pictures regardless of specific subject. An orange, a patch of sky, or a human face can be reproduced in colors in a picture, the colors having meaning as orange, sky, or face and at the same time taking their places as part of a series of harmonic chords. Once the principle of harmonic organiza-

Fig. 58.—*Road With Cypresses,* by VAN GOGH.

Painted in 1890. Broken color in lines. The artist was probably as much concerned with vibratory movement as he was with vibrating color.

tion is understood and assimilated in both production and apprecia-tion it can be applied to all pictures. In a landscape or portrait, therefore, as in the still life, the student must accept the principle, keep it in command as he practices, and so liberate himself from the easy temptation to copy facts with skill. And, again let me urge, the surest way to attain this goal is through abstraction toward gradually increasing reality—with the plastic design sense always in control.

The progression from abstraction to reality is well shown by the various portraits illustrated. The earliest figure paintings by be-ginners—Figs. 32 and 38—show the start in crude color-space sym-bols. These increase in refinement and quality in such works as those in Figs. 33 and 42. Then the Matisse and Rouault of Figs. 44 and 60 pick up the thread stemming so directly from the child and the adult beginner and play their portrait harmonies with more mature sensitivity and technique. Then Newberry and Woodruff—Figs. 59 and 62—balance reality and design and Van Gogh and Raphael—Figs. 21 and 20—complete the circle. That progression is circular rather than always ascending to greater perfection is made clear, I think, by Raphael. Even if greater mastery of the means of expression were possible it is not needed and the gain in virtuosity would inevitably mean a loss in other more rewarding qualities. It is well that progress here should return to the simple aesthetics of Matisse.

THE LANDSCAPE AND FIGURE PAINTING

The oudoor world, combining as it does the forces of construction and destruction by both nature and man, provides a stupendous array of materials and motifs on which the creative artist may draw in building his own symbolic expressions.

The old way of using this landscape material was for the artist to fare forth by car or on foot and search, sometimes long and arduously, for the perfect, ready-made picture in the actual scene. The new way may obviously include such a search but is not de-pendent on it. The creative artist can seat himself on any chance spot in the great outdoors and, looking about him near and far, find materials which he can use for a dozen pictures—or a hundred for

Fig. 59.—*Portrait*, by MARY NEWBERRY.**

The integration of line, space, color, and form has been thoroughly assimilated through long study of the exercises herein presented and gradually merged with the expression of reality. A highly personal handling of color has been preserved through all later study. Compare this with her early paintings shown in Fig. 46.

DESIGNED REALITY

***Student of Design Workshop for three years and of Umberto Romano for several summers thereafter.*

that matter—so inexhaustible are the millions of objects and details he sees. He is in command of this material; he can do with it what he will. He can enlarge blades of grass to an ant-eye scale, he can reduce trees to the height of one inch, he can make monsters out of flies or grasshoppers, grains of sand suggest a texture, as do rotting

Fig. 60.—*Clown*, by G. ROUAULT.

A brutal painting in its handling of subject but highly sensitive in its emotional organization of color and space. The felt design is the artist's chief concern; subject is dehumanized and used as a means to that end. This is a plastic painting.

PLASTIC PAINTING

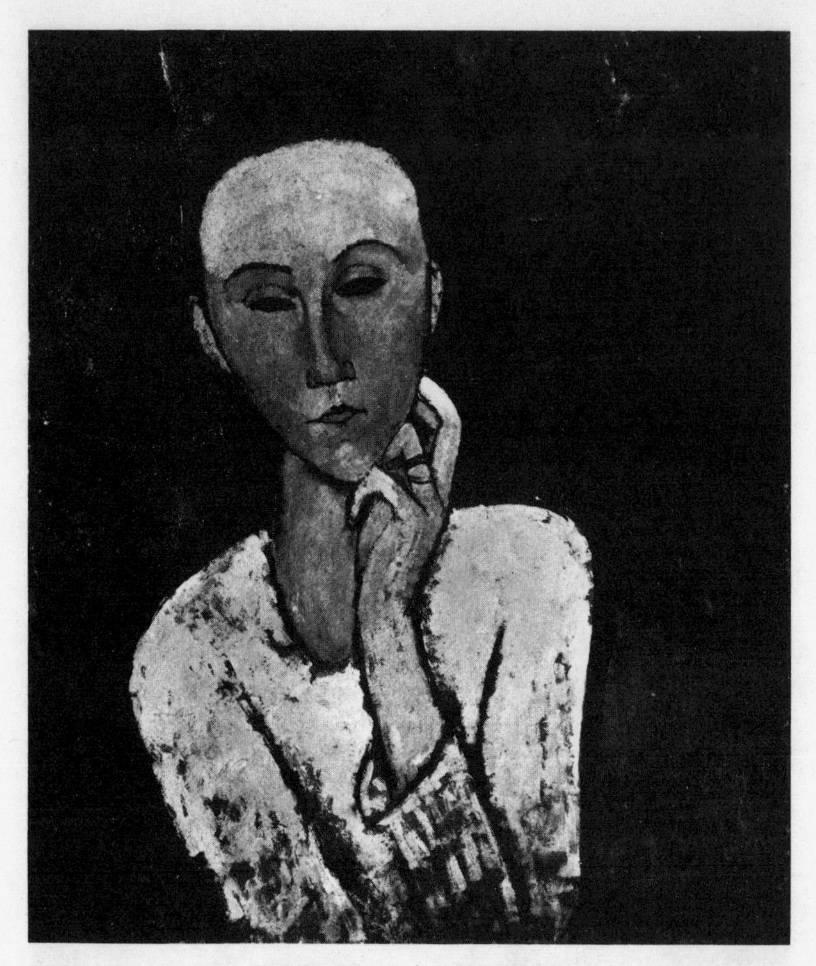

Fig. 61.—*Portrait,* by MODIGLIANI.

Note how face, hand, body, hair, and background are all translated into definite spaces and arranged or emphasized as such into a harmony. Color also is played into an arbitrary—not literal—harmony. There is distortion in the elongated head, neck, and hand yet character of the individual is not slighted. In fact, it is emphasized. This is a real person with individual as well as universal character.

DESIGNED REALITY WITH EMPHASIS ON COLOR-SPACE RELATIONSHIPS

wood, smooth, worn rock, a plowed field, foliage, a shingled roof. Taking such items as motifs he can improvise in abstract harmonies, as Stuart Davis has done in Fig. 68, or he can design reality, or play on some one note predominantly, as Benton does in Fig. 49 with textures. The world is literally at his feet; he is master of all

Fig. 62.—*Suzetta*, by HALE WOODRUFF.

A powerful expression of character. A dramatization of form, space, dark-light, and texture. Form and dark-light are dominants.

DESIGNED REALITY

he surveys; he can create his own landscape out of nature's landscape—if he is the artist creative.

In Fig. 94 a student of Hale Woodruff has so taken from nature qualities and materials and played them into rhythmic harmonies. Albert Wells has taken for his theme the rhythmic movement of naked tree forms played against the soft, wavy texture and movement of grass and the barren, horizontal form of hills. Note the staggered position of the upright forms, the variety in size and direction, the crossing of two limbs in upper left—a very significant interlocking of movement, the pickup of the curved movement across and slightly forward by the prostrate tree, the brush texture of the smaller branches, the one low stump in which is concentrated the darkest dark as, perhaps, a counterfocal point to the many lights. There is complete mastery here of every space, color, movement, and form. Texture is limited with only five or six contrasting notes and two of them, the near grass and the distant hill, repeat each other monotonously and without projection back into deep space. In spite of this weak spot, and an equal clarity of all forms which also spells

Fig. 63.—*Landscape*, by ALBERT WELLS. Morehouse College, Atlanta, Ga. Hale Woodruff, instructor. A creation in sensitive, rhythmic design in movement, texture, and color.

RHYTHMIC MOVEMENT

Fig. 64.—*Sanctuary, oil painting,* by ELIZABETH ERLANGER.**

A powerful expression of tree forms in three-dimensional arrangement contrasted with the soft fluid form of grass and coming to a focal point in the solid forms of distant house and telephone pole.

DESIGNED REALITY

monotony in that department, this is a thoroughly and sensitively organized picture. Since Mr. Wells and his teacher, Mr. Woodruff, are Negro artists, one can assume that the innate sense of rhythm typical of the Negro race has here overflowed copiously into the picture medium.

Sanctuary, by Elizabeth Erlanger, Fig. 64, strikes a mellower note. There is a foil here—the contrast of opposites which rounds out a picture or any work of art. The powerful forms of trunk exquisitely spaced and balanced are counteracted in their brutal impact by the softer forms and textures of grass and foliage. Here the single motif, tree, has its own three-dimensional arrangement of parts, the road moves in a graceful curve back into space, the eye comes to rest on the focal point of house and telephone pole, establishing another balance between the near and the far. Also there is flowing movement throughout. Directions of the parts move, the grass flows in gentle movements of rhythmic repeat and variation. The distant pole leans outward to catch the dominant countermovement of the tree. Design gives life and character to every part—and takes the same from every part.

Emy Herzfeld, in Fig. 65, has played with the motif farm and cows. What fun she has had in the playing! The cocky bull. The sleepy, slightly curious cows. The symbols for barns, silo, road, and tree. All arranged as she the artist creator, waving her magic brush, decreed. No copying of nature here. Symbols from a hundred, or one, farm scenes assembled into the one typical farm. Color, in the original, is the most rewarding of the various sensations. It is rich and deep, seeming to penetrate down into the various surfaces, not as a mere tint to stay on top of them. Also the harmony is lush, full, generous. The whole picture is generous in its sensations.

Fig. 65.—*Connecticut Valley,* by EMY HERZFELD.**

A created and designed landscape. Distance is compressed into what is nearly an over-all color-space-form pattern.

Reinhardt Galleries

Associated American Artists Galleries, New York

Fig. 65A.—*Ozark Bridge*, by JACKSON LEE NESBITT.
Student of Kansas City Art Institute, Thomas H. Benton, Instructor

DESIGNED REALITY

Associated American Artists Galleries, New York

Fig. 65B.—*Breaking Ground at Bethel*, by ROGER MEDEARIS.
Student of Kansas City Art Institute, Thomas H. Benton, Instructor

DESIGNED REALITY IN THE BENTON MANNER

Design and subject merge happily. Regardless of any technical lacks, this is a complete picture.

Thomas Benton has belittled for many years the aesthetics of painting for its own emotional values of the spirit; he has insisted that the aesthetics of design was a practical matter contributing only to the effectiveness of expression. In the last few years, however, his increasing concern with textures and the delicate minutia of plant life indicates a swing away from the stark realism of his murals to a more refined realism which comes much closer to establishing a satisfying balance between reality and aesthetics. To cross the line into the Elysian Fields of pure visual music—that Benton, apparently, can never do.

A recent exhibition of paintings by full-time students of Benton working at the Kansas City Art Institute is exactly in line with this Bentonian perspective. On his challenge to any school in the country "to produce anything comparable in the matter of all-around technical excellence" Benton probably wins. Certainly no greater technical excellence is needed by any young artist; these are masterly expressions of reality. And they are more than that. They have a creative-minded vision back of them which says something about life and nature, which dramatizes and interprets as a living art should. They all show a strong mastery of functional design. All, therefore, are mature and rounded works of modern and universal art of the realistic school. That they do not concern themselves with pure music is no fault and is not open to adverse criticism; it merely places them in one department of human activity instead of another. And another point. Whereas former work by Benton students has been so Bentonian that it could easily be mistaken for that of the master, these, even though announcing their influence, speak up for themselves in their individual languages sufficiently to be healthy, creative works. Figs. 50A, 65A and 65B are typical of the showing at its best.

MURAL PAINTING

The primary function of a mural painting is to decorate a wall. It may achieve such decoration abstractly, without specific subject, or with subject in different degrees of reality. These two functions are thoroughly established by history as well as by common sense and more or less by common practice. I say "more or less" advisedly, for in common practice in our time the decorative function is often neglected and sometimes ignored in favor of the more practical one of telling a story or portraying facts. If it is logical to assume that the two functions are somewhere nearly equal in importance it is not stretching logic too far, I think, to say that, if one is to receive preference, it should be the pleasure-giving, rather than the fact-telling, function that is in line for that honor. Presumably we pass muraled walls frequently and somewhat casually. If, in the passing, a thrill, a lift, a catch of visual excitement is contributed to the daily routine that contribution is something precious and tangible which can be taken away and used to illuminate the nonexciting hours. "This thing we call art," once said a woman dressed in mourning for a lost husband, "is something one can hold on to when all other values are slipping." The mural can bring this fresh hold on life out of the cloistered retreat into the public way. And, may I labor the point, it is not from *facts* that exhilaration flows.

To say that a mural should decorate a wall is to understate the case, because the word "decoration" has been worn thin by a long overusage with meager implications. The word "plastic" might well supplant it provided its implications are understood. Whatever the term, it is the deep sensory satisfactions of design that we are reading into the decorative function of the mural painting when we say that function should equal or take precedence over story and fact. A mural painting, whatever may be its content, must be designed.

There are several distinct schools of mural painting, each with its own debits and credits and list of ardent devotees.

THE NATURALISTIC SCHOOL

This school in mural painting is a paradox. The naturalistic picture cannot perform the basic function of the mural for two main reasons. It ignores its own picture plane or surface and so cannot decorate it. It is a stranger to the laws of design.

THE ROMANTIC SCHOOL

One school of mural painting believes it is the duty of the mural to "uplift" humanity. Its painters produce idyllic daydreams about perfect worlds where handsome youths cut hay while beautiful damoiselles sing songs and strum their lyres. This is the Romantic School. It flourished in the last century and even up to the start of the Roosevelt administration's art program, as our public buildings prior to that revolution in taste so copiously testify. The fact that mere human beings do not like to be "uplifted" and that the sordid realities of the struggle for existence are not forgotten or dispelled by immaculate concepts painted on walls did not discourage this school—it is so easy to be idealistic in paint. Nearly all the major (in size) murals at Rockefeller Center are romantic—the ones by Brangwyn and Sert being typical examples. Rivera's dynamic fresco, Man at the Crossroads, was destroyed after its installation because it dealt with realities instead of romance. This school should have died with the nineteenth century which it capably represented; it is unfortunate to find its creed of romantic escape from real life carried into the twentieth.

The Romantic School, being a product of the nineteenth century, quite naturally absorbed the naturalistic habits of its time. These habits with their ignorance of pictorial design ensured complete failure in the primary function of the mural—decoration of the wall—merely because such decoration depends on the organization of line, space, color, and form which naturalistic art lacks. The confusions which are inevitable when the naturalistic artist attempts decoration are pathetic in their futile attempts to reconcile the irreconcilables of decoration and naturalism. Oil and water do not mix. Neither does the record of fact and harmonic organization. The naturalistic artist cannot paint a mural which fulfills the primary function of mural art.

THE PHOTO-MURAL

The recent attempt to impress the enlarged photograph into substitute duty for the painted mural is dramatic evidence of this failure of naturalism to perform the decorative function. The photo-

Fig. 66.—*Mutiny on the Amistad.* A mural by HALE WOODRUFF for Talladega College at Talladega, Alabama. A highly dramatic expression of a dramatic event—the mutiny of 42 Negroes who had been kidnaped to be sold as slaves. Painted with keen insight and feeling by the leading Negro artist of the South.

DESIGNED REALITY, HIGHLY DECORATIVE

graph is a naturalistic picture made by an instrument instead of the human hand. It records all facts which were in front of the lens at the time of the exposure. Like naturalistic painting, it gives the illusion of portraying objects in deep space, as they exist in nature. It records chaos. It completely fails to organize colors, spaces, and forms on the plane of the picture into harmonic relationships. The plane of the picture becomes the plane of the wall, in a mural. The designed picture recognizes this plane and builds all materials into it. The naturalistic picture fails on both these counts.

Approval of the photo-mural or the naturalistic painting for wall decoration means that the attention is shifted from design to subject —that the art of the picture and the essence of the decorative function are ignored.

THE PROPAGANDA SCHOOL

Another school of mural painting which has grown out of the economic and political unrest of the postwar period does deal with the cold, hard realities of life and with their cause and cure. History teaches that in all periods much vital art has grown out of a natural concern with and desire to express life problems of the day, religious or temporal. It is natural, therefore, and logical that the same concern should stimulate a vital art in our time. It can do so; it has done so; it is doing so. The danger lies in an unbalanced attack by this interest—an attack which, in its concern with subject meaning, forgets the art of the picture. Reams of such art-less pictures including murals have been produced in our present renaissance both within and without the important government program. Propaganda must be balanced by art. Subject, whatever it is, must be balanced by art. That is the challenge to the propaganda artist and to all students of tomorrow and today.

THE ABSTRACT SCHOOL

It can be argued that a just balance between subject and design should result in the greatest art. The great religious paintings of the European Renaissance support this claim, as do many important paintings of today. Content gives character to form; form harmonizes

Fig. 67.—*Collapse*, by GILBERT WILSON.

One of a series of three mural panels done for Antioch College as a gift of the class of 1938. Aside from being one of the most constructive gifts a graduating class could possibly make to its Alma Mater, this is an excellent example of a propaganda mural in which *content* is well balanced by *form*.

SEMIABSTRACT, HIGHLY SYMBOLIC, THREE-DIMENSIONAL DESIGN

PANEL I: "Collapse." In the upper third of the mural, an industrial system that has got out of hand is represented as sinister, twisted machinery and tangled beams, crushing down upon Man. Bursting bombs show the imminence of violence and war. In the middle of the picture is an empty, shattered safe. Serenely unaware that the world is giving way beneath them, a dowager with a teacup and a hatchet-faced woman sewing swastikas into the flag tumble in undignified postures to destruction. At the bottom a large, putrescent, very much alive figure—the "best people" in our present society—tries to escape the ruin pouring down. Beneath him lies a human fetus—the future.

content. The two functions should blend into the mature, rounded-out expression.

But we have had a plethora of storytelling murals both in this country and in general throughout history. If decoration in its richer meanings *is* the primary function of the mural, then we sorely need a shift of emphasis to those qualities which most effectively give forth visual sensation. Abstraction is the one and only thorough means to such a shift. As explained in Chapter II, it facilitates more generalized meaning; it liberates the picture into symbolism and design. Abstraction adapts itself more easily than the real form to the organizations of design and can be enjoyed as design without the compelling distractions of real subject with its intrusive meaning. Hence it can decorate a wall more easily and completely and give forth to the passer-by its contribution of keen aesthetic pleasure (if it has such a contribution to give). For all these reasons the abstract mural is important and should be made use of much more than it has been to date. To the students of today who will be the mural painters of tomorrow I commend this thought.

The same argument, of course, applies to the easel painting and to the print—to all pictures, in fact, including photograph and motion picture. In each of these abstraction can add its rich experience values, its different interpretations of reality. The possibilities have only begun to be explored.

If there is logic in this conclusion it again approves the emphasis on, and priority of, the abstract method as the starting point for all creative painting. All that it has of value can be transferred to the real subject if so desired or its contribution can stand in its own right as an immensely important contribution to the art of our time.

In this long chapter I have tried to show the immense range of the art of painting when naturalism is taboo and emotional creation the order of the day. While claiming that emotion rather than intellect must be the source of the art in painting I have not limited illustrations to the obviously emotional type but have shown works so precise in their delineation of subject that a severe mental discipline is definitely in control. But in each such case—the mural by Davis in Fig. 37, for instance, and the works by Woodruff and his students—selection of the specific work has been made because

New York City WPA Art Project

Fig. 68.—*Waterfront Forms,* a mural, by STUART DAVIS. Oil on canvas. Above: Preliminary study for color-space arrangements. Below: The completed mural. Note the complex interplay of lines, complex and simple color shapes, brick, water, ladder, mast, rope, and other motifs.

ABSTRACT LINE-SPACE-COLOR DESIGN

I could see authentic emotion under the precision even when that approached hardness. No work illustrated in this book, except such horrible examples as are shown in Figs. 11 and 81, reveals the aesthetic barrenness of the purely intellectual product. Emotion authenticates creative painting. My illustrations, I trust, will prove the point.

DEFINITIONS OF COLOR TERMS

HUE: The kind of color, as red, blue, violet, etc.

VALUE: The degree of light or dark of a color. Light blue, dark blue, dark neutral, etc. The tone value. TINT is a value lighter than the pure color, as a pale yellow is lightened with white paint or paper diluting the original color. SHADE is darker in value than the pure color.

INTENSITY: The amount of brightness or dullness of a color. A pure yellow is at full intensity. A yellow mixed with some red and blue is neutralized or dulled to a gray-yellow.

PRIMARY: Red, yellow, blue are primary colors.

SECONDARY: Mixtures of two primaries make secondary colors. Thus orange, green, and purple are secondary colors.

COMPLEMENTARY: The complement of a color is a combination of its two opposites in the color scale. The opposite of red is yellow-blue, or green. The opposite of blue is red-yellow, or orange. That of yellow is red-blue, or purple.

NEUTRAL: Red, yellow, and blue mixed equally make gray. In all mixtures color is grayed, or neutralized. When one color is dominant in such mixtures you have a blue-gray, a yellow-gray, etc.

BROKEN COLOR: Color broken up into its constituent parts in a painting. See explanation on page 95.

FLAT COLOR: Premixed color applied uniformly. Poster painting usually assumes the use of flat color.

Fig. 69.—Abstraction, a wood engraving by PAUL LANDACRE.[1]

7. CREATIVE DRAWING

DEFINITION

CREATIVE drawing is not concerned with copying the appearance of objects as they are seen by the physical eyes in a particular light at a particular moment of time. It is not concerned, that is to say, with the accidents of light and shade falling on the surfaces of things and revealing the chaos of a multitude of visual facts and details. It is not mere craftsmanship. It is not *naturalistic* drawing. Creative drawing demands that he who draws shall be a creative artist instead of a craftsman from his first crude beginnings through all later, more mature developments.

OBJECTIVES

The major objectives of creative drawing are:

1. Perceiving and expressing the essential form-character of subject by the control of light and shade.
2. Dramatization of both subject and picture.
3. Organization of all the elements of a picture into a plastic syn-

[1] This print is one of nine recently selected by the author as among the most distinguished contemporary woodcuts to illustrate his article on woodcuts in the revised edition of the Encyclopaedia Britannica.

thesis of modern design. This includes control of line, space, texture, light-dark, planes, and forms and their relationships to each other and to the whole.

Fig. 70.—*Zorn and His Wife.* Naturalistic drawing in an etching by ANDERS ZORN. Here is a copying of actual lights and shadows as they are seen on a subject in a particular light at a particular moment of time. The chaos of nature is recorded with great technical skill. There is composition but no sense whatever of design Single lines are absorbed into the mass.

NATURALISM

In creative painting the first objective was emotional freedom and the development of the power to sense and express color and its harmonic relationships—a subjective process.

In creative drawing the first objective—the perceiving and expressing of essential form-character—is a much more tangible and practical process, which is mainly objective.

These two objectives lie in distinctly different fields with different

Fig. 71—*Cats*, by SOUTHER BUTTRICK.*

A fantasy expressing the cattiness of cats rather than their surface verities. A harmony in dark, light, and gray, also a sensitive space arrangement.

EMOTIONAL DRAWING

values and should be kept separate in early training. Later, when both are mastered and have become part of the student's equipment, they may and should merge in order to achieve the emotionally expressive drawing or painting of reality. But the merging is a subtle process and must be carefully nourished so that the values in each field are preserved without loss in either.

Since we are discarding the tenets of naturalistic drawing we can also discard such props and skills of naturalism as perspective, verisimilitude, exact tone values, etc. Perspective is an illusion of the diminishing size of objects as they retreat into deep space. It is useful only in representing actual appearances and can be used or discarded as a creative artist may desire. Since objects do not actually decrease in size merely because they happen to be at a distance from one pair of eyes, the individual illusion of their so doing may be ignored the moment an artist is concerned with realities. In Persian miniatures

Fig. 72.—A retouched photograph showing dramatic edges in the head, arm muscles, and the rope. This indicates the presence of this optical illusion in nature and its effectiveness as a means of expressing form.

DRAMATIC EDGES

perspective is often reversed with a gain in design quality and in the reality of the scene. Perspective is an unimportant tool for the artist to pick up when needed; the essentials of its use can be learned in ten minutes of explanation. The skills which can produce verisimilitude are also tools which, as we shall see, develop sufficiently when discarded from primary consideration.

Free, emotional drawing which combines expression of reality with a sensitive feeling for space and form design is illustrated in the rather crude but authentic work by Nellie M. Johnson in Fig. 12, also in the fluid interpretation of a piano by Dorothy Brake in Fig. 92 and in the highly complex St. Louis Blues by Laura Woolsey in Fig. 107. These are all concrete expressions and so limited to the concrete concept. I readily grant that there is need of the picture which goes beyond the concrete into unplumbable realms of spirit. As a means thereto, however, I prefer the harmonies of Fig. 1 (Buttrick), among students, and the abstractions of Fig. 80 (Kandinsky), Fig. 7 (Bauer), and Fig. 37 (Davis), among professionals. All these conform to universal harmonic laws. They do not register new dimensions by linear and spatial discords.

DRAWING FORM

To draw essential form consider the simplest of all forms, a cube and a cylinder. These exist in space as solids whose exterior, visible surfaces fall into flat and curved planes. These planes are revealed by variations of light and shade. The actual light falling on these planes at any particular moment may be confusing and tend to hide, rather than to clarify, their shapes and directions. Since our purpose is to draw *form* it becomes a first necessity arbitrarily to control light and shade to make them reveal these planes more clearly than they are normally seen. To do this we supplement vision with knowledge. Knowing the essential character of a cube through careful examination—hefting, feeling, perceiving, from all sides, measuring with a rule or any other fact-finding method—we manipulate light and shade in a drawing to make them say *cube* so forcefully that character is both sensed and perceived. Awareness of the result is a combination of knowing, perceiving, and sensing.

The simplest way to express form through control of light and shade on different planes is to graduate light into three different degrees on the three visible sides of cube or cylinder. Since a top light is normal, light can be thought of as falling from above like snow. All top planes will then be in full light intensity. If light comes from directly above, all side, vertical planes will receive the same degree. Better for our purpose to assume that the source is above and to one side. Then one side, vertical plane will receive more than another. Figure 73 illustrates this elemental truth on a cube and a cylinder.

DRAMATIC EDGES

More effective, however, than this simple statement is an exaggeration of observable light facts in nature based on an optical illusion.

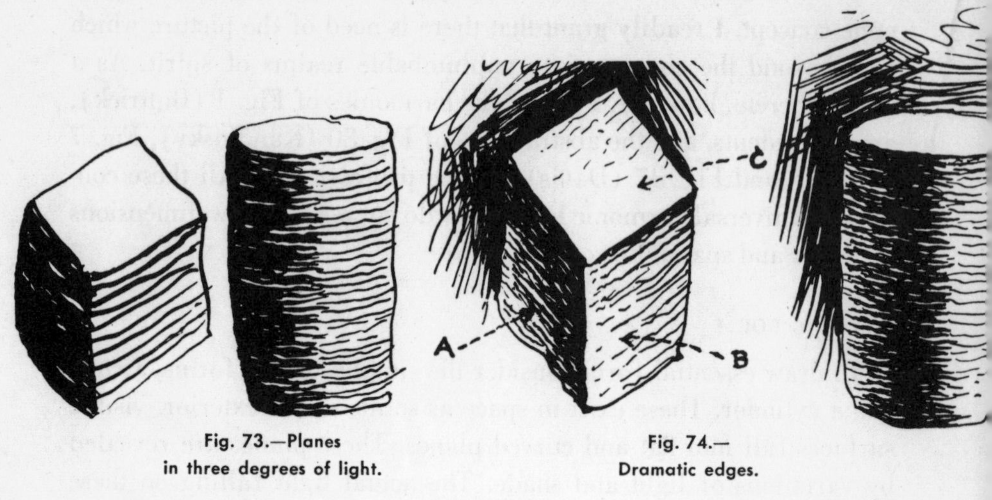

Fig. 73.—Planes in three degrees of light.

Fig. 74.—Dramatic edges.

DRAMATIC EDGES

Place a cube or any square object in a top and to-one-side light where you have the three gradations mentioned. Carefully observe the dark plane A of Fig. 74. Where does it appear darkest? At the edge where it meets the light plane C. Also at the edge where it meets the less-light plane B. And plane B is darkest where it meets the light plane C. Contrarily, it appears lightest where it meets the dark plane A.

From this optical illusion (for these planes are not actually darker or lighter where they meet each other; they only appear to be so) a law is deducible. Dark appears darker where it meets light and light lighter where it meets dark.

On a curved surface the same law holds, only the gradation is gradual instead of sharp. See cylinder in Fig. 74.

This simple law when applied in drawing or painting accentuates, or dramatizes, form. It does so through what can be called the exploitation of *dramatic edges*. The clarification and dramatization of form as form in the manner just described fulfills the first two objectives of creative drawing, except that the dramatization of the picture as a whole must include the third objective—design. Design, here as in painting and in sculpture, adds aesthetics to the conception and treatment of subject. Also it contributes vitally to the dramatization of subject and the total picture.

Fig. 75.—A drawing by STEVE BODNARCZUK* showing the application of dramatic edges to the expression of form.

Fig. 76.—Drawing by INGRID FETZ* An overstressing of dramatic edges to accent form.

DRAMATIC EDGES AS A MEANS OF CLARIFYING AND ACCENTING FORM

Fig. 77.—Free, emotional organization of forms and planes using dramatic edges, by ELLEN DONOVAN.*

Fig. 78.—*Benkei and Yoshitsune,* Japanese print, by Hokusai, showing the use of line to express varied character.

LINE CHARACTER

DESIGN—ORGANIZATION OF LINE, SPACE, TEXTURE, LIGHT-DARK, PLANES, AND FORM

In *Experiencing Pictures*[2] I have given an entire chapter to each of the above departments of design, except planes, showing the char-

[2] Harcourt, Brace & Company.

acter and uses of each in pictures. I have shown how design organization takes place and how various artists of past and present have applied it in their creations. I shall not repeat such data here. Instead I shall give examples of the organization of line, space, texture, light-dark, planes, and form as such occur in drawing, for each of these except form can best be studied in this medium. Form organization should be studied in modeling—first in clay, later in any plastic material. All, when mastered in one medium, can be applied in any other; applications, in fact, are universal. Illustrations are by modern artists and people of a wide variety in age and professions, done while they were students of a number of different schools.

FUNCTIONS OF DESIGN

In Chapter IV I outlined five functions of design as follows:

Specific and cosmic order
Placing of objects in the picture—composition
Directional movement of objects and eye—composition
Plastic movement
Plastic organization of the whole

In Chapter VI, on painting, I did not stress these specific functions, the objective there being to achieve design as unconsciously as possible and to appraise results after, rather than before, the event. In this chapter I am making the quest more conscious, thereby rounding out the attack and filling in any former omissions. The healthy blending of unconscious and conscious results should facilitate this quest.

The richly plastic picture is our ultimate design goal. Many steps take their place in a satisfying achievement, as many parts enter into the construction of any functioning machine. We shall not attempt to appraise each such part as we go; we shall only concede the importance of each to the functioning of the whole and build as best we can. Perfection, in such building, is, alas, elusive and judgment, because it relies on taste, is insecure. Empirical judgment is our right in matters of taste; we can like what we like because we like it and boldly announce the result. Only privately it is wise to examine our reasons and be sure that they are at least relevant. There can be peculiar and remote reasons for liking a work of art. Pleasure in the work is an excellent reason and, when achieved, is no mean gain.

LINE AND LINE RELATIONSHIPS

Lines, as shown in the special chapter in *Experiencing Pictures,* have a wide range in character and function. The Japanese use eighteen different types of lines, each expressing a different characteristic of subject. We, with no specific types, still have many different kinds which can be described by such adjectives as straight, curved, flowing, zigzag, firm, jerky, uniform, tapering, heavy, light, mechanical, fluid, and others. These kinds of lines, when used in a picture or an abstract design, contribute their characteristics to both subject and design, giving each a heightened meaning. Since we are less conscious of symbolic meanings than the Orientals we have hardly scratched the surface of possibilities for the enrichment of the picture which lie in this direction. In Fig. 80 Kandinsky exploits two of the above line characteristics — mechanical and fluid, or emotional — as do Leger in Fig. 7 and Bauer in Fig. 8.

In addition to what may be called their psychological meanings lines have a sensory effect on the eye which observes them as motifs in a decoration. Thus a zigzag line has a very different effect from a smooth, flowing line. So have straight and curved lines and heavy and light. These visual aspects of line are ready-made variables waiting to be exploited in a design for their sensory qualities.

There are three main ways in which lines can be used in pictures. One way is to blend lines into a mass to create a tone value, each single line being absorbed into the mass and not functioning as an entity to be observed in its own right. This usage can result in the naturalistic picture like the Zorn in Fig. 70 or in a designed picture where tone value instead of line is the means of expressing form (see Fig. 134).

A second way to use lines is to play each line as a decorative entity in its own right—the line interpreting subject, if any, and at the same time serving as a decorative motif. The Japanese print in Fig. 78 is such a work, as are also the line drawings in Figs. 80, 89, and 94.

The third way more or less combines these two. Each line does count as an entity in itself at the same time that it blends into a mass

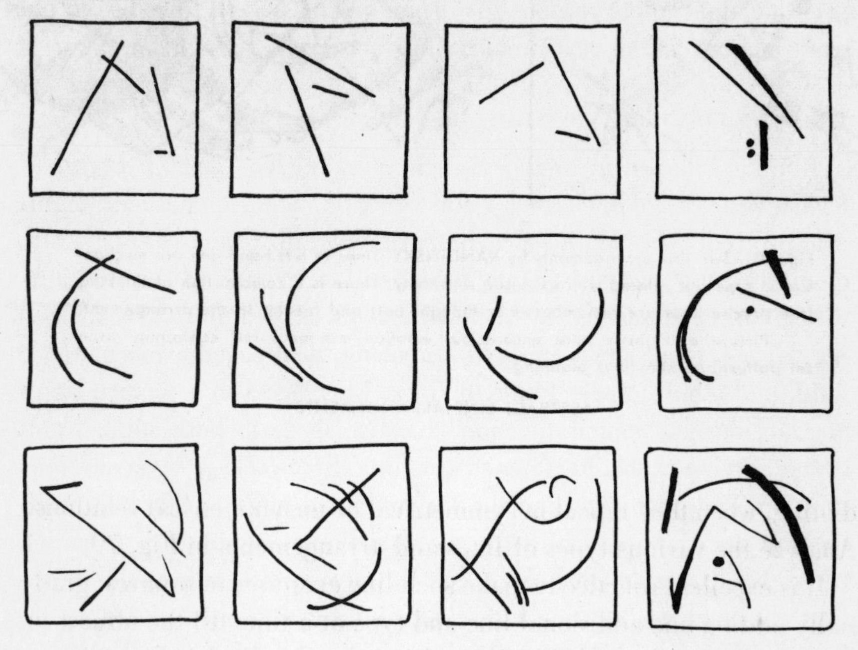

Fig. 79.—Arrangements of straight and curved lines in squares by BETTY HOWE.*

LINE RELATIONSHIPS

to express tone value and realistic subject. Such usage can be naturalistic but also adapts to the controls of design. Wanda Gág designs lines in this way in Fig. 90, as did Dürer in Fig. 95.

It is in the last two of these ways of dealing with line that we are interested.

Lines considered as elements in the picture can have the many characteristics suggested by the above list of adjectives; also they can have various relationships to each other. The simplest types are straight, curved, zigzag, flowing, wide, narrow, short, long, tapering. The relationships of such lines can be rhythmic, oppositional, parallel, repetitive, radiating, symmetrical, unsymmetrical, balanced, unbalanced. A few of the endless diversifications of such lines and arrangements are illustrated in the arrangements in squares of Fig. 79.

Rhythm begins when two or more lines, like two or more notes in music, play together in harmonic relationship. Rhythm can act when lines are in opposition to each other, when they are parallel or ra-

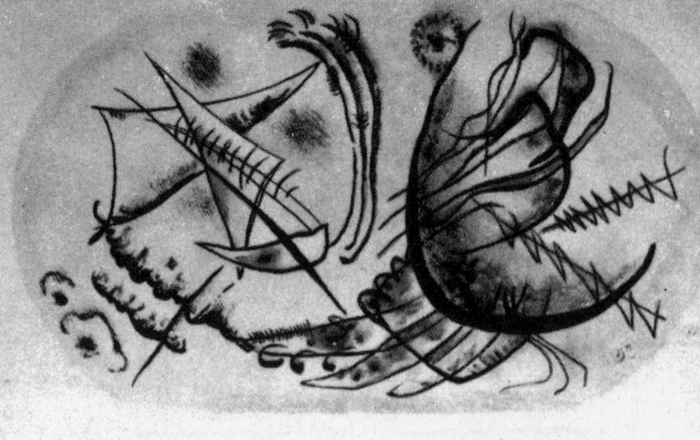

Fig. 80.—Two line arrangements by KANDINSKY. Lines in left hand one are mechanical in type but related with exquisite sensitivity. There is a combination of thinking (the precise lines are remembered or thought out) and feeling in the arrangement.

Picture at right is pure unconscious emotion—no measured conformity to a set pattern, no conscious planning.

ABSTRACT LINE ARRANGEMENTS

diating, when they repeat in symmetrical or unsymmetrical relations. Analyze the various types of lines and arrangements in Fig. 79.

It is excellent practice to make such line exercises in squares, gradually adding one additional line and type at a time till the utmost in complexity is achieved. The abstractions by Kandinsky, Fig. 80, are such amplifications, and such line motifs and arrangements have their place in the more complex abstractions of Bauer in Fig. 7.

LINE AND SPACE—CONTOUR DRAWING

Lines which enclose areas make spaces. The word "space" can refer to the limitless space of the universe or to a limited area within boundaries. Used here as an ingredient of pictures it means an area within a single plane which has limits. These limits may be defined by the meeting of two colors, in painting, or by lines as in Figs. 84 and 85. A plane may be flat like one side of a box or curved as in a cylinder. Or a plane may be considered spherical like the surface of a ball.

An outlined space may be an arbitrary, imagined shape, as is each in Fig. 84, or it may be taken from some object, as is each space in Fig. 85. Either type may then be drawn with emphasis on its character as a space and woven into a two-dimensional pattern with other spaces on the flat plane of picture surface. Or spaces may perform the double function of lying on the flat picture plane at the same time that they portray planes at different angles in deep space—as in the case of the checkerboard floor pattern in Fig. 89. When such spaces do portray objects they perform a third function; they become symbols. To state the case again in different words and with different illustrations: space can be used decoratively without concrete subject meaning in either two or three dimensions —see the Davis mural, Fig. 68. Or it can be translated into a symbol for subject in any degree of complexity and used in either two- or three-dimensional representation at the same time that it is woven into plastic design with other spaces. The black-and-white space patterns of Fig. 88 illustrate this in two dimensions, the sewing machine parts of Fig. 91 in a slight departure from two to three dimensions, and the piano of Fig. 92 in three dimensions. The color-space patterns by students of Carl Holty in Fig. 38 are more complex illustrations of this three-dimensional arrangement. The still lifes of Fig. 40 (Dreher), Fig. 48 (King) and Fig. 50 (McFee) are masterworks illustrating the same.

From these various uses in pictures it is obvious that space is as concrete an element in picture building as are the more self-assertive elements of line, color, and form.

In contour drawing a pencil with sharp point should be held vertically and, with a free arm movement, drawn around each space—the attention being focused on the space as a space to make it both interesting and characteristic of subject if there is subject. In Fig. 85 note how each space is so drawn—how the table is distorted to make it more unexpected and interesting. Distortion, it should be remembered, does just that.

TEXTURE AND TEXTURE DESIGN

Texture means quality of surface—smooth, rough, hard, soft, woolly, silky, and so on. These textures can be represented in a drawing or painting by a treatment which symbolizes each different type, and then these textural effects can be organized into textural chords of repeats, variations, and harmonies just as color, line, and space can be organized. For many years Thomas Benton gave no attention to textures, all his surfaces having the same smooth quality with a resultant monotony of effect. Recently he has admitted

Fig. 81

INSENSITIVE TO SPACE DESIGN

A plaque by a high school student (reproduced in a magazine article by the teacher as a worthy example) which shows intellectualized design. There is no feeling whatever for space quality. A bleak, barren work. Contrast it to the felt designs of Charles Virga in Fig. 89.

this lack and swung to the opposite extreme with textures featured more ardently than any other plastic quality. Pussy Cat and Roses, Fig. 49, is an example of this and can be called an overstressing of the one quality to a point where its presence becomes as objectionable as formerly was its lack. Note how every object in this painting has its different texture even to the wood of tabletop. Note also

Fig. 82.—Spaces in nature. Each flower is an ordered design as a unit. The total arrangement, however, though interesting because of variety, is accidental and chaotic.

CHAOTIC SPACE ARRANGEMENT

Fig. 83.—Textile design by a student of Cooper Union. Carol Harrison, instructor. The single unit and the total arrangement are designed.

DESIGNED SPACE ARRANGEMENT

how many textures are exaggerated as in the tufted rug and the fur of cat—an exaggeration which becomes garish because of its obviousness. In the woodcut by Dürer, Fig. 95, textures are more normal in relation to other qualities and thoroughly integrated into the design. The masters of the fifteenth and sixteenth centuries in Europe knew texture design as they knew all design and used it with masterly restraint.[3]

DARK-LIGHT AND DARK-LIGHT DESIGN

Dark and light can be used in a picture in at least five different ways. These are:

1. To model form by control of light and shade.
2. For their psychological meanings. Dark gloom, light gaiety, etc.
3. As decorative elements in a pattern.
4. For dramatic effect.

[3] Since Benton and his disciple Craven have always derided "aesthetics" and sensory experience, claiming that design is a means to an end and never should be an end in itself, this attempt to play on the sensitivities with texture effects is illuminating. If its crassness makes it an aesthetic discord, as I believe it does, it may well exemplify an intellectual attempt at what can only be emotional harmonics to be authentic. Intellect has fared beyond its depth and failed. The failure proves that intellect has its limitations in this field and explains the attacks on aesthetics as that familiar recourse of human beings to condemn what they do not understand.

Fig. 84.—Space arrangements with straight and curved lines by BETTY HOWE.*

TWO-DIMENSIONAL SPACE RELATIONSHIPS, SIMPLE

5. As an element of design.

The first part of this chapter illustrates the modeling of form. Pictures of storm, night, dark interiors and sunlight and brightly lighted interiors suggest psychological meanings. The drawings by Charles Virga, Fig. 89, are perfect examples of decorative elements in a pattern. Fig. 75 is a dramatization of the forms of ordinary blocks and practically all the drawings shown in this chapter are examples of light and dark used as material for the total design of the picture. Such use is particularly striking in the drawings by Souther Buttrick, Figs. 1 and 105.

There is nothing new about any of these qualities. Numbers 1 and 2 have probably been used in all pictures dealing with form since pictures have been made. The old masters were adepts in dramatization as have been in greater or lesser degree numerous, but not all, of their followers. And it is ironic that the earliest known pictures—the drawings on the walls of caves—have in many cases more pattern and design since than have our naturalistic pictures of today.

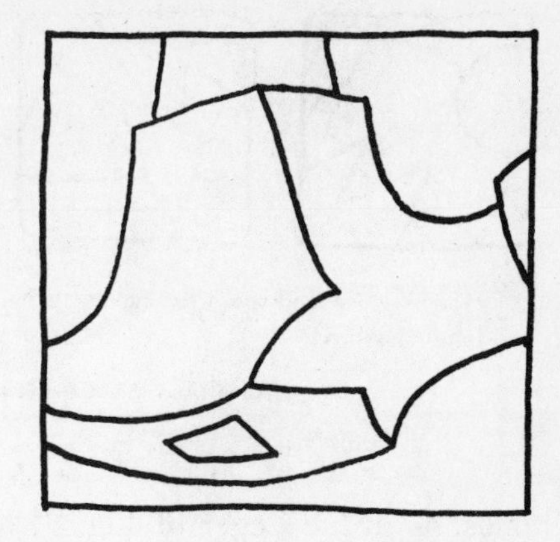

Fig. 85.—Space arrangements by BETTY HOWE.* Spaces taken from real forms.

THREE-DIMENSIONAL SUBJECT-SPACE
RELATIONSHIPS, CONTOUR DRAWING

PLANES AND PLANE DESIGN

The surface of a picture is a plane on which, or into which, all the elements of subject and the means to its expression are organized into a plastic whole. Planes which are the surfaces of three-dimensional forms, as has been explained under the heading Plastic Form in Chapter IV, perform what is really a triple function in the plastic picture. They represent subject, they decorate or design picture surface, and they can be organized into space-plane harmonics within the picture field. I say "space-plane" instead of "plane" harmonics to include the shapes of planes as well as their directional movement in deep space as a quality to be dealt with in the design. If this shape or limitation of the plane is understood as part of its quality, the word "space" can be omitted from the title.

Planes can be parallel to the picture plane, retreating into deep space away from it, or they can fall into a limitless diversity of angular movements. In the natural scene these movements and relationships are accidental and chaotic; the artist's task is to order them into a balanced harmony of pulls and stresses—into an integrated whole. He can do this with naked planes alone as in the diagrams of Fig. 96 and the plane arrangements by Bauer in Fig. 7*a* and *e*. Or he can break into the plane harmonies with supplementary lines and

Fig. 86.—Line and space arrangements by MABEL VANDIVER.* Also illustrates overlapping planes.

ABSTRACT SPACE RELATIONSHIPS, COMPLEX

tones, as in the Leger of Fig. 8; or with textures, shadows, foliage, or nitches as Survage has done in a masterly way in Fig. 112.

The diagrams of Fig. 96 illustrate a few variations of plane relationships. In *a* the planes are parallel to the picture plane but, because of their overlapping, seem to retreat into deep space in a downward curve—as indicated by the dotted line from center to center.

In *b* the planes are still parallel to each other but not to the picture plane. They are of different sizes and move back into the picture in a wavy movement as indicated by a line from center to center.

In *c* the parallelism is gone, diversity of movement begins.

In *d* shapes change as a preliminary to symbolizing objects of varied character—round, square, etc.

In *e* diversity increases with a countermovement of small planes opposing the major group of movements.

In *f* planes have been lifted from the surfaces of rocks (see Fig. 99) and diagrammed to emphasize their plane relationships. Note how the small rock and its top plane at left center become the focal point of the entire picture.

Fig. 87.—Subject translated into space arrangements by MABEL VANDIVER.*

Fig. 88.—Subject translated into sensitive black-and-white space arrangements in a square by BETTY HOWE.*

SUBJECT-SPACE RELATIONSHIPS

What makes such plane arrangements aesthetically right? Sensitivity. How is sensitivity developed? By such practice and study as we are here presenting. I am avoiding long word explanations of the functioning of plastic form and all its parts because comprehension does not come through that means. It comes through practice and that alone.

FORM DESIGN

Form in this discussion is used in the sense of volume, or mass; not in the sense of a designed structure, which it can also connote.

In nature an individual form, like a tree, plant, flower, snowflake, or animal, is a design in the sense that there is an orderly, functional arrangement of the parts. Such a single, functional design may be beautiful—that is, the arrangement of the parts may be a visual harmony pleasing to look at. This kind of design is present and can be enjoyed when the single object is detached from the general scene and observed for its own specific qualities.

When dozens or hundreds of objects in the natural scene are observed, however, the individual design with its order is lost in the chaotic arrangement of the many as these appear to the observer. Nature, therefore, is chaotic in the total picture it presents to the single pair of eyes observing it. If copied in a picture, this chaos is transferred to the picture. The task of the creative artist is to bring order into the arrangement of forms in his picture—to build pictorial *form*.

PLASTIC DESIGN

Fig. 89.—Highly sensitive creations in line, space, planes, and dark-light, based on firsthand observation of life and environment, by CHARLES VIRGA. Cooper Union. Carol Harrison, instructor.

In a picture or sculpture, as in nature, a single form or a group of forms may be designed, each being a unity.

Such forms present the most effective way of studying form design. From the single form to the group of three, five, and more is a logical development that rapidly gains in complexity as the number and variety of forms increase. In the picture the interplay of three-dimensional movements and relationships shown in Fig. 102 illustrates the possibilities and provides the plan for all manner of applications to diverse subjects. For instance, compare this with Fig. 104 and note the similarities. In the former the white cylinder is the pivot around which other forms swing; in the latter the standing man becomes that pivot. The planes of the near flat block are about the same in each, whereas in the latter the planes of walls and steps are an enlargement of the walls of the various blocks. Then the bending man becomes a complex diagonal group of movements much more complex than any block and his suspenders and the stones in the wall amplify their planes and add varied eye experiences and richer values to their areas. Note how the crossed suspenders become the most active motif in the whole and thereby center interest on their owner.

Fig. 90.—Illustration for *Snow White and the Seven Dwarfs,* by WANDA GAG. Line, space, and dark-light are woven with subject into a highly fanciful decoration which should delight the soul of children of any age. Each line functions individually and blends into the whole.

DECORATIVE LINE AND SPACE ARRANGEMENT

Form design should be studied in modeling. The simple exercises suggested in Chapter IX provide the way. They can be mastered in their basic essentials in some two weeks of practice and experiment. Once so mastered the principles involved can be applied wherever forms are organized into design.

There are three main ways of designing the placing and directional movement of forms in pictures.

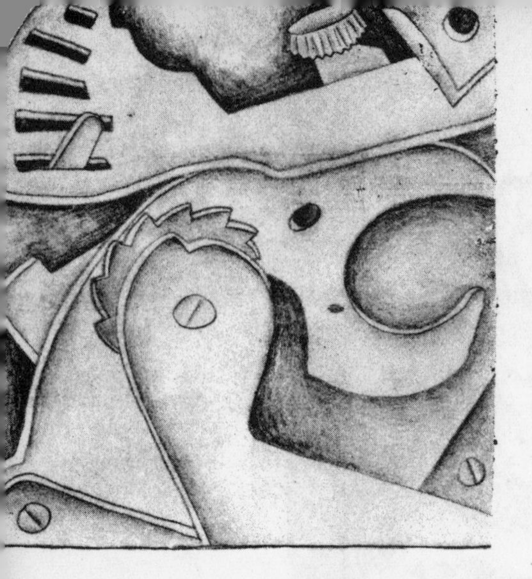

Fig. 91.—*Sewing Machine Parts*, by DOROTHY BRAKE.*
A subject space arrangement carried into three dimensions.

SUBJECT-SPACE ARRANGEMENT

Fig. 92.—*Piano*, by DOROTHY BRAKE.*
Space arrangement in a three-dimensional object where every space is woven into a felt design. Note that background space is as carefully considered as any other, also the dynamic accent of the black keys.

SUBJECT SPACE-FORM DESIGN

1. To arrange forms in a row.
2. To stagger forms all parallel to each other but at different distances from the eye, like standing trees in a forest.
3. To arrange forms moving in many directions and at different distances from the eye, as occurs in the general scene with its endless diversities, but controlling all such forms to create an integrated whole.

The first of these arrangements is too simple to be interesting. The second is too uniform to please; the eye craves variety. The third is based on the realities of nature and is unlimited in its potentialities for visual interest and excitement.

Directional movement back into deep space within the picture field, around a pivot and out again, plus any degree of added complexity of supplementary or countermovements, is illustrated in Figs. 99 and 107. In Chapter IV this movement was discussed under the head of Plastic Form and the Picture Field as one element in such form. Other elements which concern us here are relationships of planes and the quality which was there explained as "plastic movement." All these qualities as they are implemented with color (in the painting), line, space, texture, light-dark and form in the drawing, combine to create the plastique of the picture—the thoroughly integrated and mature design.

In the simple block arrangement of Fig. 102 let your eyes play from plane to plane. Take any one plane and study its relationship, in both shape and movement, to all the others, one at a time. Let

Fig. 93.—Texture exercise by JOHN McMURTRIE. Carnegie Institute, Pittsburgh. Combination of tool produced and constructed surfaces giving variety of texture scales from smooth to rough—pebbly to porous—etc. Materials used include: wood, paper, scotch tape, sponge rubber, cardboard, cereals, macaroni, washcloths, etc.

TEXTURES

your eyes follow the directional movement from one form, or plane, to the others—in, through, and around. Note the forms for their different sizes and characters in relation to each other—the square

Fig. 94.—Woodcut by ROBERT NEAL. Atlanta University. Hale Woodruff, instructor. Textures are used to symbolize textures in nature and are played into an arrangement of repeats and contrasts.

TEXTURE DESIGN

against the round, and so on. Note that the white cylinder becomes the pivot or center of interest because of its position in relation to others and because it is the lightest light. Study the different directional arrangements in Fig. 104. Then turn to the stage design of forms in Fig. 106 and study the vastly more complex but similar arrangements of planes and forms. Then note how L'Engle, in Fig. 111, has compressed form and plane arrangement into a compact picture field and how Survage, in Fig. 112, has abstracted planes from forms and played them into both directional and plastic arrangements.

The outstanding characteristic of the bureau drawing in Fig. 105

Fig. 95.—*The Virgin with a Monkey,* by DURER (1471-1528).

Note how the textures of smooth ground, rough foliage, hair, clothing, etc., are featured for their own specific qualities, then woven into a thoroughly unified whole.

MASTERLY LINE, SPACE AND TEXTURE DESIGN

is form as form. Note the clarified form-truth of box, pitcher, and drawers. Light-dark has been controlled to this end; top planes are all light, side ones are in varying degrees of dark. Note that all spaces are felt, no accidents, no chaos. The distortion of bureau end and drawers adds to interest by diversifying shapes. Note that mirror is treated as a plane instead of as a reflecting glass on the assumption that its plane quality is the more important in the picture.

The drawing or painting of forms floating in space, as has been argued, is a great liberation and invitation to design. Note how, in

Fig. 96.
THREE-DIMENSIONAL RELATIONSHIPS OF PLANES

her improvisation on a musical theme in Fig. 107, Laura Woolsey has woven a complex directional movement of forms—the eyes starting from the accordion keyboard, moving up its zigzag steps to the guitar, flowing backward along its swelling body, jumping to the violin with its turning movement backward and down, around the pivot of the vertical rod, forward, around and out through the curved bones, flowing down under the accordion to the circular knobs, up the guitar stem, deflected to the music stand, and ending in the title of the music—St. Louis Blues. In addition to this movement-theme planes play against each other in both shapes and directions, light-dark is organized to stress the important elements and subdue others, as well as to express form. A thoroughly organized picture.

Fig. 97.—Perfection of design in nature in the single plant form.

Fig. 98.—The chaos of nature in grouped rock forms.

Fig. 99.—From the chaos of rocks on the ocean shore at Gloucester a student has organized rock forms into an integrated arrangement.

a. Two-dimensional.

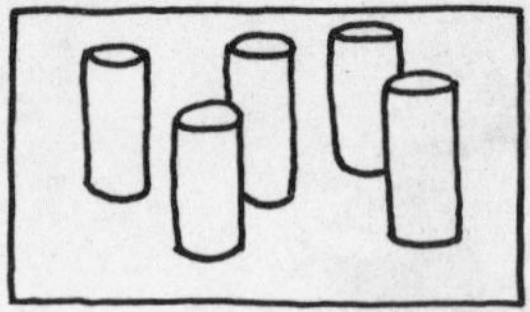

b. Three-dimensional, staggered, parallel.

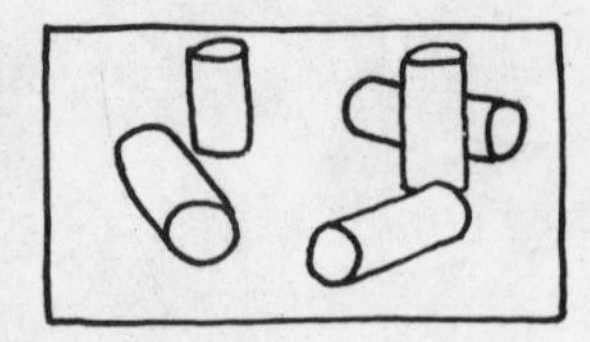

c. Three-dimensional, staggered, interweaving.

Fig. 100.—Three types of form arrangements.

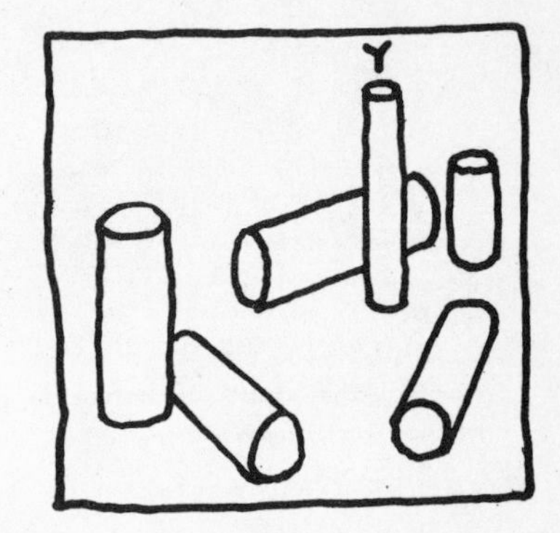

Fig. 101.—Three-dimensional form arrangements revolving around a pivot.

Fig. 102.—The same as Fig. 101 with more complex forms and movements expressed as solid forms.

Fig. 103.—An arrangement of forms in deep space, by G. H. WILDE.* An original conception. Making use of letters as interesting forms and arranging them in a three-dimensional organization.

FORM ORGANIZATION

Figure 108 of wrenches is an excellent example of form which forcefully expresses character and of character which gives its quality to design. Note how important the small form of the nut becomes as contrast to the larger forms and as a pivotal point in the arrangement.

In Fig. 1 Mr. Buttrick claims his creative right to poetic license by seeing through one form to "inner realities" and by making weird dream-forms into concrete form-realities.

The abstract forms so effectively dramatized by Paul Landacre in Fig. 70 tap a field of visual experience which is sorely needed today as compensation for the multitudes of storytelling (story-yelling, my typewriter by accident said, and shall we deny it?) pictures. A symphony, this, in form.

Figure 111 by William L'Engle is a three-dimensional, interweaving form arrangement compressed in depth into a compact design. Note how forms are enriched by variations in light-dark and texture motifs of scales, fins, and dotted areas. Imagine how empty these forms would be without that enrichment. Color, of course, completes and unifies the whole.

Figure 112 by Leopold Survage is a surrealist conception featuring the organization of planes in deep space. Planes have been detached in some areas (and not in others) from the forms of which they are, or might be, a part and played into harmonic relationships. The sky treated as a symbol, not an illusion of the actual, stops the inward movement, marks the backdrop of the picture field and completes the space-form design.

Giving priority in drawing to the expression of concrete reality is not, as I have said, the one and only educational method. I give it priority as a balance to the emotional approach to painting on the assumption that the two will be ultimately combined. Other art educators give drawing a quite different emphasis. Outstanding among these is artist, Peppino Mangravite, head of the School of Painting and Sculpture at Columbia University in New York City.

Fig. 104.—A composition in deep space. Note the lack of dramatic edges, the contrary accent on the silhouette and the consequent weakening of form expression.

Fig. 105.—The varied forms in and on a bureau dramatized as forms and as an arrangement, by SOUTHER BUTTRICK.*

THREE-DIMENSIONAL FORM DESIGN

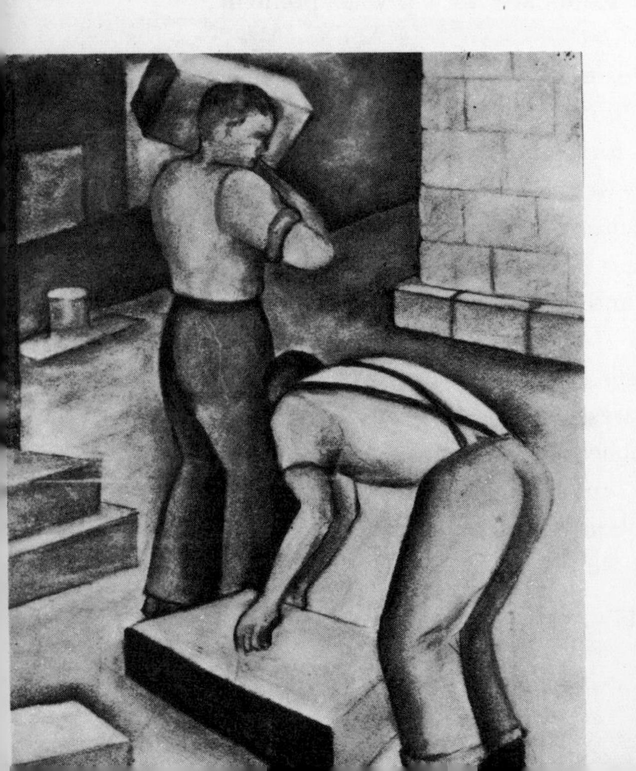

Fig. 106.—Organization of abstract form. Modeled in clay and then drawn by FRANCES ELLISON.* Such an integrated group of forms was planned for a stage set to meet the psychological needs of a certain play.

THREE-DIMENSIONAL FORM DESIGN

Fig. 107.—*St. Louis Blues.* A drawing of forms floating in space by LAURA WOOLSEY.**

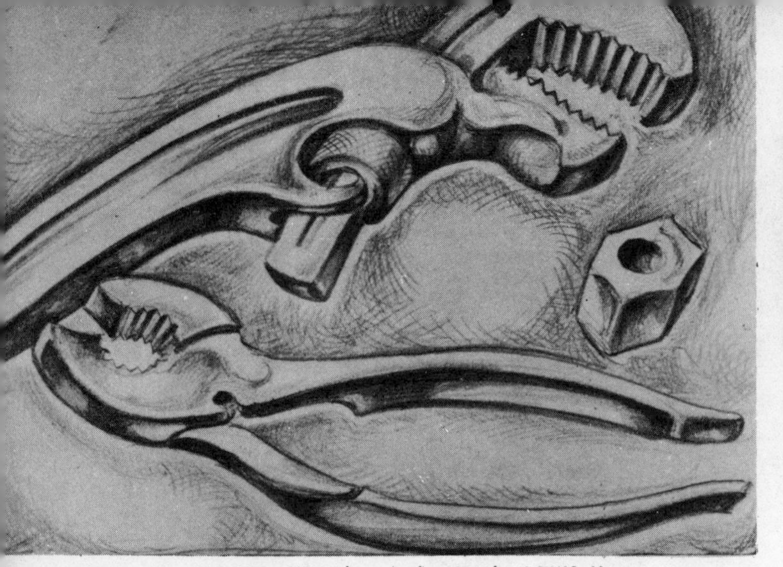

Fig. 108.—*Wrenches.* A drawing by LOUIS H. SANDHUSEN.*

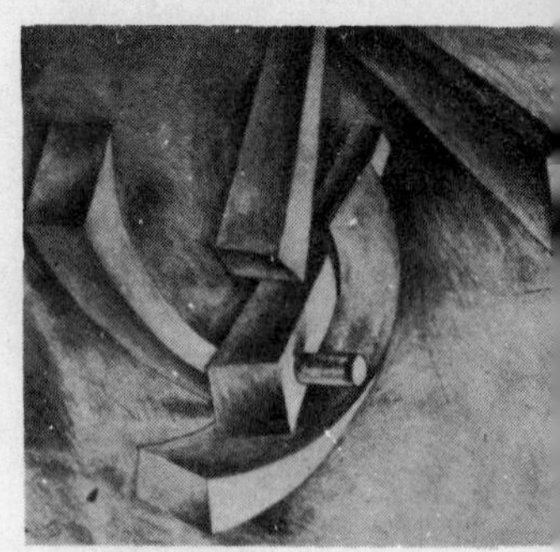

Fig. 109. — Three-dimensional arrangement of forms. By a Design Workshop student.

Fig. 110.—*Cattle,* by ETHEL MAGOFAN, former student Colorado Springs Fine Arts Center. Boardman Robinson and Frank Mechau, instructors. An effectively organized picture with subject character dramatized and giving its character to the character of the design. Functional design.

THREE-DIMENSIONAL FORM DESIGN

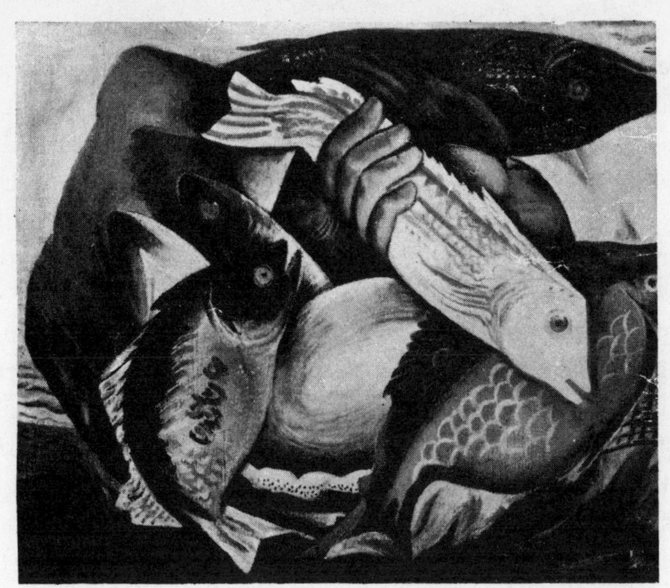

The Georgette Passedoit Gallery

Fig. 111.—*Fish Composition,* by WILLIAM L'ENGLE.

C. W. Kraushaar Art Galleries

Fig. 112.—*Landscape at Reussillon,* by LEOPOLD SURVAGE.

THREE-DIMENSIONAL FORM AND PLANE DESIGN

This school, one of the relatively few working under an harmonious program subscribed to by its entire faculty, uses drawing as an introduction to all other courses. But it does not teach "drawing from nature" via the posed still-life or model. Far from it. Starting on the preamble that "Design is the core about which all other teaching is assembled," it calls drawing the "grammar of art" and has its first-year students extract from observed objects certain elements which can best be expressed in the drawing medium. Among these are "pure line as line, shapes, tones, textures, recognition of the picture plane, getting simplified essential character of subject, sensing proportions and scale and learning space division, dissection of the picture plane and its linear and tonal unification." It even uses drawing in pen and ink to get the textural character of a subject, including the nude (not merely its silhouette), as a preparation for painting, which must also build form by a textural breaking up of color. Figure 113 is an example of this approach by a beginning student.

The emphasis on drawing as an introduction to painting, and even to sculpture, continues through three years of study with the emphasis on the synthesis of the two, or three, media and with a gradual progression into the complications of three dimensions—in form and design. The first study of the nude is via contour drawing. But that alone is not the end. As soon as a number of such drawings are made, the next step is to plan groupings of figures, still in outlines, to tie in with life and the organizational problems of design. By the third year, "life students" are organizing their drawings of the nude into compositions tentatively expressing a theme to be carried out in painting or sculpture; see Figure 113 A. Thus is the synthesis of all the parts with the art of the picture and with life realized as the normal routine of the artist. Such students, one might say, are artists from the first month of their study.

One of the many exercises given first-year students, and a significant one, might be called the *Essence of the Tree* exercise. Directions are simple—to make a drawing that will express as many as possible of the essential truths about a tree. What are such truths? Type of trunk—height, width, bark and *cross section* showing veins (an invisible truth). Type of roots, branches, foliage, flowers and seeds. One branch shows the character of foliage, hence one may suffice. The same applies to leaves, flowers and seeds. The silhouette of the total tree might be expressed by outline instead of reality. As the imagination of a student works on his challenging problem it is natural for him to see the answers in his individual way; automatically they are different from those of his fellow students. Also automatically he will assemble his answers around the "core of design" in his own way according to his unique vision. And the actual results in the finished drawings are as unique as would be expected. Figure 114 is a fair example. Drawings are enhanced, by the way, with black, white, brown and yellow pigments, thus synthesizing drawing and painting.

Sculpture, the art of form, grows naturally out of this basic training as a specialized pursuit—the emphasis, as in painting and drawing, being on design. Oronzio Maldarelli is in charge of this department, imparting to his students the plastic form he so admirably integrates in his own sculpture.

In the fourth and fifth years of this broad-visioned and effectively planned study come the more developed techniques, the social adaptations, the more detailed study of history (which has been a background reference from the start) with its analytical exploration of the works of classic and modern masters, the election and carrying out of special assignments, endless discussions of problems, from special tools and techniques to the artist's relation to tradition and to specific tendencies in contemporary art. Students choose their special fields of interest—religion, economics, portraiture, landscape, the tangibles of reality or the intangibles of pure esthetics, conduct their own research and carry out their own projects. The result is individualism disciplined by a knowledge of the constants which unify the arts of the ages. Students leave a school of this type solidly equipped for the responsibilities of professional performance and with an esthetic and psychological adjustment which should assure leadership in their chosen fields. The solidity of these foundations has in fact been externally recognized by such events as the granting of at least ten Fullbright Fellowships, from 1950 to 1952, to students of Columbia's School of Painting and Sculpture.

Fig. 113.—A drawing which extracts lines, planes, tones and textures from a still-life and builds them into a design. By a first-year student in the Foundation Course.

Fig. 113A.—A drawing tentatively expressing a theme, as a preparation for a later synthesis of drawing and painting. By a third-year student.

BASIC TRAINING AT THE SCHOOL OF PAINTING AND SCULPTURE
OF COLUMBIA UNIVERSITY

Fig. 114.—By JOHN T. QUINN. A drawing enhanced with color, expressing the essential truths of a tree. First-year student.

Fig. 114A.—By FRANK DORSAY. An advanced student project on the religious theme, carried out independently.

Fig. 114B.—By MITZI SOLOMAN. This was done by Miss Soloman, now a professional sculptor, while she was a student working under Oronzio Maldarelli.

STUDENTS OF THE SCHOOL OF PAINTING AND SCULPTURE OF COLUMBIA UNIVERSITY

8. DESIGNING THE HUMAN FIGURE

"For a few years I have exclusively drudged on the figure, to get some action and structure into it. And through that very drudgery, I had somehow lost the animation to compose and to let the imagination work." VINCENT VAN GOGH, 1883

DRAWING THE HUMAN FIGURE

The scene is a life class in an important art school at the opening session of the third year of a four-year course. The instructor, a well-known academic artist of his city, is explaining the work to his new students just starting their junior year.

"In the first year you got accustomed to the nude and studied action. In the second year you loosened up and got a sense of volume. Now here, in my class, you begin to work. Then next year, your fourth, with Mr. B you will get the aesthetics—the artistic point of view."

Student interrupting, "But, Mr. M, aren't we supposed to get the aesthetics through all four years?"

Mr. M: "No. You are not ready for aesthetics yet. You have to know your tools before you can use them. That's my job—to teach you to use the tools."

According to this philosophy, art students should spend three long years of their precious youth in learning techniques before they should begin to turn their attention to producing a work of art.

It is difficult for me to find restrained language in which to register my disagreement with this process. Crime against youth—negation—murdering of a native art at its source—these are the terms that cry to be loud-speakered to the students of the nation and to their elders who condemn them to this stagnation of spirit. To be circumspect, to be tolerant of contrary opinion, to avoid hurting the feelings of the older school, to say merely, "I disagree"—these polite ways are not enough. Obstacles to progress must be removed if there is to be progress. Removal must precede rebuilding.

Why draw or paint the nude human body?

A question, this, which every student of art should ask and answer before giving up three or four or two or even one year of his life to its study. The obvious, current answers are several. I list them. Are they valid answers?

The human body is the most intricate and beautiful of God's creations; it is therefore logical material for the subject of pictorial art.

The beauties of the human body cannot be improved on by the artist; *ergo*, he must paint them with faithful reverence.

Pictures are mainly concerned with human life and drama. To paint bodies in life-drama it is necessary to know their form, anatomy, and actions and be able to express these with technical mastery.

All three of these, it will be noted, are practical answers. Of course, the human body is intricate and beautiful, therefore, if the portraying of nature's beauty or action, or human drama is the dominant objective, skill must be developed and become the reason for study of the figure.

If, however, to create one's own beauty is the dominant objective, then other considerations take precedence over these practical ones. The Moderns and we as students and teachers are dedicated to these other objectives. We believe that plastic *form* is equal in importance to *content*. If this is granted it is at once obvious that power of expression and the design which constitutes *form* will be our dominant concern in dealing with all subject material, including the human figure.

This realignment of values does not deny that the artist must know his human figure. He must know the most important facts about it and should learn them in the order of their importance in relation to his objective—*always keeping expression and design dominant over facts and skills.*

What is the most important characteristic of human bodies? They have parts—a trunk, legs, arms, neck, and head. These parts are jointed and move as the body acts. Action and movement are the outstanding characteristics of all human beings. And of all animals. The horizontal relaxation of sleep is the one time, except death, when action ceases. Sitting is action. Lying down without sleep is subdued action. In all other situations action is dynamic and constant. Never do human beings freeze themselves into set "poses" to hold for twenty-five minutes with "rests" (which are action) of five minutes, then resume the frozen attitude and the rest alternately throughout an entire morning. "Life classes" with students clustered around such a frozen attitude to copy it on paper or canvas or in clay are not recording *life;* they are denying the ultimate logic of life.

The answer that a life class in an art school cannot draw movement is obviously absurd. Any child or adult beginner can be shown in three minutes how the parts of a body have certain general forms and sizes, how they join together, how they move as the body acts. Any person can observe bodies in action and note well what they do. Anyone can draw such bodies and such action. Figure 115 shows how one of four adults who had never drawn before learned these fundamentals and applied them, first to single figures, then to the representation of a football game within the definite space limits of a picture frame—all within the first hour of taking up the pencil. (Originals were made in pencil; these have been redrawn in ink.)

This realization of movement, of bodies in action, then, is the logical beginning of "drawing from life"; it means what the words imply. From this beginning development can be rapid in filling out these puppet, or "sausage," forms with more and more of actual body character including a gradually amplified knowledge of anatomy. But always the most vitally important truths of movement and "life" are kept dominant over the lesser truths of specific muscular and anatomic form.

When drawing from life is based on the above-described process, development grows out of a combination of knowing and perceiving —never (as in the conventional posed-model life class), on perceiving of surface facts alone. The student learns how bodies act, he formulates in his mind from such knowledge the essentials of that action, he refers to an actual human body which *performs the action* for him and then, from the total concept formed in his mind, he creates on paper an interpretation of that concept. This actually is a creative process. At no point is there any copying of facts

Fig. 115.—Drawing of bodies in action by an adult who had never drawn before.

merely seen by the physical eye. All such facts are digested and assimilated into the total concept.

To facilitate this process the student should watch the model act and move in the desired way, then the model should stop "posing" and the student should draw from his mental concept. When he has exhausted his capacity to interpret that concept the model should act again—a one- or two-minute performance which can include going through the act several times. Then again the student draws from knowledge—a looking-inward process. This is repeated as long as necessary to gain the end of an adequate expression of a certain act.

In early training such drawings should be very general and be finished in a few minutes—many being made in an hour. As ability develops, more time should be given to each with more model actions to demonstrate it. Gradually essentials are amplified and relevant details added till, after about a month of daily practice, one drawing may take an entire morning session. And in mature and

Fig. 116.—*Swimming*, a woodcut by HELEN DWORKIN.*

Sausage figures used to portray a human situation with a few props of water, trees, and boat added to complete the symbolic picture.

complex painting or carving any necessary amount of time may be spent on a single work but the method throughout remains the same.

A student working in this way, in order to understand more than he can actually see, will walk around his model, will feel the form to learn where the bony structure lies, will consult the anatomy book for all manner of hidden forms and details, will test out the overlapping of muscles or the tying of muscle to bone. He will have the model flex an arm, a leg, a muscle, or bend the neck to see what happens to the forms in flux. He learns where a muscle begins and ends, how it swells and pulls against the bones. He constantly builds up his knowledge so that easily and intuitively he can visualize and express any body in any action from that knowledge. Such a student or artist is emancipated from slavish dependence on the physical appearance of forms; he is equipped to *create.*

The great creative art of the past has always been an outgrowth of some such basic way of working as this. Primitive artists drew pictures from knowledge gained by observation; they did not have "life classes" in which wolves, bison, and warriors posed for them from nine to twelve. The early Egyptians and Greeks knew the essential truths of human and animal bodies and organized them into designs of form. So did the Chinese and Persians. The great masters of the European Renaissance drew from within out—they knew their forms and actions and bent them to their will. Imagine the difficulties Michelangelo would have had if, as he lay on his back on a vast scaffolding painting the Sistine Chapel ceiling, he had had to pose a model to copy from the frozen "life." Artists of his day would have laughed at such pathetic incapacity. They knew their human bodies in action. They had not had the misfortune to be trained in an academic art school of the twentieth century to copy only surface facts.

SPACE DESIGN

Going back to Fig. 115, there is another quality which the beginners in their first hour of drawing had become conscious of and begun in a simple way to apply. That quality is *space.* They had sensed the space around their bodies—the fact that a white space

Fig. 117.—A second panel from the mural by LAURA WOOLSEY for Brooklyn Ethical Culture School (see frontispiece) which shows the ease with which puppet figures may be controlled and built into the picture design.

Fig. 118.—A naturalistic life drawing in which the movement represented is frozen into a model's pose and copied from the life exactly as seen.

COMPLETE LACK OF DESIGN

around a black one is a definite part of a picture and that such space has to be felt or considered in arranging all the elements within the frame. None had been conscious of this before. None will forget the fact hereafter. The first hour of drawing saw them take the first necessary step toward comprehending the intriguing possibilities of space design.

The human experience called aesthetic roots in a sensory response to the qualities of elements and to the quality of their relationships. Lines, spaces, darks and lights, and forms are elements which have qualities in themselves and in their relationships. The students who felt the relationships of light spaces to dark spaces in Fig. 115 were responding to such qualities. So are any students who respond to the qualities of color in their earliest paintings. Aesthetics, then, can be a factor in art education from the first hour of creative work. If aesthetic experience is the richest value in a work of art, the comprehension of that experience is the primary concern of art education. To delay all concern with the major value in this field to the fourth year of study is, I repeat, an aesthetic crime.

Figure 118 is a straight naturalistic drawing copied from a frozen "pose" without the slightest hint of design knowledge. It does not even reorganize light and shade to express form effectively as is done in Fig. 130 where the clarified forms reflect the functional design of form which is in the human body.

The drawings of Figs. 119 to 124 represent the opposite point of view, where movement and design are the primary concern. Note how the body in Fig. 119 is wrong in proportions but expresses action forcefully, also how the 14-year-old, in his first life drawing got the essential truth of a certain action. Note also that the two heads are drawn from knowledge rather than from actual appearance of a specific model and how essential truths in both cases are dramatized.

To gain complete command over the movement, grouping, and design of human bodies in action, as has been said, the drawing or painting must be done from an inward knowledge which liberates the artist from the chains of observed facts. Only when so liberated can he find the power to bend bodies and all supporting data to his aesthetic will. Fig. 125 of the three nudes illustrates such a liberation and command over all material. Contrast it to Fig. 127 of the two nudes, which painting is obviously made from posed models and is only slightly liberated from them—the liberation being more in the color scheme and setting with its created harmony than it is in the figures which are mainly literal. Figure 126 by Bostwick was painted as a self-study but it shows a liberation from the literal fact and a dominant concern with color-space harmonics in spite of the tangible presence of subject—often a more difficult achievement than the looking-inward process with its memory or creation of subject concept.

Fig. 119.—Early drawing by ELIZABETH ERLANGER.**

Fig. 120.—First life drawing, by RONALD, age 14.

THE
BEGINNING
OF
DRAWING
LIFE
MOVEMENT
AND
DESIGN

Fig. 121.—By MARY NEWBERRY.**

Fig. 122.—Early drawing by MARY NEWBERRY.

Fig. 123.—
Early drawing by
ELIZABETH ERLANGER.**

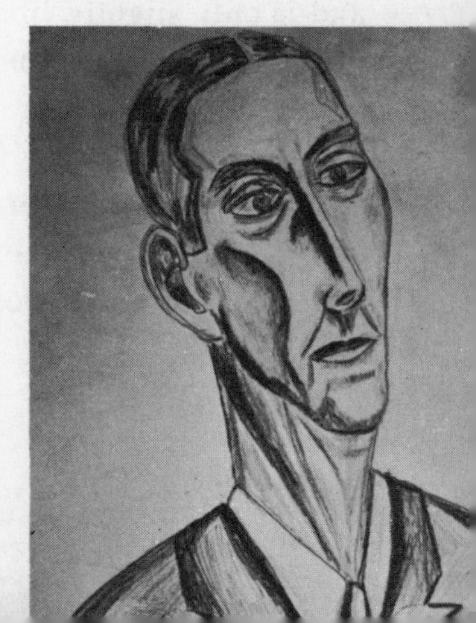

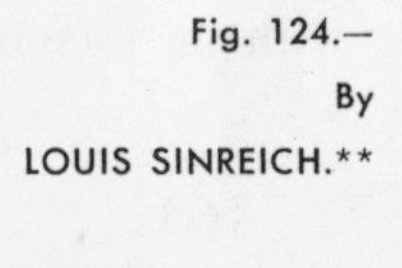

Fig. 124.—
By
LOUIS SINREICH.**

The Colorado Springs Fine Arts Center has for a number of years made a practice of engaging practicing artists as teachers in its school. Its selections have included such outstanding Moderns as Boardman Robinson, Peppino Mangravite, Arnold Blanch, Frank Mechau, and Adolf Dehn, all of them with a creative approach to their art and a knowledge of modern design in different degrees. This policy has resulted in a definite escape from the conventional art school product into a dramatic expression of real life. This living attitude toward subject seems to be characteristic of the bulk of the school work. Not all these artist-teachers, however, have stressed design, and the lack of design is frequently evident, as in the otherwise very much alive heads of Fig. 4. The theory, as I understand it, makes *expression* of subject (not copying) the dominant matter and allows design to emerge unconsciously, if at all, from the char-

Fig. 125.—*Three Nudes*, by MARIAN CORTNER.*

A group of nude body forms translated into their main three-dimensional planes and organized with supporting color areas into a unified whole. A plastic painting.

Fig. 126.—*Inclusion of Artist*, by JANE BOSTWICK.*

A thoroughly emotional integration of dark, light, color, and space. Form treatment incidental. The inner vision here translates itself into a thoroughly harmonious plastic whole.

ACTION AND DESIGN THE DOMINANT CONCERN

Fig. 127.—*Figure Arrangement*, by RUTH CHEW. Corcoran School of Art.

An example of the overlapping of naturalistic figure painting with modern creative design. This is a composed group with a sense of color and space harmony. It is an advance over the painting of the single posed model.

NATURALISM MERGES INTO COLOR-SPACE DESIGN

Fig. 128.—*The Singer*, by MARY POWER. Corcoran School of Art.

A freely painted and original conception which is different from the conventional art school study in that it slights skill for feeling and sensing. This emancipation from skills allows a forceful expression of essential meaning and a free play with color, space, plane, and form harmonies.

CREATIVE EXPRESSION

Fig. 129.—*The Dance*, by TED LITTLE. Colorado Springs Fine Arts Center. Boardman Robinson, instructor.

Life and movement is the dominant concern and is forcefully expressed. There is an unconscious and functional light-dark design that is a byproduct of the dramatic action portrayal. Design is not considered for its own values.

WASH DRAWING FROM LIFE

acter of subject; it does not give it an equal place for its own aesthetic values. This is the functional design discussed in Chapter IV and without question has its own values. The danger, when design is thus ignored, is that it will fade out entirely through neglect and undervaluation leaving only dramatic naturalism. Design cannot be spared from pictures.

Another progressive action which this school has taken is the apprenticing of its talented students to professional mural painters,

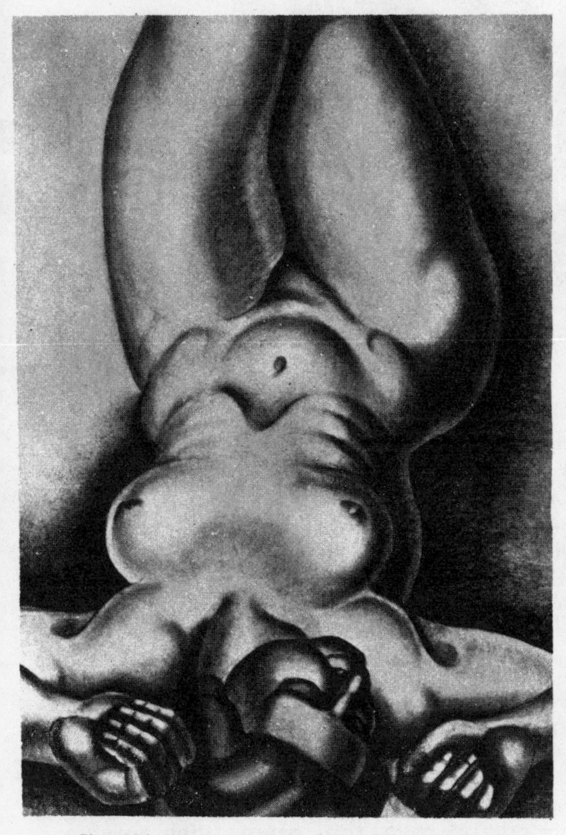

Fig. 130.—Nude drawing by a student of the School of the Worcester Art Museum showing dramatized and designed form. The design here is played into an obviously decorative treatment and so becomes, perhaps, too important.

Umberto Romano, instructor.

DESIGNED BODY FORMS

Goupil Gallery

Fig. 131.—*The Bather*, by MARK GERTLER, English. Clarified form and design merged into a unified whole.

Courtesy Museum of Modern Art, New York

Fig. 132.—*Eve*, an oil painting by MARIANO SILVA VANDEIRA, Mexican. An excellent example of a painting which shifts emphasis from physical beauty to designed beauty. The artist has used essential truth to give character to the rhythmic design which is his addition to that truth. Rendering of body form and knowledge of anatomy are generalized; superficial or irrelevant truths are ignored. Universal woman is portrayed.

DESIGNED BODY FORM

some working on the government projects, thus giving them practical training in this great field. Several such students have grown, under this system, to sufficient stature to take project commissions on their own.

The remaining illustrations in this chapter add range and validity, I believe, to the central argument. All portray designed human action.

From the collection of Messrs. Bernheim-Jeune

Fig. 133.—*Odalisque on a Green Divan*, by HENRI MATISSE.
Plastic design is dominant over specific facts of the human body. Knowledge of anatomy and skill are subordinated to the art of the picture.

THE BODY A PART OF A DESIGNED WHOLE

Fig. 134.—Wood engraving by LYND WARD. An extraordinarily sensitive and versatile creation in black and white with lines, dots, and black-and-white masses the means to the expression. From *Vertigo, a Novel in Woodcuts.* (Random House, New York, 1937.)

A MASTERPIECE OF PLASTIC FORM

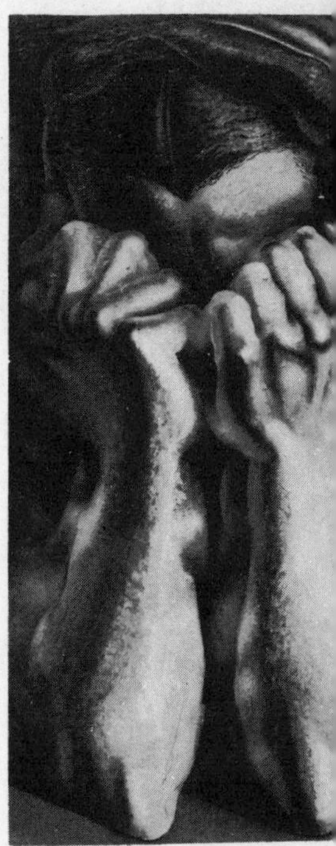

Fig. 135.—*The Sob,* by DAVID A. SIQUEIROS.

One of the triumvirate of painters, Rivera and Orozco being the other two, who initiated the Mexican renaissance. Powerful form (expressed with dramatic edges) here portrays powerful emotion.

EXPRESSIVE POWER

Courtesy Pierre Matisse Gallery

9. CREATIVE MODELING

OBJECTIVES

THE objectives of a study of creative modeling are threefold:

1. To realize the nature of form.
2. To organize or design form.
3. To combine these two experiences with the expression of subject.

To do these three things is to experience the art of sculpture.

REALIZING THE NATURE OF FORM

To realize the nature of form one must think first of form in the abstract—of form as form, of chunks of clay, stone, or wood for their mass, bulk-weight, or volume. Then one carries over this form perception to subject—to the bulk-mass of a mountain or an arm. The form of a tangible object has volume even if surfaces alone can be perceived by the eye. In the art of sculpture it is necessary first to sense that volume and then to express it effectively.

When this bulk-mass is realized—first in the mind, then in applications in a material like clay—perception of it goes beneath surface; in fact, surface is ignored or seen through to gain that end. There can be no art of sculpture without the understanding of this elemental process. When a student or a famous sculptor of the academic school copies surface facts he is not dealing with sculpture as an art of form; he is dealing with it as the craft of making a replica of something seen with the physical eyes. This craft is a technical matter depending on skill of hand and little if anything more.

Fig. 136.—*Neighboring Pews.* A naturalistic sculptured group by JOHN ROGERS, who made 87 such groups between 1860 and 1900 which, in cheap plaster casts, were bought and displayed in over 100,000 American homes. This straight copying of surface facts represents the lowest aesthetic ebb to which the great art of sculpture has ever descended or can descend. There is a total lack of the realization of form as form and of form design.

FORM DESIGN

Most people are capable of sensing the play of forms in controlled relationships to each other. But in many the power of sensing, feeling, and enjoying these relationships or formal harmonies has been

Fig. 137.—A first attempt at free, emotional, bulging form in interesting arrangement of parts. By ELEANOR O'HEARN.*

BULGING FORM

allowed to atrophy from long neglect. Formal harmonies in music and poetry can be enjoyed but are missed in sculpture and painting.

In order to sense form relationships as quickly and easily as possible it is necessary at first, in sculpture as in painting, to eliminate subject because subject, with its irrelevant interests, distracts attention from design. First lessons for adults should deal entirely with form as form; later ones can then apply the findings to subject, merging the two into an harmonious whole. For children this may or may not apply. The natural interest in expressing subject should be humored; form realization and design can be encouraged as a means to that end. The bodies of dogs and elephants are firm roundish masses but you have to see through the dog's hair to the body

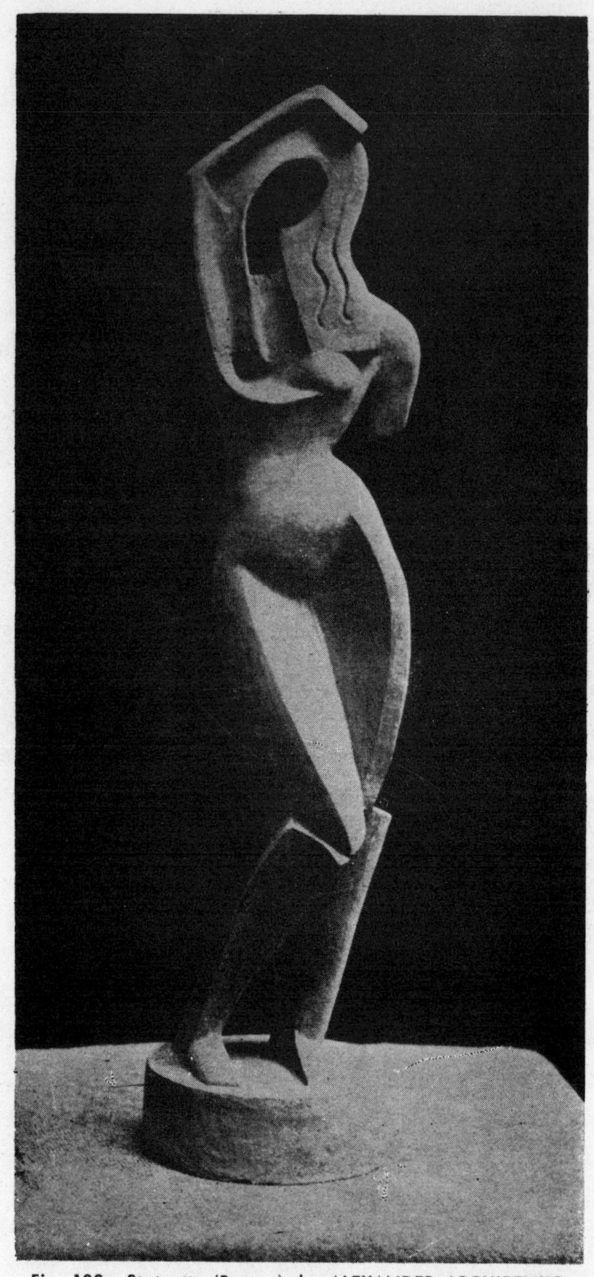

Fig. 138.—Statuette (Bronze), by ALEXANDER ARCHIPENKO

THE HOLLOW AND BULGE COMBINED

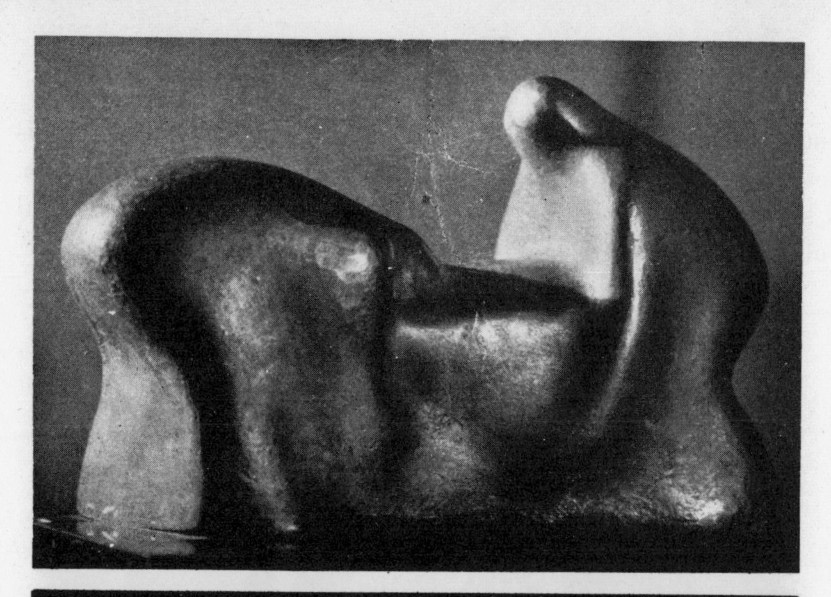

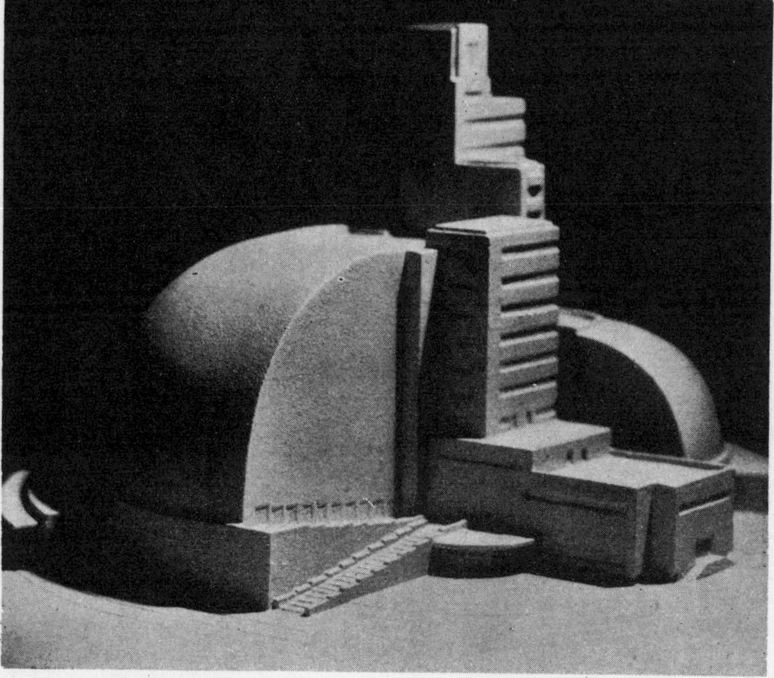

Fig. 139 (above).—*Two Men Lifting,* by SAUL L. BAIZERMAN.
Semiabstraction combining subject and design. There are transition hollows here between bulging forms.

Fig. 140 (below).—*Repertory Theatre,* by NORMAN BEL GEDDES.
Bulging curved forms and square forms combined.

underneath. Children can get that point. The surface of the hair is not the real dog. The application to subject is *one* field of expression, it should always be remembered; abstraction is another of equal and sometimes superior potentialities for aesthetic experience.

Fig. 141.—Modeling the human figure. The first step. The body is made of parts which bend as the body acts.

THE BODY IN PUPPET OR SAUSAGE FORMS

FORM DESIGN APPLIED TO SUBJECT

The application of design to subject is not too difficult a process to comprehend. In fact, its essentials can be grasped in less than a week of creative modeling. Applications can then grow in richness and complexity forever after. The new values thereby added to subject are their own reward for two main reasons. They give both

Fig. 142.—*Head,* a wood carving by SOUTHER BUTTRICK.* Semiabstract bulging forms.

Fig. 143.—*Grandfather and Child,* by DOROTHY BRAKE.* Distortion which heightens reality and creates compact design.

DESIGNED FORMS

Fig. 144.—Essential truth plus the pleasing arrangement of elementary design. By ELLA S. CLAYBURN.*

Fig. 145.—*Head,* by ALICE BUSCHER, former student at Cleveland School of Art.

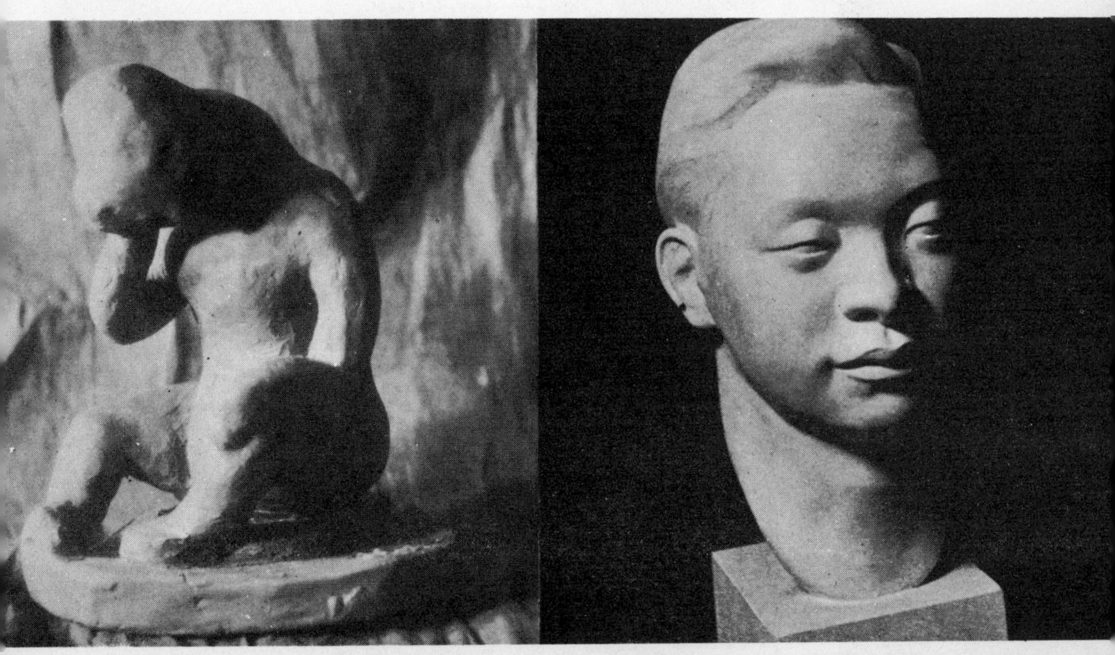

artist and observer the keen experience of enjoying visual form-music, when it exists, and to the bare facts of subject, as these are seen by the ordinary eye, they add the increased effectiveness of dramatic control.

New York City WPA Art Project

Fig. 146.—*Guitar Player*,
by JAN DRELICH, age 13.
Done in an Art Project class at Madison Square Boy's Club. Bill Barrett, instructor.

A WORK OF SCULPTURAL ART

METHODS—EXPRESSING FORM

Form, as has been said, implies three-dimensional mass. Mass is effectively expressed by a bulging outward—a fullness which seems to swell with inner energy. A hollow is the negation of form—an empty space filled with air. The bulge is the essence of form.

The sphere is the perfect form because it is all bulge, no flat planes, no hollows. Other geometric forms, the cube, the cylinder,

ig. 147.—*Cello Player*, by MAR-
ARET CUMMINS, advanced sculp-
re student of Cooper Union Art
chool.

Fig. 148.—An interesting arrangement of body forms by JO E. HILL*—the arrangement being considered of more importance than body truth.

DESIGNED ACTION IN BODY FORMS

Fig. 149.—
Composition,
by ALICE BUSCHER.

Former student of Cleveland School of Art.

A distinguished form design.

Fig. 150.—*Child*, by MARJORIE CARTER, student of Chicago Art Institute.

Georgette Passedoit Gallery

Fig. 151.—*Cat*, by RHYS CAPURN, former student of Archipenko Art School, New York City. The essential form of cat body sensitively expressing motion and determining the character of the design.

DESIGNED FORM AND MOVEMENT

the pyramid, are solid forms when considered as a whole but less obviously form when the surface alone is observed. To make the flat planes of a cube swell slightly outward accentuates form character. All bulges heighten and dramatize form.

Cup your hand and you see a hollow (air space) surrounded by a series of forms or folds of flesh, each of which bulges till it meets its neighbor. So, in human or animal bodies, do all forms bulge. This fact in nature can be made the basic law of form expression in sculpture. When it is applied the expression has power; when absent it is weak.

Assuming that this is the basic law of form expression, the student should start with experiments in bulging form in clay with all hollows eliminated. These should be made freely and emotionally to avoid stereotypes, to achieve the surprises which normally occur when the hand is released from the domination of habit and intellect. Bulging forms in the abstract, which are *interesting as forms,* should be the goal of a number of initial exercises for the student of sculpture.

For a considerable period of early study this word "interesting" can take the place of the word "design." If a form is interesting it is more than likely to be good design. Interest implies the characteristics of good design—variety of relationships, dominance, rhythm, etc. It is important to make *interesting* forms. It is important to watch them take shape under the tool or hand and to sense when they are interesting. Alertness to quality is inherent in this process. Awareness is the beginning of the aesthetic experience.

To get bulging form in clay a chunk may be roughed into free variations of parts; it should be punched, jabbed, twisted, gouged with tool or hand till interesting forms emerge—till a large part plays against a small one with different movements and directions and different character of curves *vs.* angles, or any freely made surprise effects. With flat, square-end tools, in different widths, the rough forms can then be molded into bulges. A bulge starts where it meets the table or one bulge and ends where it meets another. There should be no ditches or hollows between two bulges; the junction should be a clean meeting of the two planes, curved or flat. Bulges can be made of quick or slow curves or they can flatten out into a flat or near-flat plane. Figure 137 represents such bulging forms.

This law that form is forcefully expressed by bulges does not mean that the opposite of the bulge, a hollow, cannot be used in sculpture. It postpones such complications till the essential form-truth is mastered. It divides the learning process into single steps instead of confronting a student with the vast problem of creating and designing form and combining it with subject simultaneously —an impossible task. In good time all single steps can be combined into the mature expression. In good time hollows may be used as a definite contribution to the visual aspect of sculpture either in the abstract or in the semiabstract expression of reality—as has happened in the Statuette by Archipenko (Fig. 138). Hollows in such examples are a foil for bulges and by contrast heighten their effect. In the

Courtesy Weyhe Gallery

Fig. 152.—*Hail and Farewell, No. 3,* by ANITA WESCHLER.

One of a series of five sculptures in artificial stone showing the emotional and spiritual relationship between men and women. Note the fullness and richness of the bulging forms. Also that action is portrayed.

DESIGNED FORM AND MOVEMENT

expression of straight reality in human or animal forms, at least, it is difficult to think of a way in which hollows can be used, except as an opposed motif in environment, because they express the negation of form instead of form itself. When used carelessly by sculptors they express weakness rather than strength.

Exercises in form design should start with the single abstract form, making it more and more complex and perfect in its interrelationships. Then there should be the progression toward two detached forms, so organizing them in relation to each other that every form, plane, and movement blends, across the intervening space, into the unified whole. Then three and five forms can be so dealt with. Then the abstract forms can change to free distortions of subject—rocks, houses, or even body forms. Stage sets can be a means to this end as they logically allow distortions and abstractions in their function of creating a psychological atmosphere for human action. Figure 106 shows such a group of abstract forms sensitively interrelated, which might well serve as a set for a stage play.

FORM DESIGN AND REALITY

In order to keep design dominant over the reluctant material of reality when the two begin to be combined it is necessary, as has been said, to make subject facts secondary in importance to the relationships of design. The easiest way to do this is to distort or abstract subject with complete disregard for truth and to center all awareness on the design. When this is done with dozens of creations through several weeks of time and with increasing complexity and finish the habit of design awareness becomes so developed that it works with increasing fluency. Then gradually more and more attention can be shifted to essential subject truth. This program is solid and sure as a foundation for all later growth.

In Fig. 139 Mr. Baizerman has concentrated on an action, lifting, and has given the feeling of that action with only a generalized impression of bodies built into an arrangement pleasing to the eye. He thus gets essential truth without the limitations of specific truth. And he is left free to organize forms to please the eye and to express the general concept. In Fig. 140 Mr. Bel Geddes has designed forms with the utmost freedom within the general limitation of his subject, Repertory Theater. Such general limitation is no check to the creative spirit; it merely channelizes creation within one functional field.

PART III

APPLICATIONS

Fig. 152A.—Hand-wrought sterling silver ash tray. Won $100 first prize in silversmithing at the 1948 National Decorative Arts Exhibition at Wichita, Kansas.

Fig. 152B.—Hand-wrought sterling silver and ebony creamer "in suspension."

Both designed and executed by RONALD H. PEARSON**

Fig. 152C.—Hand-wrought sterling silver water pitcher, sugar and creamer. Designed and executed by LORNA BELLE PEARSON.**

10. APPLICATION OF THE CREATIVE MIND TO THINGS OF USE

"In India, in the 8th century, the artisan or artist possessed an assured status in the form of a life contract, or rather an hereditary office. He was a member of a guild and the guilds were recognized and protected by the king. The artificer was also protected from competition and undercutting. 'That any other than a Silpan (artificer) should build temples, towns, seaports, tanks or wells,' it is said, 'is comparable to the sin of murder.'"

From *The Dance of Siva*, fourteen Indian essays by Ananda Coomaraswamy.

To liberate the sensory enjoyment of design from the practical habits of mind which have engulfed us today is a colossal task. People who tolerate and live with white lace curtains, rococo rugs, pseudoantique furnishings, tan-colored walls, and drab and dreary towns do not appraise these things with their senses alert and *like* them. They do not *sense* or *feel* their qualities at all. They cannot do so; their senses are dulled. Instead they accept unperceivingly or their conscious mind says, "Oh, here is a familiar curtain or rug; everybody has its like, the stores and papers praise it so it must be all right." Or, perhaps, the familiar curves and swirls even register the thought "pretty" because that thought is associated with such types of design. The liking of atrocities in design, in other words, is thoughtless habit or a judgment imposed from without and accepted because native sensitiveness and inherent creative abilities are undeveloped and cannot resist the imposed opinion with a counterassertion of genuine individual taste.

On the upper economic levels the blindness and the deference to accepted authority tolerates living with "antiques" in spite of the

Fig. 153.—Evidence of our spiritual poverty and divorce from the creative arts. A "period" room advertised by an American dealer for sale to wealthy American citizens. The assumption back of all such period furnishing is that money can buy imported distinction of an aristocratic age of the past—that by living in a room from some "royal palace" a businessman of today can somehow himself become *royal.* The fact that such masquerade is considered *proper* and respectable instead of an escape from the challenging responsibility of creating our own environment *in harmony with ourselves* exposes the fears and aesthetic ignorance back of our divorce from the arts.

obvious discord with the individual and with contemporary life.

This so widely typical deference to standards of taste imposed from without is exploited by the vast business interests which deal in applied art merchandise because standardized styles which can be mass-produced guarantee profits. Business, it cannot be stated too often, is business. It functions for profit, not for education, quality (unless profitable), enjoyment of life, or national distinc-

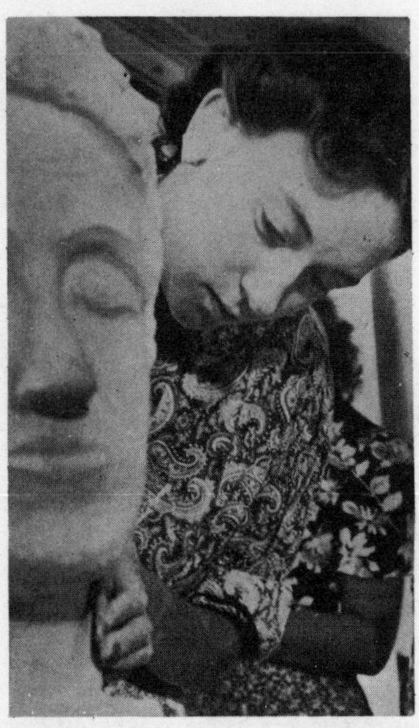

Fig. 154.—Discords in everyday life. Two art students wearing smocks which violate every principle of the creative mind applied to life which should be the objective of their training. The near smock is a copy of an East Indian design completely out of harmony with a twentieth century American girl; the other is of naturalistic flowers, the most debased type of all so-called "design."

EDUCATION BEGINS AT HOME—EVEN WITH THE STUDENT'S SMOCK

tion. The dictates of business in the matter of styles and qualities are not impartial; they are partial. And, because determined by profit, they are aesthetically corrupt. The business of "interior decoration," it should be noted comes under this head.

In the field of applied arts, good, contemporary design and profit have been, and still are, on large-scale (but not necessarily on small-scale) production irreconcilable. In the field of machines they are, on the other hand, reconcilable. Good, functional, modern de sign helps the mass sale of automobiles, iceboxes, stoves, airplanes, radios, and clocks. Good, modern design in architecture, furniture, textiles, and dishes is on the gain but still ensures minority sales only to the enlightened or adventurous few. This situation means automatic profit censorship. We get good machines because a major-

Fig. 155.—Colonial designs for woven textiles. These were outstanding creations of their day that do credit to the design tradition of America.

The *Index of American Design,* a WPA Art Project, has done immense service to the tradition of American design by recording in exact detail a vast number of historical designs which make up that tradition.

HISTORICAL AMERICAN TEXTILE DESIGN

ity will buy them; we get copies of antiques or rehashes of previous best sellers in textiles for exactly the same reason.

The first step in education for the art of living is emancipation from this corrupt force surrounding us on every side. The fact that there has been a steady, if slow, gain in design quality during the past fifty years proves that taste, with or without education, somehow does improve.

I have no space here to give a fair survey of designs by artists

Fig. 156.—*April*, by CLAYTON KNIGHT.

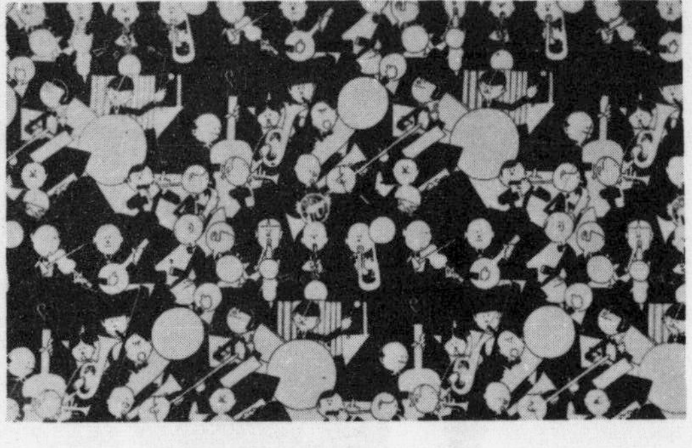

Fig. 157.—*Rhapsody*, by JOHN HELD, JR.

Two of the most original and distinguished trade silk designs of our time. Produced for silk dress goods by Stehli Silks in 1928.

Bach Magnificat

Moon and Clouds

Fig. 158.—Two textile designs by HENRIETTE REISS. The Bach design was never produced. The Moon and Clouds was one of a series by Miss Reiss produced in raw silk drapery material in 1929.

DISTINGUISHED TRADE TEXTILE DESIGNS

Fig. 159.—Silk screen textile design by RUTH REEVES. One of a set produced for W. & J. Sloane in 1928. *The American Scene*. One section from a large nonrepeating design with motifs taken from country life and played into free, emotional, color-space harmonies. This set of creations of today, done as the great art of the past was done—portraying contemporary life—are among the few most distinguished textile designs of our time.

of things of use. The following examples by students and professional artists will give, however, an indication of a vital trend. They cover several different fields and products of both hand and machine.

The Design Workshop has always included both machine- and handcraft in its program orbit but has lacked facilities to extend research, teaching, and production into these immense and diverse fields. In one field, however, that of the hand-hooked rug, it has called in leading modern artists to design floor coverings that are an expression of our own time and has produced and sold rugs totaling some twenty-five designs. The artists who cooperated in this venture were John J. A. Murphy, Thomas Benton, George Biddle, Buk and Nura Ullreich, John Storrs, Winold Reiss and Henriette Reiss, Ruth Reeves, Blanche Lazzell, Aladjalov, Helen Turquand, Mary Tannahill, Emily Reist, and the author.

The set of rugs so produced was the first in this country to be

Fig. 160.—*Accordion*, by LAURA WOOLSEY.**

HAND-HOOKED RUGS BY DESIGN WORKSHOP STUDENTS FOR THEIR OWN USE

Fig. 161.—*Birds*, by MARY NEWBERRY.**

Fig. 162.—*Fishermen of the South Seas.* A wall hanging in fine worsted yarns designed by GEORGE BIDDLE, executed by JEAN CHAMBLIN.

Fig. 163.—*Animals,* by GEORGE BIDDLE.

HAND-HOOKED RUGS DESIGNED BY AMERICAN ARTISTS AND PRODUCED BY THE DESIGN WORKSHOP

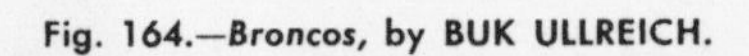

Fig. 164.—*Broncos,* by BUK ULLREICH.

ig. 165.—An architectural or "floorscaped" rug by VINOLD REISS. Assembled by Frances T. Miller.

Fig. 166.—*Railroads,* by THOMAS H. BENTON.

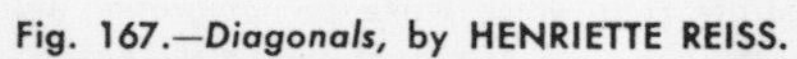

Fig. 167.—*Diagonals,* by HENRIETTE REISS.

Fig. 168.—*Points and Circles.* A hand-hooked rug designed by RALPH M. PEARSON. One of three separate rugs which make an integrated design. Produced by the Design Workshop. One of a set of rugs designed by American artists.

RUGS DESIGNED BY AMERICAN ARTISTS

designed by contemporary American artists. It made American rug history. It received wide publicity, numberless invitations to exhibit (which could not be fulfilled), and the tangible support of over two hundred individual rug buyers. But, without working capital, it could not enlarge or survive the Depression. Figures 162 to 168 show several examples of the rugs which made up this set.[1]

[1] John J. A. Murphy, the artist, advanced the funds which made possible the production of this important set of rugs designed by American artists. He did so on principle because he believed it to be of great social importance to allow the modern, creative artist the opportunity of functioning as a designer of things as well as of pictures and sculptures.

Fig. 169.—*A Bed of Flowers*, a hand-hooked wall hanging, by MARGUERITE ZORACH. Made with old-fashioned curved hook on hand-loomed linen with wool material. Design was "freehand," not worked out in advance. Made in 1927. Property of the artist.

A MODERN MASTERPIECE IN A HAND-HOOKED WALL HANGING

Such penetration of the artist into the designing of things of use should be the goal of the new art education. Training of *artist* designers and of all art students to stimulate public support for such a program is its definite responsibility.

FABRIC DESIGNS BY ARTISTS

COMMISSIONED BY ASSOCIATED AMERICAN ARTISTS GALLERY.

PRODUCED BY RIVERDALE MANUFACTURING COMPANY IN 1952.

Two of a set of eight designs commissioned from among its artist members by A.A.A. This is another example of the infrequent but very important instances of designs by genuine artists getting into production and use. These prints sell for from $2.25 to $2.75 a yard, the artists getting a royalty on all sales. Two of the set were reproductions of paintings — by Luigi Lucione and the late Grant Wood—a very questionable proceeding; textile designs should be created for their flat-pattern decorative function, as these are.

Fig. 170.—*Shell Chest*, by WITOLD GORDON.

Fig. 171.—*Curio Cabinet*, by DORIS LEE.

Fig. 172.—Distinguished design of highways and bridges, from a Long Island Parkway. Note simple, functional lines of bridge and drive—a perfect synthesis. Also rustic light poles and lamps.

DISTINGUISHED PARKWAY DESIGN

11. A ROUNDED ART EDUCATIONAL PROGRAM

THE creative philosophy and method here presented applies to all art education. It applies to professional training in its many departments. It applies to the training of the child, the youth and the amateur. The applications, as has been said, are foundational rather than complete; one might generalize and say that for the serious student a year of planned guidance and practice would establish the fundamentals on which specialization can then build endlessly. For the less serious, or where condensation is necessary, the same fundamentals can be brought well within experience in as few as thirty working sessions, as long personal experience has amply demonstrated. And the child can thrive on the excitements of creation with guidance that will release his internal natural resources, almost from his first wielding of brush or crayon. In these latter cases it is the start as a grand emotional spree that matters, with its happy, riotous whoopee and chaos; the disciplines will grow automatically—under the right leadership. Then come the applications to life in endless procession.

For a substantial part of our foundational material and for an inspired guidance in applying it to life, we owe a heavy debt to the original Bauhaus of Weimar, Germany, and to its two former members—Dr. Walter Gropius, now Chairman of Architecture at Harvard University, and the late L. Moholy-Nagy who founded the School of Design in Chicago. The Bauhaus philosophy, through the dedicated practice and teaching of these two men has penetrated far (but not yet far enough) into our thought and education.

Both have given us books which make tangible their messages.[1]

In the book, *Bauhaus 1919-1928,* published by the Museum of Modern Art, Alfred H. Barr of the Museum comments as follows:

> The Bauhaus is important for the following reasons: Because it courageously accepted the machine as an instrument worthy of the artist. Because it faced the problem of good design for mass production. Because it brought together on its faculty more artists of distinguished talent than has any other art school of our time. Because it bridged the gap between the artist and our industrial system. Because it broke down the hierarchy which has divided the "fine" from the "applied" arts. Because it differentiated between what can be taught (technique) and what cannot (creative invention). Because its building at Dessau was architecturally the most important structure of the 1920's. Because after much trial and error it developed a new and modern kind of beauty. And, finally, because its influence has spread throughout the world and is especially strong today in England and the United States.

This statement of a program for applying art to contemporary life, as it was formulated and practiced by the original Bauhaus, and as it was imported to our shores, thanks to Hitler, stands as the extension of vision and practice which the new art education must adopt if it is to lead its students and its communities into new dimensions in the art of living.

The specific teachings of Moholy-Nagy have been absorbed into a fair number of schools; among them, according to Mrs. Moholy-Nagy (who is carrying on the educational program), the Design Departments of Yale University and Brooklyn College, the California School of Fine Arts, Pratt Institute of Brooklyn and The Institute of Design of The Illinois Institute of Technology of Chicago. Without criticizing its program, one should still note that the Bauhaus slant in general has been toward industrial art; it has not been deeply concerned with the fine arts.

A SCHOOL OF THE FUTURE

If an education which leads its students into new dimensions in art and the art of living does embrace the ingredients I have

[1] *The New Architecture and the Bauhaus,* Walter Gropius, Museum of Modern Art, New York, 1936.
The New Vision, L. Moholy-Nagy. First edition, 1938. Fourth revised edition, Wittenborn Schultz, Inc., New York, 1947.
Vision in Motion, L. Moholy-Nagy, *Paul Theobald,* Chicago, 1947. Fifth edition, 1952.

mentioned, it will outline the main characteristics of the School of Tomorrow. The Department of Industrial Design of Pratt Institute, headed by Alexander J. Kostellow, and the departments of Advertising and Textile Design and Illustration, have developed such an outline from internal growth over a long period of time. If my diagnosis is correct, they become one of our valuable pilot plants which must by its native logic cause some radical demolitions and reconstructions among conventional art schools—when and if the said native logic is discovered. Our cultural communications system being what it is, however, antiquated structures will still be safe from the curative scalpel for a considerable time to come—far too safe in fact for the welfare of their students.

Mr. Kostellow's and these other departments have a carefully selected faculty which is harmonious in esthetic essentials. That happy event is not a blessing from on high; it was deliberately planned. Its students, therefore, are not distraught by conflicting ideologies as they travel from class to class. They can grow and blossom peacefully under the sunshine of an integrated program. The first year of that program is given over entirely to training in basic principles—of creation and design. The selection and clarification of these basic principles are the outgrowth of years of experiment, of testing every available resource, including Dynamic Symmetry. The testing was via experience, not confined to theory.

Kostellow's department is supposed to, and does, train students to take their place in industry as designers of mass-production wares and of interiors, exteriors, showrooms, advertising layouts and the like. The first year's "Foundation Course," however, ignores these objectives, rules out the influence of ulterior motives, such as profit, and concentrates on an uncontaminated experience in pure esthetics. Original creation and design in many materials in addition to drawing and painting—clay, plastics, wood, glass, metal, etc., all embodying the component elements of line, plane or surface, positive and negative space (volume), value, light and dark, texture and color—are used with or without subject content. Says Mr. Kostellow:

We decided to start with the simplest and clearest elements of design and structure. From the primitive's point of view, but using the language of today, we aimed at establishing definite meanings by converting moods into terms, and by regarding each graphic and plastic element in the light of the student's own empathic and rhythmic reactions and sensory perceptions based on his personal experiences.

At the very beginning we endeavored to establish a balance between the various subjects, allotting sufficient time for experimentation and investigation. To achieve this we have eliminated every trace of practicality in the problems of the foundation year. Abstract conceptions and inner compulsions expressed in terms of graphic and plastic elements are stressed; experiments in creative expression rather than in techniques are encouraged.

But such training applies to "fine" as well as "applied" art. Exactly. That is the intention. Industrial design is also, or can be, a fine art. The two are combined. And on this foundation, specialization is built. "Our school is like a pyramid," says Kostellow, "broad at the base, specialized at the top."

The second year continues this process but begins to have students recognize the cold fact that industrial design cannot be an inspirational proceeding—a creative expression of emotional origin to please the artist, or a limited number of people. It must recognize the "practical" problems of industry, manufacture and sale—and the prevailing taste of the consumer. After the inculcation of its valuable Foundation Course, the biggest problem of the school appears to be the need of solving this basic conflict between the high standards of the artist-designer and the "practical" standards of industry, always keyed to the prevailing taste of the buying public.

To meet this conflict, the school aims at a middle course with the least possible compromise. It gives students a course in "functional esthetics" and it invites designers and executives in the outside business field to come to the school for short introductory study of its esthetic goals. And they come—and refresh themselves, as individuals, from their steeping in the sterility of conformity. Another innovation is the inviting to the school of permanent exhibits of their wares from manufacturers so these, the wares, can go on the laboratory table for dissection and study from both angles. It is a brave attempt to solve a devastating impasse and probably the best one available today. Behind it, of course, looms the dominant

STUDENT WORK, DEPARTMENT OF INDUSTRIAL DESIGN,

PRATT INSTITUTE, Brooklyn

THE FOUNDATION COURSE

These problems are all designed to acquaint the student with these structural design forces which, when controlled, can produce an infinite variety of effects.

Fig. 173

Fig. 173A

Two drawings showing a variety of dynamic planes in space organization.

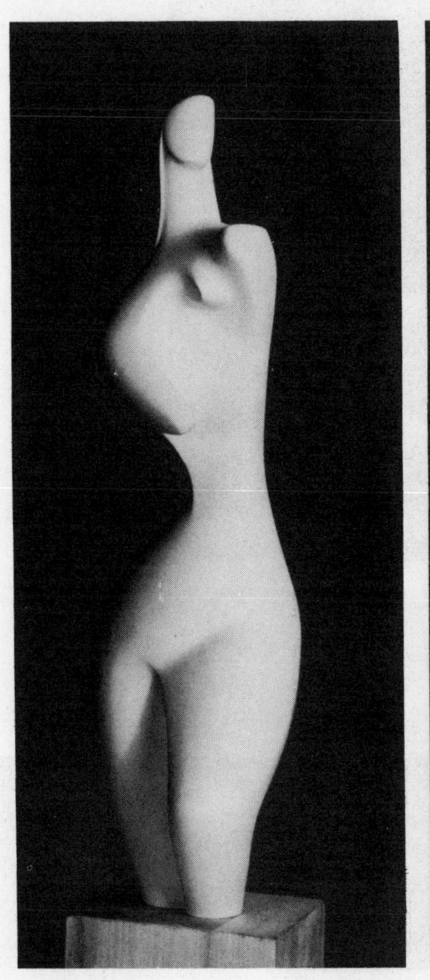

Fig. 174.—A sculptural problem to demonstrate form design and the contrast between convex and concave form.

Fig. 175.—Three rectilinear volumes. One of the first problems carried out in three-dimensional material to produce an integrated unit of three diverse volumes.

STUDENT WORK, DEPARTMENT OF INDUSTRIAL DESIGN,

PRATT INSTITUTE, Brooklyn

Fig. 176.—Organization of forms, planes and movement in deep space.

Fig. 176A.—A variety of studies from beginning and advanced classes showing how the basic design learned in the first-year Foundation Course is applied to mass-produced items.

problem of how to raise the average standard of popular taste so it will demand better design. This problem remains the more unsolved the more esthetics are involved. However, it is to the industrial designer in this country that most of the credit must go for the remarkable advances in design quality and public demand in things of practical use—machines, cars, busses, bathtubs, office furniture and the like. Pratt Institute is here plowing fertile ground.

The outstanding characteristics, then, of this particular school are its Foundation Course, its unified approach, its emphasis on the individuality of students and their unique inventions and manipulations of all available elements and tools, the identification of art with the needs and life of the community, the attempt to establish a fertile ground for cooperation with industry and the basic emphasis on the organizations of design which grow out of our time and place. For his school and associates Mr. Kostellow ends a remarkable article on these issues (from which I have quoted) with this summation of their creed: "*As designers, we express our todays and build the taste of the tomorrows.*"

There is considerable scattered but very weighty evidence at hand to indicate that our most progressive art education is correctly assessing the dominant trend in today's professional art and building on its enduring values. For instance, the high school art shown in the Greater New York Scholastic Art Awards Exhibit of 1952 included more spirited, original, high level creations which tamed youthful, honest exuberance with the (often unconscious) controls of felt design, than is usual in these annual showings. Correspondingly, adult imposed skills with their genius-killing distractions from a creative art, were much less in evidence. This marked a decided gain over the contrary trend in child art of a dozen years ago reported on page 217. The largest number of exciting creations in this 852-piece show came from the Abraham Lincoln High School of Brooklyn and the High School of Music and Art in New York City. But much creditable work also came from a number of others of the 68 high schools represented. The gains, in other words, were fairly widespread.

12. CHILDREN ARE CREATIVE ARTISTS

CHILDREN are born creators and remain so until their native art impulses are killed by the imposition or imitation of adult standards concerned with skill and literal fact. For the young child creation is joyous adventure. It is a game using color or any medium as a means to saying something in pictorial symbols with a happy recklessness which tosses skills and truth out the window without a quiver of hesitation or regret. It is automatically original because it flows with such bubbling freshness from within out. It is unself-conscious. There are no conflicts. A flash of vision melts into concept and concept into expression. Whatever that expression is is right. There is no wrong. From such divine self assurance creation must be born.

Then comes the devastation. Conflict begins. Doubt enters. Self-confidence wavers. Attention is diverted from the inner urge to the outer compulsion. Grownups must know better. Maybe my way is wrong. My, but that certainly does *look like* subject. Isn't it wonderful to have such skill? Look, everyone likes that kind of picture. I want to do what teacher likes, what everybody likes. I can be skilfull too. And so does creative art die.

Before me lies a newspaper clipping from a large midwestern city. The headlines are:

NURSERY SCHOOL AT UNIVERSITY LEARNS ABOUT ART

Let me quote (the italics are mine):

The children—ranging from 20 months to 5 years old—were introduced to expert instruction in art. . . . Miss ——— ————, a graduate of the Smith College Dept. of Art (and I think a teacher training institution should take the responsibility for its products) directs the art work and sits at the children's easels *to guide their work by example.* "It is interesting to see," commented the principal of the school, "how the four year old children eagerly reproduce the simple sailboat, tadpole or airplane *drawn by the instructor,* while the two year old's reaction is delayed. Two or three weeks later the two year olds will surprise us with a figure dating back to the earlier model." . . . About half the tiny students are children of faculty members. The other half is drawn largely from the families of business and professional men in the neighborhood.

So a large and famous university is starting the children of its faculty members out on the sad road of divorce from the arts. It is actually teaching nursery children to copy adult concepts. It is instilling respect for and encouraging the copying habit. It is doing its best to ensure that future citizens of the university community will continue the present policy of escape from the responsibilities of creative practice, which escape is so usual in university architecture, furnishings, and visual art. It is normal for five-years-olds to create lustily in their own idiom with supreme contempt for the irrelevant ways of the grownup. The university is throttling that healthy vitality at its roots. It is killing native art.

Children have a native sense for related harmonies of color and space which only needs to be protected and encouraged to grow into a flowering art. They can invent freely and happily. They are alert to environment, like their friends the animals, and are quick to take hints and suggestions from any source and weave them into their own creations. To them, while still unspoiled by adults, a painting is an end in itself. It is a picture language. It is directly "spoken" in color; there it stands—a new thing under the sun to be looked at for its own values. It is not, as the dumb grownups would have it, a replica of nature. It is a *creation.*

The first step in the teaching of art to small children is undoubtedly to let them alone to do what they want.

When they have done that, when they repeat themselves over and over, or when they are "stuck" and don't know what to do, then suggestion is a fertile stimulant. Let me report a conversation between an artist teacher, Miss B, and Margaret, an 11-year-old girl from a working-class family, who came to a Saturday morning class in a social settlement in New York City.

Miss B: Good morning, Margaret. Well, what are you going to paint today?

M: I don't know what to paint.

Miss B: Oh! Paint something that happened to you.

M: But nothing ever happens to me.

Miss B: I don't believe it. Something happens to you every day of your life. Come, now. Didn't something happen to you yesterday?

M: No. Nothing happened to me yesterday.

Miss B: How about your family? Didn't anything happen to your family?

M: No. Nothing. Except that my father didn't get home till midnight and mother was very cross.

Miss B: Why was she cross? What happened?

M: Oh, my father drives a truck over in Jersey. And he got stuck in the mud. And he didn't get home till midnight. And mother had to sit up and get supper for him. And she was mad.

Miss B: Well I should say that was some happening. Why don't you paint that?

M: Paint that? You mean paint that? [Thinking] Well, all right. I guess I can. All right, I'll paint that.

And Margaret went off in a corner and worked steadily all morning. Then she brought to Miss B the painting shown in Fig. 177. In it we can see the truck and father with his shovel, mother at the stove cooking supper. A table is set for one with a clock saying twelve. And at bottom a frieze of rather obscure figures.

Miss B: Margaret, this is wonderful. It's a mural painting. I like the colors. And the spaces. It tells the whole story. I can read it all. But what is this frieze down here at the bottom?

M: That's people making bullets.

Miss B: But why did you put in people making bullets?

M: Because if people didn't make bullets they would have money

Fig. 177.—*"My Father Got Stuck in the Mud,"*
by MARGARET McARDLE, age 11. Greenwich House, New York City.
Helen Beach, instructor.

This four foot wide mural painting done at one sitting in response to suggestions by Miss B. is one of the most remarkable child paintings that I have ever seen. It grows out of personal life experience. It creates its own symbols and weaves them into design with feeling dominant over thinking. It is original, courageous, and self-reliant. Skill as such is ignored giving way to more important qualities but is sufficient to implement the concept. In its functional blending of story and design this creative painting is completely within the Grand Tradition of the ages.

AN 11 YEAR OLD MURAL PAINTER

to fix up the roads over in Jersey. And my father wouldn't get stuck in the mud and get home at midnight.

Here, I should say, is the ideal relation between artist-teacher and child student. Suggestion which stimulated thought and vision into a concept was the teacher's contribution on the spur of the right moment. Her previous contribution had been guidance in exciting play with colors and spaces, which, as outlined herein, unconsciously developed power in the child to do with them as she wished. There were no inhibitions or fears in Margaret. She had the courage, when she thought *truck,* to paint truck directly, freely, forcefully, watching the colors and shapes and instinctively (which means unconsciously) choosing those which seemed most pleasing. A truck is a squarish shape; so she painted a squarish shape as symbol. Father

Fig. 178.—*Self-portrait,* by a five-year-old. The technical knowledge of this child artist was very limited. She knew that she had a body, head, arms and legs. These facts of life she painted with directness and confidence. Then the picture did not seem complete. Perhaps teacher asked questions. "Would it look better with more colors?" Yes, it would. So more colors went in to fill the paper. "Would it be interesting to make the colors more important with lines?" Yes. In went the lines. There was suggestion but no dictation. Result: a designed picture.

AN INSTINCTIVE DESIGN SENSE

as a shape is not squarish; he has rounded sausage forms for body, legs, and arms. So she paints such shapes and the symbol Man emerges. The same happens with other data. Each symbol flows into its own place, its own shape, its own colors. A vision organizes itself

Fig. 179.—Two crayon drawings of cats by third-grade children. Attleboro, Mass., Public Schools. These are frankly symbols in geometric patterns—probably suggested by teacher. But every symbol in the room was as different as these two.

THE CHILD USES DESIGNED SYMBOLS

Fig. 180.—Crayon drawings by EPIPHANY MAISANO (left) and GENE FARNESE (right), both aged 11. Paterson, N. J., Public Schools. Miss Claire Frazza, teacher.

Fig. 181.—*George Washington Cutting Down the Cherry Tree.* Color-space-subject arrangement by ANNABELLE MELLINGER, age 9, State Teacher's College, California, Pa. Betsy M. Hazen, instructor.

SYMBOLS IN COLOR-SPACE DESIGN

Fig. 182.—*Trucks,* by JOHN LE MAY, age 13. Paterson Public Schools, Miss Gladys Grundy, teacher.

INTUITIVE ORGANIZATION OF FORMS

into a concept. The concept is expressed with feeling. The design sense functions. A work of art is born.

Suggestion may be even more specific than this; it may stimulate the painting of a picture in the child's mind. "Now, let's have a story about a king," the canny teacher will say. "Does anybody know what a king looks like?" Yes, yes. Everybobdy knows what a king looks like and all the hands in sight plead for the chance to tell. "What kind of clothes does he wear? What does he have on his head? What does a crown look like? Where does he sit? What does a throne look like? Like a kitchen chair? Does he live in an apartment? No? Well, what does a castle look like?" And so on, and so on. Each young brain is painting its own picture and a bit later when turned loose in the art room each transfers that mental picture to paper. And all the transfers are different. Originality is rampant. Originality is normal. The creative spirit in man cannot, at this age, be downed.

A young child should not be made conscious of terminology. The words "design," "balance," "rhythm," "dominance," "harmony," should not be inflicted on it; to do so tends to hamper the creative process by forcing it out of the wonder-realm of the unconscious feeling and sensing into the practical realm of thinking and so burdening it with all manner of impedimenta related to skill, facts, truth, adult standards. An excellent horrible example of adult standards and intellectualism in the use of color is provided by A. H. Munsell in his book *A Color Notation*[1] when he prescribes a course of study for secondary school children. I quote (italics are mine):

> Previous work with *measured scales,* made by the tuned crayons and *tested* by reference to the color sphere, have so *trained* the color judgment that children may now be trusted with more flexible material. They have *memorized* the equable degrees of color on the color sphere and in general gained a *disciplined* color sense. *Definite* impressions and *clear thinking* have taken the place of *guess-work and blundering.*

Fig. 183.—*Snowstorm,* by DORIS VAN SETERS, age 13.
Paterson Public Schools. Miss Helen Stanley, teacher.
This is a snowstorm and the snow is made of bright color flakes. Is snow white in nature? What of it? Colored flakes look bettet and Doris therefore painted colored flakes.

CREATIVE SELF-ASSURANCE

[1] See Bibliography, page 249.

Against this advice I pin my complete faith on the proscribed "guess-work and blundering." Strange how educational ideals change.

The qualities back of a complex art terminology can, however, be encouraged as they emerge in the child's work. "Ah! These colors look well together, don't you think?" Or, "With all this red don't you want more different colors? Does the green look well against the red? See how important this brightest color becomes. Is this space too large for all the others? Do you like all spaces the same size? Do you like large and small spaces in contrast to each other? Are all animals in the world the same size? Are all men the same size? Would you like to see all such the same? Would you like all shapes in a picture to be square? Or round? Do you like a mixture of both in one picture? Is that more interesting?" That word "interesting" can be substituted for all the qualities of design. Good design is visusally interesting. Bad design is uninteresting. A creation is more interesting than a copy. A symbol is normally more interesting than an inventory of visual facts, a copy of nature. Such questions and comments make the child artist conscious of qualities in his painting—*after they are achieved*—and so help to bring them within experience and make them a part of normal equipment where they can and will be used normally, freely, and subconsciously. Children quickly respond to the stimuli of these qualities in painting. They can even get excited by abstract painting which stresses only such qualities. Creation and design, therefore, can be constantly developed both as an end in themselves and as a means to the dramatization of subject. Children can be, and normally are, creative artists.

There are at least five ways of teaching art which can be guaranteed to kill the art impulse in children. One is imitation or outright copying of other art forms or styles. One is copying nature—naturalism. One is the imposition of adult standards, including skills. One is intellectualism, even within the modern, creative field. And the fifth may be the integrated curriculum where art becomes a mere handmaiden to serve loyally and self-effacingly other subjects such as history, sociology, and geography. I say "may be" deliberately, for integration of art with other subjects need not be a negative influence on the child—*if the art is master instead of servant.*

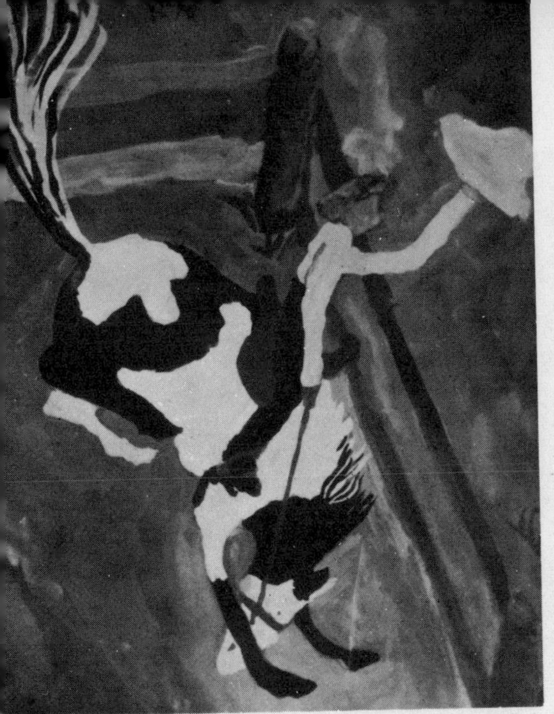

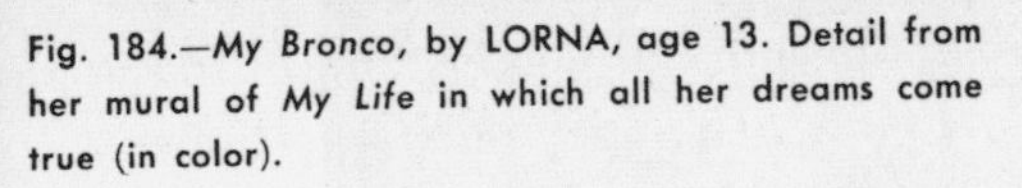

Fig. 184.—*My Bronco*, by LORNA, age 13. Detail from her mural of *My Life* in which all her dreams come true (in color).

Fig. 185.—*Gloucester*, by RONALD, age 14. Symbols of the sea life which he loves are translated into color-space arrangements.

Imitation and copying have been sufficiently pilloried herein to need no more castigation as the reverse of the creative process which comes naturally to children.

Adult standards imposed on the child or young student are deadly. They produce skilled automatons. Pleasure is then limited to craft achievement. Of itself craft has none of the above values. It is a practical matter, a means. It can and should be valued as a contributory element but it must be kept in that place. Values of the spirit are more important than any means to their realization.

Teaching should never be limited to a process of passing on information or skills from teacher to student. It should be a process of stimulation, encouragement, of drawing out and developing what is already within the student, a partnership in a building task to

Fig. 186.—A painting in oil by MARILYN LIPSON, age 16.
Abraham Lincoln High School, Brooklyn. Leon Friend, instructor.

SKILL ASSIMILATED INTO THE YOUNG ARTIST'S CONCEPT

which both contribute. Black Mountain College, near Asheville, N. C., was founded precisely to re-form education into that creative process.[2]

[2] In an exhibition of some 1,200 examples of high school art held several years ago at Rockefeller Center in New York City I made a rough, general survey to see how many of the exhibited works were original in the sense of being a genuine expression of the age represented. The rough count gave some 20 such works about which there could be no doubt—works which were fresh-visioned, alive, and obviously an expression of first-hand experience. The proportion was 1 to 60: 1 original to 59 which were dominantly the victims of adult standards in point of view and in their pathetic striving for adult skills. Commercial art was strongly represented and showed the least originality; the

Art should integrate with life; it should not be taught in isolation. But the impulse to create, symbolize, and unify is an imperious one. It must give orders. It must remake, redispose, reinterpret. Like King Do-do it must airily wave to the Lord High Executioner to do his duty on the slightest whim. Then, having eliminated, it must also build—and to its own design. Of course, it can "interpret the family life of the Greeks." But it must do so according to the dictates of the child's rampant, frolicking vision. How do Susie and Jamie imagine Mr. Phidias having breakfast with his wife? They have studied Greek history. They know what kind of house it was and have seen the chairs and tables, oil lamps and urns. They will more or less use such data. Then they will create. Their fancy will be turned loose on this material. They will interpret history. And the important thing *above all others* is to nourish and protect their vision, *their* interpretation.

The teacher should show curiosity about the vision. She should respect it, should build self-confidence to stiffen and authenticate the imperialism of the creative ego. For in this direction lies the courage which will allow art to combat the negations all about it, to assert itself and change environment for the better. Without this courage art ceases to be creative art, ceases to have value to the child.

The other method, where the history teacher calls in the art teacher, requests the art classes to illustrate life in Japan next week

vast bulk of such work was imitation of prevailing commercial standards.

In May, 1940, I made a much more thorough study of 567 paintings out of a total of 1,500 in the exhibition called Young America Paints, held at the American Museum of Natural History and including work from elementary and junior and senior high schools of the entire United States. The results were as follows:

	Total studied	Original	Adult standards	Percentage original
Elementary	174	144	30	83
Junior High	116	34	82	38
Senior High	277	48	229	17

Such a count cannot be exact, of course, because there are many doubtful cases, but it does show a definite decrease in originality and creative power as education advances through the various age levels. In startling contrast to these proportions was a group of paintings by Mexican children in the public schools of Pharr, Texas, where, out of a total of 26 works shown, the entire number were original creations interpreting the life the children knew.

Fig. 187.—Illustration by HERMAN LETTERMAN, age 16.
Abraham Lincoln High School, Brooklyn.
Creative imagination has here had free play both in treatment of subject and in design. Leon Friend, instructor.

ABSTRACT CREATION

and then herself does the dictating—This temple must be accurate; a ricksha has two wheels, etc.—reduces art to the level of the accurate illustration. It becomes day labor—a task to be done like so many pages of geometry. All the joy and excitement are gone, all the thrill of playing Lord of Creation. And *all the value is gone*—except, perhaps, such value as attaches to a clearer visualization of certain historical facts.

By the very nature of creative art it must do the integrating of an "integrated curriculum." In so doing it can deal with subject after subject, in murals, in book illustration, in subject matter for textile design, stage sets, and so on. And in this process with its emotional drive behind it there will be more incentive to look up factual data and use it than there possibly can be when the drive is merely on learning and imposed by authority from without. To give authority to the art impulse in our professional artists or in our children is evidence of the civilized life. When we integrate art with other school interests by granting it authority we shall be setting a pattern for, and hastening, the achievement of that goal.[3]

THE CRITICAL AGE

In the years below ten children create with unabashed confidence in the rightness of their own vision. Then comes that critical period of growing self-consciousness where outside authority and the adult world begin their devastating conflicts and where the tendency to conform is born. How shall the art teacher bridge this period? The question is undoubtedly one of the most crucial in the educational program for children.

As I see it, there are two important answers. One has been ably stated by many progressive educators under the heading of Personality Development. In *Art Education Today*,[4] from 1935 to 1939, there are at least a dozen articles whose arguments for the arousing of interest through vital experiences and their expression without the imposing of outside adult standards include the dealing with this critical age.[5]

All these articles agree, and the point is obviously valid, that expression of experience per se is valuable and developing regardless of other issues. All of them agree that the organization of the statement of experience for the sake of effective expression is like-

[3] In *Art Education Today*, 1938, published by Teachers College, Mr. Thomas Munro states the case for the above type of integration very fully, giving detailed evidence of the decline of art quality in the work of the children of Mexican schools when the goal was changed from free creation to imposed historical illustration.

[4] Teachers College, Columbia University.

[5] Among such articles are the following:
L. Thomas Hopkins and H. Rosabelle MacDonald in 1935.
Edith L. Mitchell, Florence Cane, Caroline B. Zachry, and Mary E. Albright in 1937.
Furman J. Finck, Thomas Munro, and Mary E. Ragan in 1938.
Fred Strickler and Jane Driver in 1939.

all creative drives, if they are to be authentic, must come from wise valuable and developing. Most of those listed, however (I cannot be too exact in this appraisal but am sure of a majority), give no place to design for its aesthetic values or as one rewarding path for personality development. In other words, they grant the practical function of design as order but ignore it as an aesthetic emotional experience; they ignore the art in expression.

The other answer includes the first. But it also stresses technical problems and design as a heavier diet and an arresting challenge to the eager young mind. Is it "sissy" just to paint for fun, just to get exciting colors and harmonies to enjoy? "I'll do that easy stuff in my dotage," said one 12-year-old boy referring, if you please, to simple black-and-white woodcuts freely drawn with no worries about truth or skill—in which expression he had found himself and done delightful work. "All right," the resourceful teacher can say; "let's make it harder. Go ahead and make the human bodies and houses and pigs have real form. Deal with top and side planes in varying degrees of light. Organize your lines, spaces, dark-lights, colors, and forms into a pleasing picture, into an effective design. Get reality with increasing complexity." Then, if the aesthetics of design is also sissy, the dramatic effectiveness of design (a practical matter) can be stressed—as a shifting of emphasis but not as an abandonment of aesthetics. Or pattern of color and shape can be indulged, not for the exquisite pleasure involved, but for the very practical reason of increasing eye interest in an object of use. Use can include a design for the school magazine, a window curtain, an illustration for a history thesis, a wall hanging of sports for the assembly room, or a stained-glass window (on paper) for a Christmas celebration—all practical matters. So, the practical motivation being given its place, perhaps the emotional excitement or the pleasure from pure visual sensation can also have its place and even become respectable through association with such respectable company.

The argument that creative design has a potential cash value in merchandise or machines may increase its respectability and provide the green light to further practice in its production. But never should this irrelevant material interest be the *source* of the will-to-produce; all creative drives, if they are to be authentic must come from within, not from without. But block signals must be removed or changed.

A FEW CONCLUSIONS

The power to create is born in children. In tender years it is self-assertive and happily triumphant. Later, unless protected and encouraged, it will surrender to adult standards and gradually wither and die. The creative teacher will treasure and stimulate it through suggestion. She will avoid the conflicts of intellectualization —she will not try to make the creative process conscious by verbalization or terminology. She will not talk about "creation" and "design"; she will keep her students doing the thing the words mean. The words "interesting" or "exciting" can stand for design for a long time. And finally creative power must have free reign over subject in and out of the integrated curriculum.

The methods for creative designing herein discussed are not adapted for young children. They must be omitted, changed, or diluted to meet their needs. Subject normally interests the child. Subject, therefore, should be his starting point instead of abstraction as with the adult. As a side issue and as a supporting enrichment abstract design qualities will find their place, if encouraged. The design sense is in the child and it will out. At the difficult ages between ten and fifteen design problems along with problems of expressing reality will bridge the gap in the art impulse created by growing intelligence.

The teacher of children must be a creative artist in her own right. She must know from *doing* the experience she is to teach. She must have the creative as against the copying attitude of mind. She must know design. She must have power over materials. She must have the ability easily to translate concepts into symbols. She must have the enthusiasm which will quickly catch and stimulate the enthusiasm of her charges. And, of course, she must know child psychology and have the pedagogical training which our present teacher-training institutions supply—often to the neglect of the above-mentioned qualities. Of the two necessary fields of teacher equipment I give the former—the creative attitude and knowledge of design—first importance. The creative spirit will somehow find its own way of imparting experience.

13. CONCLUSION THE CREATIVE MIND AND THE WORLD IN WHICH IT LIVES

"It seems to me that Expressionism returns art to livingness, to aesthetic evocation, to revealment of those values which feed the spirit."

SHELDON CHENEY.

IN this last sentence of his book, *Expressionism in Art*, Sheldon Cheney crystallizes the faith back of his life experience as writer and observer of the art of the ages.

In contradiction of such faith comes the following letter from an art student deeply disturbed by the barbarities of war:

> Yes, I know there is a big creative idea of which you and we are all a part. But how can it or we help save the world? Give me one good solution to the world's problems through art and you will have done better than Wagner, Beethoven, Titian or Michelangelo. Look at Germany and Italy today. How have the great men of art of the past helped modern Italians and Germans to love their neighbors? I am afraid art is an effect, not a cause—except in war posters and band music. I don't know why men kill each other and destroy the work of years. Jesus didn't stop them, nor all the Catholics and Protestants; how then can I do so armed only with "creative living"?

You are right, dear student. Neither you nor I nor all the artists of past or present, nor all the religions and the prophets, can *stop* the brutalities inherent in the animal nature of man from cropping out like a pestilence of old when dominant forces in the man-made world nourish evil instead of good.

But—and there always is a "but" as a symbol of force opposed to force—life is conflict. All life in nature—all animal and vegetable life, including that of man—is conflict. There is the eternal conflict between growth and decay, between nourishment and destruction, between rival powers—the wave against the rock, the strong against the strong, the strong against the weak, the evil against the good. The rain and the wind through aeons of time defeat the mountain, wearing it down to a mere stump of its one-time glory. Animal defeats animal, is nourished by his victim and, in his turn, is defeated and gives nourishment to his enemy. Man defeats man and is defeated in turn, over and over again through all the ages of recorded life. The universe is a conflict of thrusts and pulls of planet against sun, of suns against other suns. But here balance has been achieved. Balance which endures and avoids the catastrophe which would follow the victory of one gravitational pull over the delicate poise of all.

Balance is the answer, not victory. Victory and defeat may be fleeting; balance endures. Evil is victorious over good. Good, at times, defeats evil. But always good opposes evil—checks it, ameliorates its effects, lessens its power. So, too, does evil oppose good and check it and lessen its power. The fact that neither can win complete victory over the other, anihilating it, the fact that the balance shifts as the opposed forces gain or lose—this law of the universe proclaims balance of power to be the crucial matter. And in that balance each one of us infinitesimal units in the Great Scheme has his place. We contribute to the balance. We tip the delicate scales just so many notches in the direction we want them to go, in the direction of the particular good in which we believe. That is our victory. That is all the victory we can hope to achieve. That is the victory which checks just so much of the opposing force, which helps to maintain the balance in which life and growth can endure. And life and growth have endured through five thousand years of known history; they have endured and they have gained. Slowly and painfully but steadily, in spite of many reverses, the forces of construction have gained over the forces of destruction.

Creative living, then, is a weapon in this never-ending battle of forces into which we were born and in which we must live and, in our turn, die. It is a powerful weapon. It has won its victories through all of man's history and they are impressive victories. The pyramids of Egypt, symbols that man's works can endure against all the ravages of man-measured time. The temples and sculptures of ancient Greece, the cathedrals of medieval Europe, the paintings, carvings, the decorated things of use which have come down to us from all manner of places and all periods of time. Each one of these is a cumulative victory and an enduring contribution to the balance of power.

Who are you, art student, to imply that Wagner, Beethoven, Titian and Angelo have failed to "solve the world's problems" in some degree? Remove them from history and you remove whole mountains of weight from the scales of the forces of life and hand them over to the opposed scales of destruction. Who are you to say that you and I and the living creators of today have failed to throw our ounces of the positive where they would oppose the negative? Who are you to deny to all religion its contribution to the sometime triumph of spirit over matter? Where would we be without the great total of these positive forces? That item of epochal importance you forget to answer.

The totalitarian state with its dictatorship over the free spirit of man is the major enemy of the creative mind and the civilization which it has slowly and painfully built against all negations of man and nature through five thousand years of time. With it there is no quarter. Death and devastation will be the fruit of the conflict. The only consolation for him who hopes for the better life is the sure knowledge that the forces of destruction cannot win in the long, long run. The forest fire does not kill all the trees nor scotch all the seeds in the ground. After the fire has passed rebirth begins. Seeds germinate and rear a delicate green life among the blackness. Other seeds are blown or carried into the blighted area by nature's agents —wind, bird, animal, man. The rain slowly washes away the charred wood. Fallen trunks rot and merge with the earth to nourish new life. In good time Life reasserts itself; the devastation is gone. So it will be with the devastations of Barbaric Man.

From the major dangers of barbarism and imprisonment of the human spirit it is a welcome relief to turn to the lesser dangers on all sides of us against which the fight can be fair and democratic and where any large or small, temporary or permanent victories can be chalked up and enjoyed.

Education, we can say with certainty, effectuates creative living. Education which liberates the human mind from the blind faiths, the bigotries, the taboos of the ages, which teaches it to combine feeling and thinking, to control emotion with reason, to deal creatively with all the materials of the environment—mental, physical, material, and psychological—this is the kind of education that is a force in man—a powerful, constructive force. It is at work in progressive schools in all fields. It is at work or can be at work in the arts and in schools of the arts.

Creative living, if believed in and practiced with conviction and courage, affects first the one life of him who does the acting on his beliefs. Positive living becomes a force generating energy which is transmitted to and affects others—a friend, a member of the family, a fellow student, perhaps even a so-called teacher. With growth—and such dynamic energy cannot remain passive—its power grows, its orbit of influence spreads. A friend-student is dissuaded from selling his soul to the average standard, to the corrupt goal, to the easy way which happens to lie at his feet. The vital spark which lies dormant in all human beings is kindled, the fire burns, eagerness for the difficult quest is roused, the life of the temporary or enduring victories and the wide influence is begun. And the results no man can foretell.

THE POSITIVE AND NEGATIVE FORCES—SCHOOLS—ART SCHOOLS

Different types of art schools and art departments have different virtues and defects. In this country the virtues are more than likely to stand to the credit of an individual teacher or executive who has sufficient vision to swim against the tide. The defects are more catholic than that; their causes spread into the general attitude of mind, into the folkways of the American people as a whole. Since these ways are definitely divorced from the experience of creative art, it is hardly to be expected that the educational instruments which they set up to teach their children will rise much, if any, above their source. The individual can rise above his source; the general average of many individuals measures those who never care nor dare to try.

THE LARGE INSTITUTIONAL SCHOOL

The large institutional art school, especially one under the auspices of an art museum or a university, attracts the largest number of students because of the overwhelming dignity and bulk-weight of its impressive Gothic cathedral or Greek temple plant, the size of its student body, and the long list of members of its faculty. Can so impressive a school in a cathedral or in a vast museum filled with the great art of the past be wrong in its teachings? A hard question, this, for the young student trained to respect for his elders to answer.

The great institution can be many things. Its greatest asset undoubtedly is its plant—a place to work and study with every conceivable facility, with funds to engage every needed instructor, with congenial surroundings and the inspiration of the great art of other days. Its greatest liability is the cultural lag which is inevitable in a large institution where conservatism is more than likely to be entrenched both in a board of directors composed of businessmen chosen for other virtues than their comprehension of creative art and in a staff many of whose members date back in their training to a decadent period from which they have not rescued themselves. To such staff members change means economic danger and is automatically resisted — a resistance likely to be supported by the board because of friendships, humanitarian motives, or lack of understanding of a new philosophy. If, by some chance, a progressive director is projected into this situation his task of reform is well-nigh hopeless. He cannot discharge old stand-bys en masse and a few dismissals or retirements cannot cure the malady. He can bring in new blood to hold its place precariously but the resultant clash of viewpoints creates discord and confusion both for the school and for its students. "There are many points of view in art," said one progressive director recently, "and the one-man school can be dictatorial in choosing among them. But we, with a thousand students and 67 teachers, cannot. We must be tolerant. We have to face the fact of divergent opinion and satisfy it. Some students want skills. Some want the more creative. Some want design. Some want commercial art. Well, we give them all these different ways and let them choose."

Even the acknowledged progressive institution does not as a rule escape this dilemma. In one such large teacher-training college the required courses in educational theory function independently from the art department and its practice and applications of teaching method with the result that the integration preached in the former is not applied in the latter. This elemental conflict is heightened by additional conflicts of viewpoint among the art department staff. Just as the philosophy of education has come from one professor and art methods have come from another, so has one taught painting, another drawing, and still another designing—each with his own point of view and different emphases and methods. Then, assuming that all these varied points of view have at least a common educational progressivism, there is another department—interior decoration—which, because a grave surgical operation has not been successfully accomplished, teaches a complete denial of the creative philosophy of the other departments through a creed of copying past arts. What is the poor student to do under such conditions? In spite of the apparent advantage of meeting "many points of view," he or she is more than likely to graduate with a confused philosophy and no independent, personal point of view at all.

The weakness of such conformance to demand lies in the lack of any basic standard or philosophy and of leadership in presenting it.

Are creation and design the least common denominator of all the arts or are they not? Is skill in craftsmanship art or is it not? These decisions are basic. They can form a foundation on which small or large educational structures can be built. To date the majority answer has been an affirmation of the second question: skill is art. It is on that platform that most of our large educational institutions have been built and it is on it that most of them still function.

The minority voice, however, is continually gaining in authority —the voice that has learned from history that creation and design are the art law of the ages, that skill is craft, not art. But the permeation of this voice does not solve the problem of the large school; it only creates confusion.

We need the large art school. Mass education is a necessity in a democracy. But its value depends on its character. Education can be negative, destructive, or passive. Also it can be positive, constructive, and effective. Tolerance is an admirable virtue in some human relations and in some aspects of education. But its value in the matter of choosing foundations on which to build for present and future is a crucial one and must be carefully considered. The primary responsibility of education is to youth; tolerance should not make of the art school an old teachers' home.

One of the by-products of the lack of leadership involved in "satisfying divergent opinion" is the general surrender to the average standard which it encourages. "That's all right, but it's arty," the instructor in the illustration class will say to an aspiring student. "You're getting too arty. Better get back to the solid commercial stuff." You should not aspire; you should not be original, this is to say. It doesn't pay. You should accept the decadent standards of the commercial magazine in its effort to please the average taste. Or, the teaching of applied design is geared to that of current commercial wares. Clipping files are kept by the school library and by the student and it is to these the potential creator goes to smother his divine gifts in the sad process of lifting a suggestion here and another there from the successful artist who has gauged the average taste sufficiently to sell his pictures or designs to business. In such commercial classes and in thousands of high school classes in design the prostitutions of business are accepted without question as the goal to be achieved. And the reason for the surrender is to train "to get a job."

Unity of basic philosophy can be achieved in a collaborating group—in sports, in business, in research, in science, in war, and in many practical tasks. Our complex modern civilization could not run an hour without such basic unity of purpose in the many fields of communal activity on which its very existence depends. The authoritarian state imposes this unity by force, destroying all opposition. We refuse that barbaric way. We choose the much more difficult democratic way. But democracy must not deny the right and necessity of leadership or its conflicts will cancel out its gains. Leadership and basic unity of plan are the minimum essentials of progress.

In these pages I have outlined the basic standards which I believe provide the foundation for unity in art education. The standards are not my property or my discovery. They are widely distributed in time and place. The are internationally acknowledged. Once they are accepted as the foundation of a plan and instructors in any school are chosen for their acceptance of their basic implications there will still be room for all normal diversities in individual application. Such divergencies are healthy and a challenge to the student to find his own individual path to a general goal. It is the contradictions in basic philosophy and the conflicting pulls of opposed goals that are devastating and generate only confusion.

Since practice based on these new foundations means a great saving in time through the elimination of endless exercises in skill development, a radical change in program in a conventional art school becomes inevitable. Roughly this can follow a plan which gives the first year to a training in the fundamentals herein outlined. Then any number of succeeding years may be given to practice in their application to usable creations in any media from pictures and sculptures to things of use. The year of drill in exercises to develop a sensitive power in the organization of line, space, dark-light, texture, color, planes, and form is ample to make such power an integrated part of individual capacities to be used automatically in all situations where these elements come into play. The same period is ample for drill in establishing the creative, reorganizing attitude of mind toward subject. Skills, discarded from primary consideration, will develop faster than before and will prove ample to take care of all aesthetic needs as they arise. And at the end of such a preliminary year the turn to production which can be used in many fields, which has an immediate social value, provides a driving energy and an enthusiasm which can never be approached when the only drive is skill and the remote financial allure of "getting a job."

What is the answer to this crucial question? Students do have to get jobs. Families have made sacrifices to pay school expenses and must be relieved of money pressure. Funds are exhausted. Earnings must begin. The school is right in its concern with jobs. But should that concern translate itself into a sellout of all ideals —a sacrifice of the body and soul of youth to the cynical moloch of profit, a training to accept and participate in, and thereby authenticate and entrench, the corruption?

It need not do this. There are other ways of meeting the practical need.

In the departments of the easel picture, print, mural, or sculpture there is no pressure today toward corrupt practice. Once skill as a goal is discarded the student is free to create according to his lights, and the school should back such creations by commissioning murals for empty school walls (first at no fee but expenses, then to the outstanding young artist, a modest fee above expenses), by exhibiting and selling at low prices such selected works as deserve support and by soliciting outside commissions.[1]

In the department of the cartoon and illustration, the pressure toward conformity to the naturalistic picture does operate since the great bulk of illustration of magazines and books, including children's books, is still on the naturalistic level.[2]

Advertising art, in spite of its unearned reputation for leadership, still keys its pictures to the aesthetically starved twelve-year-old mind (the supposed average intelligence level of all American citizens) and so cries aloud for the leadership and education which will advance the average at least a few notches.

It is in the great field of applied design, however, that the greatest need for reform lies and the greatest opportunity for the young

[1] The school of the Colorado Springs Fine Arts Center is training its advanced students on actual mural commissions and some have already received Art Project commissions as a result.

[2] The field of children's book illustration provides one of the richest fields for the modern creative artist. A recent investigation showed a bare half dozen creative artists in evidence here, with dozens of confused imitations of the modern and the bulk of the work naturalistic. The child is an adventurer, a creator. He should have adventurous, exciting, designed creations in his book pictures. Among the very few artists who are giving him such creative fare are Wanda Gag, Ludwig Bemelmans, Wm. Pene du Bois (outstandingly), and James Daugherty, Lois Lenski, and Helen Sewell (with reservations). The balance of the field sorely needs renovation.

student-artist to earn his way. Also the greatest responsibility and opportunity for the school to help him do so.

All technical standards required by industry to meet production limitations, price levels, and so on, can be met in school training, so the student is equipped to illustrate or design within them. These are legitimate requirements of business to which no exception can be taken.

Where industrial design is not depraved, as in the general fields of the machine (automobiles, airplanes, typewriters, vacuum cleaners), of business architecture (modern factories, skyscrapers, some restaurants, stores, banks—which have discarded their false, Greek temple fronts, silos), kitchen and bathroom fixtures, women's dress (which has undergone a remarkable regeneration since it stopped copying Paris and acknowledged American designers), there is already an open way to creation and to honest, functional design. Even if modern design, in some of these departments, has fallen into conventional "streamlined" stereotypes (as it has), there is no impregnable reason why another new conception cannot make its way. Teaching can be honestly creative in these directions.

Where design still is dominantly corrupted by profit or ignorance and fear, as in the general fields of home and public building architecture (with increasing exceptions), of furnishings, including textiles and rugs (with some exceptions in furniture but practically none outside of plain colors in either textiles or rugs), in jewelry, advertising (exceptions too rare to locate), teaching can avoid the humiliation of the aesthetic sellout in two effective ways.[3]

It can train for the creative design growing out of contemporary life, can honor it, exhibit it, use it in the school environment, educate for its public approval and for the support of such minority examples as do get into production. Then it can frankly tell its students

[3] Modern furniture should be designed by the creative artist designer. Industry has recognized this in its show pieces for modern exhibitions in a few isolated instances but has turned more frequently to architects of modern tendency—witness the Exhibition of Contemporary American Industrial Art at the Metropolitan Museum in New York in 1940, which had on its cooperating committee in charge of the exhibit eleven architects, nine industrial designers, and no artists (painters and sculptors). This happened in spite of the fact that the design-conscious modern artist is aesthetically the best equipped for designing things of use.

of the commercial decadence which still dominates mass production, advise them to find the rare quality job if possible or to take a job, if that is necessary, in a depraved field and to design to meet its standards as a temporary expedient but all the time to be watching for the break which will allow a finer product its chance and all the time to be advancing the cause of the finer work in every possible way.

Or, secondly, it can educate to the highest possible creative standard and then, in competition with the depraved business field, try to find outlets and public buying support for small-scale production which does not compromise, which allows the creative artist to function at his best. If that involves a salesroom in the school building, so much the better; the process of selling the distinguished product makes the whole educational process more functional in that it completes the cycle and puts into use the things its students produce.

If, within a single year, all schools or school departments which teach art would accept and put into practice such a constructive program, the higher standards of public demand would be felt by business almost immediately and within five years the present strangle hold of the corrupt standard would be definitely broken. When the great American public, holding as it does absolute power over business through its own buying demand, allows itself to remain sunk in its own fears and ignorance at the behest of its own instrument, business, the dilemma is tragic. And when education fails to accept the challenge and combat the decadence, the result is a cultural tragedy.

COLLEGES AND UNIVERSITIES

One such cultural tragedy which exists in many colleges and universities and stridently proclaims our national divorce from the arts is the frequent failure of the authorities to allow their own art department (when it is progressive) to apply its teachings to the school environment. For instance:

In a large university in New York City the building of the Faculty Club was furnished in an antique period style *without consulting the Department of Art and Architecture.*

A large university recently built a new girls' dormitory. The building was simple, functional, and modern in feeling, if not consistently so in design. An interior decorator was allowed to furnish the huge main-floor reception room with imitation Chippendale furniture and curtains with naturalistic flower motifs typical of commercial design at its lowest level of decadence—*without consulting the Art Department.*

The alumnae of a famous eastern women's college furnished their alumnae house in Spanish antiques (I don't know where responsibility lay in this case—except, presumably, with the alumnae).

In a far western college the president allowed the contractors to sell him imitation Chippendale furniture for the reception room of a new girls' dormitory of good modern design and, perhaps even worse than that, accepted a bargain offer of carpet of the 1890, commercial, pseudoantique design (than which no American rug design has been or can be more depraved)—*without consulting the Art Department.* And, when the head of the Art Department heard what had happened and protested that these furnishings violated every principle he was teaching and that he would have to tell his students to practice the opposite of official college practice, the president apologized but excused himself by saying he had been very tired that day and this bargain offer allowed him to get the matter settled easily.

This negation in official practice of the teachings of their own departments is a sinister educational blunder. It is sinister, not only because it means discord within the organization and confusion for the students, but because it involves a surrender to commercialism and its depraved standards and a complete failure to put into practice the leadership which a great educational institution is supposed to assume. On the student this public insult to the Art Department, with its flouting of any cultural advance which may be struggling for expression therein, can only be negative and destructive.

To put it bluntly, ignorance in high places is, of course, the cause of this failure to integrate institutional teachings. Faculty members have to tread softly in protesting such a situation; they can be punished in various subtle ways. Who, then, can help the institution out of this dilemma? The enlightened student? Perhaps that is the answer. Perhaps the student should take the responsibility of educating, first, himself and then his Alma Mater.

HIGH SCHOOLS

The most potent negative force in high school art teaching is the imposition of adult standards including skills which cause the steady decline in originality from the elementary grades through junior and senior high, as that was revealed in the percentage table on page 217. This, plus the deference to commercial standards, the training to such standards as a means of getting a job and the almost complete lack of training for leadership explains the mediocrity of the great mass of high school art.

Responsibility for this negation of the normal creative powers of young people is probably divided between the general practical attitude of mind typical of our time, the state syllabi which, in so many cases, make that practical attitude official and impose it on teachers and students alike, and the tendency to imitate and please which is certainly not far under the skin of the average child. Leadership in creative doing would overcome all these pressures, as is amply proved by the small but significant proportion of genuine creation which does come out of the high school mill under the encouragement of those teacher-geniuses who somehow get around their state syllabi and inspire their young charges to be themselves. When there is a preponderance of creative work in one school, or under one teacher it does not mean that child talent is concentrated in that particular corner of a city; it merely means that a creative teacher is functioning. To entrench and support such teachers and widen their influence and number is the heavy responsibility of school boards throughout the country—a responsibility which will need the clearing out of much deadwood both in personnel and in rules.

There are other handicaps under which the public schools in general must work—too short an art period (a double period in high schools should be the minimum), difficulty in getting supplies of the right amount and quality (I know of teachers who buy supplies for their children out of their own salaries because the official ones are inadequate), too-large classes which make any individual contacts almost impossible (and in creative art the individual contact and understanding is a necessity), and finally the conflicts with authority which the creative teacher, under present conditions, can avoid only by a miracle if she lives up to her ideals. These are lesser evils, however, than the all-pervading adult standards which penetrate even into the perfectly equipped art room and vitiate the teaching program at the expense of youth.

One other malady in the high school art field is the contest or exhibition, with or without prizes, staged under the auspices of some business institution for its own advertising purposes. Soap sculpture contests staged by a soap manufacturer, the national exhibition, Young America Paints, staged by a manufacturer of art supplies, the art prize contests by the *American Magazine* and others like it, are examples. Since these are business enterprises, it is a foregone conclusion that they are going to set up the accepted average standards, call in school authorities who represent those standards, honor with prizes work that excels in mediocrity, and dishonor, by implication, work which explores the different way or dares to assert itself as swimming against the tide. Every item on such programs is educationally bad. The deference to business and the granting it authority in such matters are bad. The honoring of the average standard is bad. The general idea of prizes for "the best" is devastating in its negative effects on the sensitive creative minds which are far too different ever to be acclaimed as "best" and which must then, by inference, be less than best. The prize is an evil influence also in its arrogant assumption that there is a "best" when such a label only means that three or five people who happen to be a majority of the jury think so. Who are the jury? What are the backgrounds of its members? Is their opinion worthy of respect? These questions should nullify the jury award, but they do not. They do not even get asked. The great mass of people accept the verdict: this romantic, naturalistic painting (which won a recent prize in the *American Magazine* contest) really is "the best." The influence of such reactionary awards is tragic as it affects youth and the national culture.

School authorities should never abdicate to business their educational responsibility. If there must be contests they should be staged as an enterprise of associated schools or under public or governmental auspices. Thus will the cheapness, the humiliation, and most of the evil effects of abdication to profit be avoided. Even if reactionary school officials dominate school contests and give the same caliber of awards, the result will be more healthy. It will presumably be democratic and the taint of commercialism will be removed.

THE ELEMENTARY SCHOOL

In the lower elementary grades children are still the creative artists they were born. Protection, encouragement, and a sympathetic attitude on the part of the teacher is all they need to produce voluminously original works of symbolic art. The heavy task of our educational system is to keep the rich qualities here native and to develop them without loss. We have kept them fairly well in the lower grades but the carnage has been progressively higher in upper grades as our intellectualizations and our adult concern with technicalities got in their deadly work. The one spot in our great educational system where creative art has flourished consistently and widely enough to approach folk-art proportions is in the lower grades of elementary schools.

THE PRIVATE SCHOOL

Progressive private schools, as a class, have probably taken and held the lead over all other types of schools (if not over isolated, progressive classes in the public schools) in this first half of the twentieth century in stimulating, developing, and preserving a genuine, creative child art. So far ahead of professional art schools have they been in discarding copying for creation that our national art would be infinitely more developed and significant if the large professional schools had been closed for a quarter of a century and all their art students routed through "progressive" schools from kindergarten to college. The credit for this unbelievable situation lies with the general progressive philosophy stemming from Dewey and, in the art field, probably as much from Arthur Dow, who taught at Teachers College of Columbia University in the early years of the century, as from any one individual. In art education Dow was the first to break with skilled copying of nature at the opening of the century and to throw the emphasis the other way toward decorative design. He did not get very far toward what is now known as pictorial design but he did blaze the trail and in forty years countless numbers of art teachers and so-called artists have never learned the A B C which he was teaching that long ago. The power of the human mind to insulate itself from contemporary knowledge, even in its own special field, is a truly amazing thing.

TEACHER-TRAINING INSTITUTIONS

Many teachers' colleges including state teachers' colleges, in absorbing and applying progressive educational principles, have also absorbed a progressive attitude toward art and so, like the private schools, have conserved and developed the native creative powers of their students and through them of youth in general. Credit for this progressive philosophy and practice where it has penetrated into college teaching seems to belong to individual heads of art departments more than to the institutions themselves. Progressive individuals imbued with the new ideas in their own training have put them to work for thousands of students when they reached positions of authority. All this stemming backward to a source in a few individuals is an impressive display of the potentiality of ideas to propagate and grow in fertile ground and to flower and fruit in generations without end. Unfertile ground is the dead loss and here, as in horticulture, something must be done about it.

CURING THE NEGATIONS

WHAT CAN THE SCHOOLS DO?

A number of suggestions have already been made as to how schools can conserve rather than destroy the natural creative resources of youth. I shall not repeat these suggestions. Once the school has done its grounding in fundamentals (of the new kind) and has become forward-looking and idealistic, one matter is self-evident: there should be collaboration between teacher and student in solving all problems both aesthetic and practical. This spirit of collaboration should exist at all age levels but, as age increases, more and more should responsibility and initiative be shifted to the student; more and more should the teacher become guide and consultant rather than autocratic authority. And the school should back student idealism as far as it possibly can.

WHAT CAN THE INDIVIDUAL STUDENT DO?

He can exercise judgment from the very beginning of his art education, first by deciding what kind of education he wants, second by choosing teachers and schools, so far as that is possible, in accordance with his goal. He can avoid the Naturalistic School and training as he would taking a walk on a treadmill; both are identically the same, they get nowhere so far as art is concerned. Once on the creative educational path he can take the initiative, and keep it, in planning, in doing, in study, reading, and research and thus develop self-confidence and the power to think and act creatively. For the creative mind functions in multitudes of directions other than that of making a picture; it can come into play in just about every waking activity from buying a smock to decorating a room or choosing a wife or husband. Practice and initiative in using one's creative mind is the best possible means of achieving the art of living.

Fig. 187.—By DONALD ALLEN, age 12. Birmingham, Ala. Public Schools, Phyllis Korth, teacher.

Showing how a 12-year-old can make his own original Christmas cards or decorations.

Fig. 188.—By JEAN LUND, age 14. Same school and teacher as Fig. 187. A crayon drawing showing an exuberant native power to create and design in symbols with unconscious originality—which power can be directed to designing things in endless profusion.

Interior decoration is a field long overripe for rescue from the hands of prostituted commerce, including the conventional "interior desecrators" who play the business game and keep their customers engulfed in their own ignorance and fears merely because copied antiques are stable merchandise ensuring a generous profit. The modern creative artist is the most resourceful designer in color, space, and form. Interior design is design of color, space, and form. So is furniture. So are furnishings in general. The creative artist is the logical designer of all things of use.

Once liberated from period styles and all copies of past arts, we can have a veritable renaissance in the art of living. Color harmonies can be played in the walls, textiles, and furniture of a room —harmonies in gay colors, if one likes gay colors, in neutrals, if one likes neutrals, in heavy ultramarine blues with contrasting vermilions, if one likes powerful color. Furniture can be functional, comfortable, honest, and our own creation. Rugs can be semiabstract creations by artists, famous or amateur, or complete abstractions in harmonic design. When such products are not available, rugs can be hand-hooked and the local cabinetmaker can be called in to carry out furniture of the artist's, the student's, or the amateur owner's design with a result which will warm the heart with its personal flavor and original quality. Again the school store can function as agent to educate, exhibit, commission, and sell. Or, if there is no school store, the adventurous student can do his own soliciting, can sell himself, at first, the redecorating of his own room to make it express himself. Then he can sell the family on one new room, then a friend, a neighbor—anyone, anywhere, to get a chance to use his creative powers.

In furnishing a room he must buy materials. This means search and research and search again. Is there merchandise on the market rich in color or design quality? Yes, there is—if he can find it. Plain-colored textiles and rugs. Some kitchen utensils and dishes in color and good functional design. (Jug-town pottery is an example). Well-designed stoves and iceboxes. Judgment is needed. Excellent critical training. Paint is cheap and will do wonders in room design. Rich-colored curtains can replace the negative white lace ones which can still be seen at some American front windows. A dining table in full color is infinitely more rewarding than an all-white one. And so it goes. New arrangements, new creations throughout the house, throughout the environment. The pleasure in living is enhanced. A vital lesson is learned and passed on to others. It is the task of the creative artist to design in color, space, and form wherever color, space, and form are used.

To make a living there are countless additional creations which can be made and sold. Tombstones today are hard-boiled, cold-blooded conventional stereotypes, entirely commercial. The sculpture student or young sculptor has a field here ready-made for the personal monument of originality and distinction. Bookplates can be designed to order at from $25 up. Christmas cards of the commercial breed are an insult to the recipient in their brazen announcement that the sender does not care enough for his friend to write a personal greeting and so sends a cheap (or costly) impersonal, stereotyped, and meaningless nonentity printed by the hundreds of thousands. A vast field here for personalized creations. Posters and signs can be made and sold wherever such are used—in competition with the commercial atrocities which disgrace store windows and other public places. Advertising art is a field waiting to be conquered by the creative artist; ads can be works of art as they rarely, if ever, now are. Stage sets for the school or the little theater—sets which create a psychological atmosphere for the setting of a play through abstract or semiabstract designs with symbolic, instead of literal, meaning. Pottery, jewelry, metalcraft made either by hand or by machine all await the magic touch of the artist to bring them to life as works of art as well as merchandise. All these fields as well as many others need reforming. And all offer the making of a living to him who wins buying support for the creative way.

In contrast to the widespread use of folk art in other ages our divorce from such use is startling and a disgrace to a so-called civilized nation. The garish intrusion of commercial billboards into city, village, and country landscape, the cheap, sentimental, naturalistic, picturings on such billboards, the medley of raw primary colors and of whites and tans on houses, the false-front stores and public buildings, the garish interiors of most theaters, hotels, and clubs, the hard, barren, tan, interior walls of schools, the mediocre, naturalistic pictures for sale in "art stores," the outlandish, meaningless junk (usually imported from Japan) sold at high prices in "gift shoppes"—all these prove the divorce and the aesthetic illiteracy behind it.

These and the other negations already mentioned cry aloud for the crusading spirit to tear down the old and rebuild the new. Frontiers, did you say? Are there no frontiers left for the youth of today to conquer? Here, dear student, is a frontier which begins at your very door, in your own room, in your own dress, smock, or necktie and extends to the fartherest corner of this great country waiting hopefully to be conquered. All these fields need the young and pioneering artist to rescue them from their commercial decadence and make them again a credit to the nation and part of a developing national culture.

The fact that much of the regeneration here envisaged can come under the head of folk art is a significant thing. One of the cultural dangers of our time is the increasing vicariousness of the average experience of life. More and more we become passive spectators of the activities of others. We *listen* to the radio, *watch* television or the play, movie, prize fight or ball game. We *buy* everything we use; nothing anymore is *made by hand.* We call in specialists to do repairs and odd jobs around the house. We do not sing, dance (other than social dancing), compose music or poetry or paint for pleasure. We do not *practice* either the crafts or the arts. And we need to do just that to save ourselves from somnambulism as a way of life. We need to keep our spirits awake with creative doing.

In the late 1930's occurred a series of events which, more than any others in the entire history of our country, tended to counteract our habitual cultural lag and vicarious relationship to the arts. I refer to the production and educational events sponsored by the federal government under the Roosevelt administration. The Federal Art Projects, which started as a relief measure during the depression and later developed into a combination of relief and a definite cultural program, and the commissioning of murals and sculptures for government buildings under the Fine Arts Department of the United States Treasury, actually created a renaissance in American art which could never have happened under any other auspices. Artists were allowed to work at their profession; their productions went into all manner of public buildings—to cheer the sick, to entertain and instruct the well, to make living richer by opening doors into the experiencing of the arts for the millions who had never before realized that art, in its many media, was a thing to live with and by rather than to gaze at with awe and curiosity in the pillared walls and glass cases of an art museum. Practice classes were held for all ages, thus allowing the participation that ensures understanding.

Standards, in the government program, were confused between the creative and copying schools; in the mural program there was far too much emphasis on the realities of subject and too little on esthetics. Mediocre talents were subsidized along with discovered and undiscovered genius—but such negations are inherent in the democratic process and so are justified as an expression of our way of life. Beyond this the gains to the civilized life were epochal.

As a nation we came of age in these events. We demonstrated our belated discovery of the historical fact that achievement in the arts measures civilization and that there can be no widespread production, understanding, and using thereof until artists have been freed from the uncertainties of private patronage and the corruptions of commerce and allowed to create for the enjoyment of the mass of their fellow citizens. It was this discovery and the action taken to implement it that made the Government Art Program the most constructive cultural event of the past century.

Since 1940 there has been no revival of the program and none by the United States Government is yet in sight. The United Nations, however, is demonstrating an international interest in the same cultural goals; we await developments here with palpitating interest.

As indiviauals, we of the older generation have done what we could to hasten the national arrival at these goals but the gains to date are only a beginning. There are more of you—the youth of today. Your foundations are surer—if you find and adopt them. There are, or will be, more segments of society to give you support. You can tip the scales a good number of notches toward the creative way. You can do your part along with Wagner, Beethoven, Titian, Angelo, Cézanne, Orozco and their followers to solve the world's cultural problems in some degree, to oppose the forces of negation, to make art again a living thing.

Success to you, Student. The task is hard, honorable, and rewarding. The world sorely needs *creative artists.*

Fig. 189.—*"How I Feel After Reading a Pulp Magazine,"* by JOAN VILLA, age 15. John Marshall High School, Chicago. Marguerite Pearce, teacher.

NOTE. All the illustrations shown with this chapter, other than the above, are by recent students of the Design Workshop who, with four exceptions, were amateurs painting for pleasure. Of the exceptions—Burgess, Fritzinger, and Moore are art teachers and O'Connor a college student.

These are experimental, learning creations, the result of from five to thirty lessons by mail, rather than finished works of art. Some of the students have had previous conventional academic training, some have not. None of the work has been exhibited; this is its first public showing.

14. TEN YEARS LATER

WHAT has happened, during the past tragedy-packed decade, in art and art education? Obviously a great deal, some of the events being negative in influence, some positive. The time is opportune to appraise these influences with an alert eye and mind and see what we shall see. That is the purpose of this chapter.

Both content and "form"[1] are supposed to inhabit pictures. For many decades, in theory and practice, it has been assumed that content and form not only cohabit in pictures and sculptures but that they are approximately equal in importance—the content supplying the building materials, the form contributing the plan or structure which gives them character. So well established has been this assumption, it has the effect of an axiom.

In present practice at this halfway mark of the twentieth century, however, we are sadly mixed up, not only about the axiom, but also about the individual and relative merits of these two ingredients. So muddled are we in fact that some people (including some artists and art teachers) forget one or the other—and sometimes both—of these basic elements and try to make pictures or sculptures without them. When content is entirely eliminated we get complete abstraction. When form is by-passed we get message, if any, and perhaps skill. When both are tossed out the window the contribution to the observer is—chaos. And chaos is not art.

Since muddled thinking on this issue seems to be the outstanding dilemma of our art world, it behooves art education to inquire into and try to resolve the matter as one demanding priority. It must do so in the interest of its own health and to establish its own

[1] The word "form" is used in its sense of order or orderly arrangement, as an alternative to the word, "design."

leadership out of this cultural morass. Since content is a contribution of individual choice, whereas form is a universal element, the focal point of the discussion obviously should be on form.

In this matter of form in art, as well as in other matters, and in spite of the fact that there are six published books on modern art to my credit, I make no claim to being a final authority. The correlated study of many inquiring minds is needed to separate the wheat from the chaff in all art, including our own, to reappraise all values and decide which are authentic and durable. Particularly necessary are cooperative study and agreement as to what are the few basic values on which others depend. If and when there can be such agreement, then other contributory values can take their related places in a sensible perspective. Complete agreement, in other words, on all matters is as unnecessary and undesirable as it is impossible; no one, I am sure, desires such monotonous conformity. Variety, here as elsewhere, is the spice of life. But agreement on the few *basic* issues would provide the solid platform from which other minor and personal opinions could with logic and zest diverge. We need both the agreements and the divergencies. It is for such basic agreements that I argue in these pages.

As one reads and ponders the characteristics of a living art and art education which presumably will survive the ravages of time, a series of questions springs to mind which demand careful answering. Among them are the following:

ARE THE EDUCATIONAL GOALS AND METHODS PRESENTED IN THIS BOOK DATED? DO THEY NEED REVISION DUE TO THE PASSAGE OF TIME?

No, the goals and methods are not dated, even though the specific evidence used to support them may be. They are as old as the hills. No, I retract. They are only as old as picture-making man—who has been roaming over various hills for more than 20,000 years. The Cave Men knew how to create and design symbols which conveyed meaning. They somehow understood the standards of excellence for which we are here arguing. The millennium will have arrived when we of today—all of us—equal their understanding. For evidence, see Fig. 13.

HAS THE GENERAL SITUATION IN ART EDUCATION IN THIS COUNTRY CHANGED IN THE LAST DECADE? IF SO, IS THE CHANGE FOR BETTER OR WORSE?

HAVE THE VALUES AND METHODS HERE ADVOCATED BECOME MORE WIDELY UNDERSTOOD AND USED?

HAS NATURALISM, THE DOMINANT ART PHILOSOPHY OF THE NINETEENTH CENTURY, CONTINUED ITS WANING INFLUENCE, SO MARKED IN THE FIRST FOUR DECADES OF THE TWENTIETH CENTURY, IN THE FIFTH DECADE?

Obviously it is impossible to answer questions like these with exactitude—without undertaking a prolonged and costly survey of all art schools in the country, a project far beyond the capacity of any individual investigator. I have made no such survey. From first-hand evidence I know there has been a remarkable gain in the understanding of basic values in a considerable number of specific cases where an individual artist-educator, or in some instances an entire school, has had the opportunity, without devastating conflicts, to teach these values. The influence of such teaching has spread and will continue to grow as its fortunate students in their turn exert influence on their individual world and its future students—provided they are not corrupted and disenfranchised by later counter-influences. Then, as always happens, there have been and are a goodly number of independent souls, of many ages and positions in life, who are capable of making their own decisions in this matter of values regardless of the mass of confusions which plays on them and around them continuously from every side. All honor to these independent ones. They are the stuff out of which culture grows. Frequently unhonored and unsung because they are of the minority which the majority does not understand, they keep up the good fight regardless of personal gain—and in the end, in some degree, win. From among the artists in their ranks come the geniuses who make history and ultimately are rewarded with fame. From among those who are educators or patrons who support in various ways the actually out-in-front, creative programs, comes that elusive thing called progress. All of these human forces have

Fig. 190.—By SISTER RITA.* The first step in drawing the human figure—to get living action.

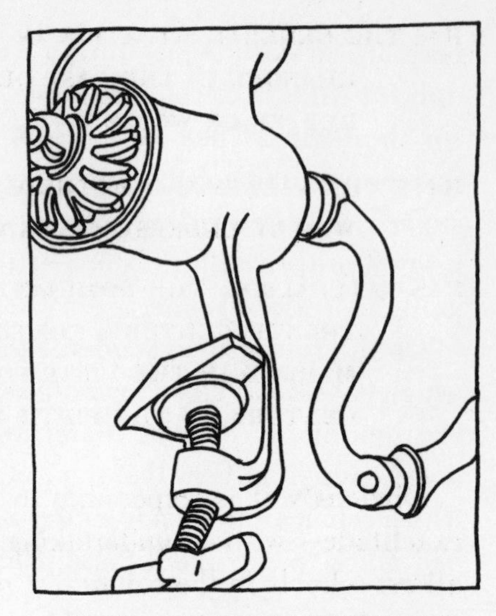

Fig. 191.—By DOROTHY WILLIAMS.* Line and space design extracted from a three-dimensional object.

Fig. 192.—By JOYCE SWANNELL.* A fantasy based on nature and drawn in three dimensions.

Fig. 193.—Imaginary forms expressed by means of dramatic edges. By a Design Workshop student.

been at work among us during past decades and will continue their difficult roles in decades to come. They have changed art education for the better. They have made the timeless values more widely understood and used. They have helped to push naturalism, that superficially rewarding refuge of the masses of our citizens, back into its proper cultural perspective. To them we owe such cultural gains as we have made.

On the retrogressive side of the ledger are those copious forces which have delayed and corrupted the national culture; their names are Ignorance, Inertia, Materialism, with its emphasis on skills, and Commercialism, that dry rot eating at the heart of any culture which catches and then tolerates its corruptions, as does ours. I have had much to say about these potent negative forces in Chapter 13.

HAS THAT CRUCIAL ELEMENT IN THE ART OF THE PICTURE OR SCULPTURE—ORGANIZED FORM, OR DESIGN, GAINED OR LOST IN PRESTIGE AND USE?

Here is the focal point of the situation existing in our art world today where two basically opposed ideologies, the one championing form, the other formlessness, meet in deadly conflict. From this conflict there should be no retreat till the issue is resolved. No solution based on a sweet and reasonable toleration of formlessness or formal trimmings as a minor virtue along with techniques and skills can be a basis for compromise. The issue cannot be compromised. Either the contribution of the thing we call "art" is concentrated mainly in the felt organizational control and interplay of all the parts for practical and esthetic purposes, or, conversely, expression can cohabit with chaos. Our art world desperately needs a decision on this issue in order to pull itself out of the morass of confusion in which it is now floundering. Even if confusion is the order of the day in many aspects of contemporary life, the work of art should not express that current theme by means of a like confusion.

The trouble with this brave argument for a resolving of confusion, the sad weak spot therein, is that a large proportion of the opposition does not know that a conflict of ideologies exists. They do not know they have chosen sides and are supporting formlessness—

Fig. 194.—By BELL WORSHAM.*
Details of a room built into three-dimensional form and plane design.

Fig. 195.—By ULDENE TRIPPE.*
A three-dimensional design organization of forms floating in space. "Dramatic edges" are used to accent form.

Of Fig. 195, the artist says:

"This was fun—especially because I was always surprised at the way things turned out—never at all as I had visualized them. In the beginning my idea was to contrast square blocks with cylinders knocking about against each other. Then I felt the need of a large flat form and something different in the way of a small center of interest. Without being conscious of it, I added a streak of dark behind the latter that made it look something like a comet—and wham!—I was off on a new set of ideas. Each picture begets others—to me one of the most interesting aspects of this work."

Fig. 195A.—By ULDENE TRIPPE.*
An organized re-creation of data observed on a stroll through the north woods.

Fig. 196.—By MAUDE SUMAN.** A fantasy based on plant life. The main charm is the sensitive rhythmic movement and the extremely subtle vibrating color.

Fig. 197.—*Storks,* by GILDA LOZITO.* The birds and their environment are woven into an integrated whole.

because they do not realize the meaning of the word "form." This sounds incredible and would be in any other art field, but in our visual arts it actually is true. They are concerned either with skilled rendering of subject into a good "composition"—the beginning of form—or they just drift in happy contentment with things as they are. Many artists among them do present their subjects in an orderly factual array; their formlessness is limited to the lack of designed, or plastic controls, inherent in the very process of copying nature.

A minority of the chaoticists, however, do know, or think they know, that an ideological battle is on; they courageously announce to the world they have "renounced Bauhaus formalism" or "certain clichés in modern art of the late 1920's," that they "communicate psychologically," that they are "the avant garde of modern art." This is much better. Here the opposing lines are drawn and can be recognized; the conflict can proceed to its important conclusion.

To answer these claims one need only remember that form, or "formalism," cannot be dated, or tied to the Bauhaus, or reduced to a "cliché." It is timeless and placeless and without it, communi-

Fig. 198.—*War*, by GERTRUDE BURGESS.* Here is the spirit of bombs bursting in air.

Fig. 199.—*Atomic Bomb*, by CAROLINE FRITZINGER.* It tells its own story.

cation may perhaps be psychological and factual, but little, if anything, more.

However, if one judges by current exhibitions and the types of work now frequently winning awards and publicity, it is at once evident that this minority movement has pushed itself, and been pushed, into the limelight with an amazing effectiveness. An emotional spree, in other words, such as that here advocated as ideal for the first step of a beginner in painting, is actually featured as a new movement, is called an "advance" in modern art, is invading exhibitions in a proportion of up to a third of the total exhibits and is receiving prize awards, including several firsts in national showings. And, among its supporters are certain well-known art critics, several art magazines and some leading museums. Thus is a movement which can logically be called, "The Cult of the Professional Beginner," acclaimed as something new and progressive in spite of its abandonment of both meaning and form. A debacle like this can happen only in a veritable jungle of ignorance of fundamentals. But, to date, in spite of a growing momentum, the Cult is still a minority diversion from the Grand Tradition.

Fig. 200.—*Breakfast,* by LOTTIE SOBEL.
A three-dimensional improvisation on the theme of Breakfast.

Fig. 201.—*Feeding the Pigs,* by ETHEL DAVIS.*
An experienced incident from daily life dramatized into a designed picture.

Fig. 202

Fig. 203

Both by MARGUERITE N. PADDOCK** illustrating the organization of all the parts in a figure painting or portrait. On such a structural foundation any degree of pictorial complexity and character interpretation can be developed. These show solid foundations, in other words, rather than a finished work of art.

DESIGNED REALITY

One interesting side light on this debacle and its popularity in some quarters is the fact of its being a release into an *emotional* spree. Emotion has come into its own—with an explosive abandon. A dozen years and more ago, as earlier argued, the intellectualisms of the Modern School had the widest appeal as it then seemed; the more authentic emotional approach was not widely understood or valued. Perhaps our present emotional explosion is a delayed protest, among other things, against the limitations in art of the conscious mind. Other artists have been learning about such limitations and the rich rewards of emotional creation ever since the Armory Show of 1913. Our professional beginners have had to compensate for their tardiness by noise.

The majority of the devotees of formlessness probably are still found in the Naturalistic School which teaches the skilled copying of subject facts—the external, visible facts—on which our nineteenth century decadence was based. Since these good craftsmen are unaware, as has been said, of what is happening around them and of their own relationship to the art of the ages, there is nothing

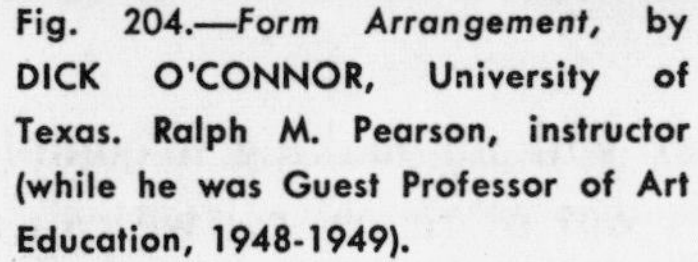

Fig. 204.—*Form Arrangement*, by DICK O'CONNOR, University of Texas. Ralph M. Pearson, instructor (while he was Guest Professor of Art Education, 1948-1949).

Fig. 205.—*Flowers*, by BESSIE MOORE.*

THREE-DIMENSIONAL FORM DESIGN

much that can be done about them. The next generation *presumably* will know better.

WHAT IS THE DOMINANT TREND IN THE ADULT ART WORLD OF TODAY AND HOW DOES IT RELATE TO, SUBSTANTIATE, OR DISCOUNT, THE EDUCATIONAL PROGRAM HERE ADVANCED?

This question can be answered with considerable confidence. Our current dominant trend, it appears, inhabits the middle ground between the two extremes just noted—of formless naturalism and the chaos of the emotional spree. It includes the works, that is to say, of the many artists who do know and practice in varying degrees the controls of form. Here lies the solid core of our contemporary production and the works which, granting other timeless and timely merits, will endure. Within its ranks are the actual, if often unspectacular, leaders in our art—the real avant garde. It is into the company of this serious and hard-working group that the much publicized professional beginners will disappear when and if they ever learn the A B C's, or next higher attributes, of their art, and become adults therein. (Quite naturally they will delay the growing-up process as long as possible—if immaturity continues to bring them fame and fortune.) This middle ground we can presume to call the source of our dominant trend, not because of an inventory of the actual number of significant works produced —such works are always a minority in any general showing—but because of their solid worth, fairly widespread distribution and provable leadership. It is better to allow such characteristics to determine dominance than the mere superior quantity of mediocrity.[2]

IS TODAY'S ART EDUCATION CORRECTLY ASSESSING THIS DOMINANT TREND AND IS IT ABLE TO KEEP ITS BEARINGS IN THE FACE OF ANY ABERRATIONS FROM, OR DEGRADATIONS OF, THAT TREND?

This is a hard question to answer without making a complex and widespread survey. Since this is out of reach, all we can do is hazard guesses as to what is happening. As a guide there are several facts.

We know, for instance, that a profound knowledge of design or form is rare and limited to a few artists and art teachers. We know that the basic design sense, on the other hand, is native to all men and has been so through man's history back to the Stone Age; hence some degree of this native sensitivity will come through in man's products without conscious teaching—unless it has been killed by neglect, evasions, or contrary teachings (as much of it has). We know, furthermore, that design, in the visual arts (and all others), has many degrees of complexity, from a four- or five-note color harmony,[3] to the organizational maturity of a Cézanne, Renoir or El Greco. From this fact it follows that design awareness will be equally diverse among artists and art teachers, each being limited in production and teaching to the range of his own vision. And, finally, we know that unawareness of design is almost total on many low and high levels of our art world. The evidence is the

[2] Mr. Pearson has written a series of articles on some fifty of our leading artists under the title, "The Modern Renaissance in the U.S.A.," which his school, The Design Workshop of Nyack, N. Y., has published as Critical Appreciation Course II.

[3] Such as the painting, "Cyclops," for which Baziotes won the top money prize in the National Exhibition of American Painting at the Chicago Art Institute in 1947.

continuing popularity of naturalism on the low appreciation levels of the masses and the support of chaos or near-chaos on the "high" levels of some critics, art officials, art magazines and well-known artists.

The impact of these known facts is clear. The teaching of design will be equally fragmentary and diverse and its comprehension by students equally limited.

HAS THE PENETRATION OF A GENUINE ART INTO INDUSTRY, MERCHANDISE, AND ENVIRONMENT GAINED OR LOST? AND DOES SUPPLYING CULTURAL NEEDS IN THINGS OF USE STILL OFFER THE MOST FERTILE FIELD IN WHICH THE YOUNG ARTIST AND ARTIST-DESIGNER CAN START HIS CONQUERING CAREER WITHOUT UNDUE COMPROMISE, AS SUGGESTED IN CHAPTER 13?

This is another tough one. And yet, economically and culturally speaking, it may be the most important from a broad viewpoint for the young art student or artist, and for society itself, to have answered. As outlined on page 237, it deals with Curing the Negations and Earning a Living, the latter being more pressing for the individual, the former for society.

Indications are plentiful that there has been a quite remarkable gain. The Good Design program of the Museum of Modern Art has penetrated the sacred precincts (sacred to profit) of Chicago's Merchandise Mart, thereby making "good design" news that finds a place, and is often featured, in the columns of newspapers and magazines. The fact that the Museum, in choosing its "good designs," does not make the necessary distinction between the artist and the commercial designer, means that its judgments are superficial, that they do not get down to the roots of society's illness in this great field. It plays the game along with industry. It dares not, or, perhaps, is not equipped to, *lead*.[4] Pratt Institute's Department of Industrial Design does better; it achieves leadership. (See Chapter 11.) And the brave attempts of single manufacturers like Steuben Glass and The Riverdale Manufacturing Company (page 195), perhaps a little more frequent now than a decade ago, are

[4] No artists have a voice in formulating museum policy.

potent minority proclamations that artists as designers add distinction to merchandise. But these timid and infrequent, though important, events point the way to the future rather than solve the present dilemma of our mass-production merchandise. The field is still wide open to the young artist who prefers precarious independence to the usual dry rot of a safe job with industry.

A GENERAL ANSWER

If a general answer to all these questions can be extracted from the single ones, perhaps one event which does mark a definite educational gain of great present and future importance can serve in that role. Unity of approach on basic issues within a school, and a year of foundation training for all students, as advocated a decade ago on page 229, have come to pass and are already standard practice in some schools, of which the School of Painting and Sculpture of Columbia University (page 152) and the several departments of Pratt Institute (page 200), are outstanding examples. How many other schools have arrived at and put into practice these same conclusions, the writer does not know. Whatever their number, they are our insurance that American art will carry on within the time-tested framework of the Grand Tradition. And an indication that the School of Universal Art, proposed on page 44, may possibly yet materialize.

If our blueprint of constructive developments is valid, the inevitable conflicts with conventional art teaching need endless, relentless stressing and pressing to a solution.

THE CONVENTIONAL SCHOOL

Take New York's famous Art Students League as an outstanding example of the conventional school. Its fifty or more artist-instructors are all individualists representing endless shades of uncoordinated, and often conflicting, theory and practice. Cohesion among them in agreeing on basic principles is obviously impossible. There is, therefore, no first-year course in fundamentals. Beginning students choose their masters and flounder amidst the conflicts, "usually taking at least a year to get their bearings." Then the conflicts continue as long as they study, except as they may be able to reduce them by their own trial and error decisions. (One student whom I know did this by studying all three years with one artist.) The school, under these conditions, cannot give constructive orientation help. In effect this means that students must educate themselves from fare offered them cafeteria style. Responsibility has its challenging values, but to dump all of it on inexperienced youth seems a wasteful process.

The fact that many of our leading artists have survived this training and in good time found themselves, does not disprove the waste but tends to ensure its continuation. Also the success story of the relative few, by giving prestige to the process, insures the continuation of the confusions which bedevil today's art world.

The issue, it seems, urgently demands inquiry.

TRAINING THE AMATEUR

That the painter for pleasure should have the kind of training which ensures the keenest enjoyment from the act of wielding brushes would seem to be a matter of obvious logic. What kind gains that end? The answer of this book is—creation tempered by the esthetics of design. Therein lies excitement, release, thrills, a sense of power over materials, sensory or emotional satisfactions and the like. Sunday painting becomes a much-needed antidote to the boredom of the materialistic routine. It relaxes tensions, then stimulates and refreshes.

In the 1952 Art News National Amateur Painter's Competition, the two top prizes (for oils and water colors) went to two works of hard, tight, painstaking, technically proficient realism. One, depicting a Chinese soup tureen on a table, by Sophie Regensburg, was so meticulously painted, showing every detail of dish, red tablecloth, and darker red wall, that, in gaining fidelity without imagination, it rivaled a kodachrome slide. The other, by Arnold T. Goldwater, did the same with a broad sweep of city streets, every office building stone, window, etc., being duly recorded. But, fortunately, there were just enough mistakes in perspective to testify to hand painting instead of the color camera. Both attained realism rather than naturalism—their one merit in addition to skill. Both represented long, tedious hours of work without a hint of the rewarding excitements of emotional release into designed creation. The jury, in effect, by these awards, was telling several hundred thousand amateur painters that facts, and skill in reporting them, should be the goal of their art experience.

In conclusion, again a warning. The human mind is indeed a strange instrument—with its two aspects of "knowing" and "feeling." Frequently, in a given person, one of these departments does not seem to know what the other is doing, or, one may be way over, and the other under, developed. A creative art, to be absorbed into experience, needs at least a fifty-fifty response from both mental areas. We have scholars, scientists, and cultured gentlemen whose intellects are so highly developed in this art field at the cost of feeling sensitivity that they may know all about the thing called art *without knowing the thing itself*. Since many of these persons are in positions of authority and write books, they tend to fortify the domination of intellect and the prevailing subversion of feeling. A recently published book about the creative mind, for instance, is such an amazing compilation of facts and statistics that one who tries to read it is lost in admiration of such knowledge. But when he looks at the illustrations for examples of the creative art which the statistics are about, he finds it has been almost entirely lost by the wayside. There are plenty of pictures but little art.[5]

Another recent book exploits feeling, thus delving into the opposite approach. It bases the art experience on emotion, sensing, enjoying and thereby stimulates unguessed, *un-thought-out,* personality-expanding adventures—a fertile soil for creative art.[6]

There is a school of thought, and it may draw on either one or both of these extremes, which gives primary importance to "personality" or "self-expression" in art training regardless of age, art values, or any other thing. (See page 15.) Any inner-motivated act, according to this thesis, is *self-expression* and therefore develops personality. The goal is to encourage the inner drive and release of energy—and let things happen. Whatever does happen, no matter how amorphous, flamboyant, or crude, is regarded with

[5] *Creative and Mental Growth* by Viktor Lowenfeld. Macmillan, New York, 1947. Revised edition, 1952.

[6] *The Artist in Each of Us* by Florence Cane. Pantheon Books, New York, 1951. (See reference to Mrs. Cane on page 34.)

reverence as a precious experience. Art, if it materializes, is a happy accident; if not, no matter; chaos also expresses personality.

The philosophy and method here presented reverse this approach. They give art priority and let personality bite into it—first for esthetic excitement, then for the experiencing of many other diverse values which gradually devlop. The esthetics, in other words, is the central theme which guides and nourishes personality from the first compulsion to visual communication through all stages of a rounded growth.

This book goes only part way in its attempt to aid in resolving these confusions. To summarize, it encourages creation, then concentrates mainly on a series of primary steps which facilitate awareness of the ingredients of design—colors, spaces, textures, lines, tone-values, planes, forms, and subject transformed into malleable symbols rather than lifted from nature in the raw,—*and with their welding into related harmonies*, or *plastic* organized controls. The idea is that if these building materials are recognized as basic elements (which they are not by thousands of artists), and if their simple relationships are *sensed* for their quality as well as recognized, then an ever-growing complexity of the elements and their relationships can build solidly and without foreseeable limits on this foundation. The assumption is, in other words, that if the foundation is solid so will be the structure reared upon it. To chart a specific path into the complex structure would be to present one artist's concepts when others may well own equal or superior validity. Which explains why in this book we hold to the simple foundation steps of creation and design.

DEFINITION OF TERMS

ABSTRACTION: Extracting from subject one or more elements or qualities and using them as a means or an end. Can be partial or complete. Can express inner realities. Can be used for purposes of design, emphasis, symbolism.

CREATION: Building. Bringing into existence. The opposite of copying which is a reproductive process. Re-creation of subject in a picture into a subjective expression.

DESIGN: The organization of all elements of line, space, color, texture, light-dark, planes, form, and subject into harmonic relationships—into a visual symphony.

DESIGN: FUNCTIONAL. Design which takes its character from the character of subject. As opposed to abstract design which imposes its own character on subject, if any, or plays its own harmonies unhampered if there is no subject.

DISTORTION: Tearing or twisting or manipulating into exaggerated shape or form. Used for purposes of design, dramatization, humor, emphasis.

EXPRESSIONISM: A term used by Cheney and others to label the Modern Movement. See footnote on page 10.

GRAND TRADITION: The tradition dating back to the beginnings of art history, which includes the universal qualities of creative expression and design.

MODERN ART: All art produced in our time is modern in the sense of being contemporary. But the term "Modern Art" has come to have specific meaning as describing that work which has grown out of the Modern Movement fathered by Cézanne and Van Gogh. Its fundamentals are creative expression and design. Since the great art of the past has normally been a personal or tribal expression and has been organized into design, Modern art is within the Grand Tradition of the past. It is universal art. It is the opposite of naturalism and the copying of observed nature.

NATURALISM: The copying of superficial facts and the chaos of nature as these are seen by the physical eyes without reorganization into the artist's expression and design.

NONOBJECTIVE ART: That art which has no reference to recognizable subject or concept but deals only with the harmonics of line, space, color, and form.

PLASTIC FORM: The organizations of design into a plastic or modeled whole. *Form* as opposed to content. The plastic picture is that which acknowledges and decorates or molds the flat plane of the picture's surface into an harmonic color and space unity at the same time it portrays subject in either two or three dimensions.

REALISM: Expression of essential, rather than superficial, truth.

SYMBOLISM: Subject translated into signs or symbols in any degree of reality instead of into a replica of surface truth.

A FEW AXIOMS OF CREATIVE ART PRODUCTION AND EDUCATION

1. *Emotion, feeling, sensing* must be the foundation of all creative art practice and appreciation. Practice which is controlled by conscious mind will be automatically limited to what is consciously *learned* or *known.* It can entirely miss the world of sensory experience from which the art experience springs.
2. *Sensory experience* is most easily developed when not complicated by subject or the idea or considerations of skill. *Abstract painting or modeling,* therefore, is the logical start of all art education. It develops native powers which, under present conditions, are the least developed. Once these powers are functioning healthily they can be applied to all types of objective expression.
3. Craft and technics must always be given secondary importance to *creation and design.*
4. All copying from nature or other works is *craft,* not *art.*
5. *Design* is the common denominator of all the arts. It is timeless and placeless. Without it man's expression in any medium may be informative, may exhibit technical mastery, but it *cannot be art.*
6. All people have *creative powers* and a rudimentary sensitiveness to *design* which can be developed. All art history proves this statement. The work of children and savages prove it.
7. *Art* is present in the work of a child or amateur adult the instant a personal expression is played into a harmony of line, color, space, or form—no matter how crude the harmonic expression may be. From such a crude beginning to the greatest masterpiece lie hundreds of different degrees of achievement; *all can be works of art.*
8. *Applied design* is not separate from *fine arts.* All are similar harmonic expressions in color, space, or form.
9. *Creative painting* and *creative designing* are both natural expressions of the creative spirit.
10. The *creative artist,* as professional, amateur, child, or student, should normally apply his design sense to his *environment*—to

creating color schemes for his home, to designing textiles, rugs, metalwork, etc., for his own use or for sale. This was normal practice in the Middle Ages and in the European Renaissance. Artists painted murals, designed an alterpiece or a gold chalice or any other thing which came to their studios as a commission. We should revive that natural and healthy process.

11. This counteracts the *commercialism of industry* which normally, in the applied art field, prostitutes design to meet the average demand.
12. *Living with antiques,* no matter how distinguished they may be as an expression of the art of their time, creates a situation that is in discord with the individual who is a product of *today*.
13. The individual should *express himself* in creating his own environment. If his mind is attuned to the past rather than the present it can be argued that the above discord will disappear and he can live harmoniously with the art of other ages as his imported physical environment.
14. *Teachers of art* must be creative-minded, must free themselves from all clichés of concept and practice, must develop a sensitive alertness to the qualities of things, both animate and inanimate, in their environment, including the personalities of their students, must be able to practice what they preach and inspire enthusiasm through contagion from their own. The creative attitude of mind and a participating awareness of design *are at least of equal importance* with pedagogical knowledge. Without the former the pedagogical knowledge is barren in art teaching.
15. The *art teacher* must avoid pressing students into his own or any mold. He must expect and encourage differences. He must encourage the personal point of view and expression. He can teach design and encourage art.
16. The title "*artist*" should always be modified. What kind of artist? There are amateur, professional, naturalistic, modern, creative, and design-conscious artists. There are popular, romantic, realistic, abstract, original, and derivitive artists. There are commercial artists. The term "artist" used without definition is so general as to have no specific meaning.

17. The term *art* needs similar definition.
18. An *intellectualization* of the processes of creation and design can result in art production and teaching that is aesthetically barren.
19. *Modern art* can be as *academic* as is that of the Naturalistic School which is currently called academic. This results when an artist allows his expression to be frozen into formulas, set patterns or stereotypes, or when he imitates another artist's style.

BIBLIOGRAPHY

Art and Education, by John Dewey. Barnes Foundation, 1929.

The Dewey philosophy applied to art education.

Art as Experience, by John Dewey. New York: Minton, Balch & Company, 1934.

The philosopher explains the art experience, its sources and values. A valuable widening of the horizon for the artist and the educator.

The Artist in Each of Us, by Florence Cane. New York: Pantheon Books, 1952.

A book filled with life wisdom and educational insight, featuring the creative life, the importance of feeling and emotion and the need of expressing life experiences.

Mrs. Cane's philosophy is based on her long experience in teaching children and adults.

The Arts in the Classroom, by Natalie Robinson Cole. New York: John Day, 1940.

This book takes the reader into the concrete classroom experience of the art development of little children. It brings the art experience of the children down to a small *a*—makes it a part of individual experience and growth. Back of it is a creative approach in harmony with the argument of these pages.

Expressionism in Art, by Sheldon Cheney. New York: Tudor Publishing Company, 1934.

A profound and authentic explanation of the Modern Movement in art which Cheney labels Expressionism. Demonstrates forcefully the earned place of this movement in the Grand Tradition and explains the reasons. A valuable book.

The Meaning of Modern Sculpture, by R. H. Wilenski. New York: Frederick A. Stokes Company, 1933.

Defines the artistic creed of the modern sculptors and the influences which have formed it. Also attacks the methods of archaeologists and historians of Greek sculpture, whom Mr. Wilenski describes as "professional propagandists for the reputations of certain sculptors in ancient Greece, whose works no longer exist." A refreshing and challenging reappraisal of Greek sculpture from the modern viewpoint.

The Modern Movement in Art, by R. H. Wilenski. New York: Frederick A. Stokes Company, 1928.

A thorough analysis of the Modern Movement written by an English artist who knows the modern art experience firsthand and explains it with authority.

The New Vision, by L. Moholy-Nagy. Fourth revised edition. New York: Wittenborn Schultz, 1947.

An explanation of the philosophy and practice of the old and new Bauhaus of Dessau, Germany, and Chicago, Ill., and its program of using the machine as a design medium for mass production, of bridging the gap between the artist and industry, of winning recognition and authority for the artist-designer, and of breaking down the artificial distinction between "fine" and "applied" arts.

Vision in Motion, by L. Moholy-Nagy. Fifth edition. Chicago: Paul Theobald, 1952.

Vision and Design, by Roger Fry. New York: Brentano's, 1921.

This is one of the pioneer explanations of the basic principles and points of view back of the Modern Movement to be written in English. Mr. Fry wrote as an artist who understood from firsthand experience. It is still authentic.

World History of Art, by Sheldon Cheney. New York: Viking Press, 1937.

A history written from the modern viewpoint. A reappraisal of the arts of history in the light of modern design knowledge with a consequent realignment and unification of basic values. A history which supersedes other histories or definitely supplements them. Should be standard in all schools.

INDEX